Anonymous

Essays on American art and artists

Anonymous

Essays on American art and artists

ISBN/EAN: 9783337716172

Printed in Europe, USA, Canada, Australia, Japan

Cover: Foto ©ninafisch / pixelio.de

More available books at **www.hansebooks.com**

Essays

on

American Art and Artists

by

F. Hopkinson Smith
Alfred Trumble
Frank Fowler
Nym Crinkle
William McKendree Bangs
William J. Baer
Henry Eckford
George Wharton Edwards
Henry Milford Steele
William Howe Downes
George Parsons Lathrop
Alexander Black
Marguerite Tracy
Perriton Maxwell
Frances M. Benson
Allan Forman
Charles McIlvaine
Lillie Hamilton French
Charles de Kay
Frederick W. Webber
Charles M. Skinner
Charlotte Adams
Edgar Mayhew Bacon
Arthur N. Jervis
Cromwell Childe
John Gilmer Speed
W. Lewis Fraser
Clarence Cook
Elizabeth W. Champney
Royal Cortissoz
Will H. Low
Henry Russell Wray
Henri Pene du Bois
Hillary Bell

Eleven Hundred Illustrations

by

Celebrated American Artists

Eastern Art League

Temple Court, New York

1896

Introduction.

THE rapid progress of American Art within the last decade has created a demand by the art-loving public for extended information on this subject. And as the *fin-de-siècle* way of acquiring knowledge is through talks and lectures, we have arranged with thirty-three of the brightest minds in the art world, including such well-known lecturers as Hopkinson Smith, Clarence Cook, George Parsons Lathrop, William Howe Downes, and others just as well known, to prepare a series of essays on American Art and Artists, and they have discussed three hundred and thirty-one artists and eleven hundred examples of their work. The process of illustration employed shows up the painter's craft as perfectly as it is possible to do at this advanced stage of mechanical reproductions. Biographies of well-known painters and draughtsmen are scattered through the series. Here are Nym Crinkle on J. G. Brown, the painter of street gamins; George Parsons Lathrop on Military Artists; and Gilbert Gaul, the painter of scenes in the Civil War. One artist may also discuss another, as Frank Fowler on the late Wilson de Meza, illustrator of *de luxe* editions; Miss Benson on the Moran family, a group of artists like those of Flanders three centuries ago or of Japan in this century, who seem to have the tendency toward art in all members of the name. John Gilmer Speed discusses the National Academy of

Design; Charles McIlvaine, the Pennsylvania Academy of Fine Arts; and Charles de Kay, the Art Students' League of New York. Charles M. Skinner brings the studios of New York into our ken, and Harry Fenn sketches the summer haunts of painters.

These articles are by men who know the art world well and speak from sympathy as well as knowledge.

Nor are our women artists forgotten. The ideal children of Maud Humphrey and charming women of Maria Brooks alternate with the dogs and horses of Marie Guise Newcomb. Then, as we are all more or less interested in the personality of these artists, the series of portraits, which exactly reproduce their photographs, is most entertaining. William M. Chase, Carleton T. Chapman, Julian Rix, Thomas Hovenden, Frederic Remington, George Wharton Edwards, William Sergeant Kendall, Thure de Thulstrup, Mrs. Rhoda Holmes Nichols, Robert Reid, Malcolm Fraser—all of these artists are active workers whose drawings and pictures may be met at any moment, and whose lives are worth knowing. There are also sketches and bits too many to be mentioned, by young artists just rising into fame.

Such an epitome of national art as this cannot fail to meet with an enthusiastic reception and further the cause of American Art.

ELIZABETH THOMAS MORSE.

CONTENTS

	PAGE
ALL AROUND ARTIST, AN. By F. HOPKINSON SMITH, With original illustrations by Charles S. Reinhart.	41
AMERICAN ART AND FOREIGN INFLUENCE. By W. LEWIS FRASER, With original illustrations by Albert E. Sterner.	121
AMERICAN LANDSCAPIST, AN. By ALEXANDER BLACK, With original illustrations by Julian Rix.	69
AMERICAN MILITARY ARTIST, AN. By GEORGE PARSONS LATHROP, With original illustrations by Gilbert Gaul.	57
ARABS OF NEW YORK, THE. By NYM CRINKLE, With original illustrations by J. G. Brown.	233
ARTISTIC DISCOVERER OF LONG ISLAND, THE. By LILLIE HAMILTON FRENCH, With original illustrations by Charles H. Miller.	183
ARTIST IN BUSINESS, AN. By HENRY MILFORD STEELE, With original illustrations by James Symington.	144
ART STUDENTS' LEAGUE OF NEW YORK, THE. By CHARLES DE KAY, With original illustrations by prominent members.	48
BOHEMIAN ART CLUB, A. By HENRY RUSSELL WRAY, With original illustrations by many members.	217
BOSTON ART AND ARTISTS. By WILLIAM HOWE DOWNES,	265
CLEVER WOMAN ILLUSTRATOR, A. By FREDERICK W. WEBBER, With original illustrations by Alice Barber Stephens.	65
DECORATIVE ARTIST, A. By ROYAL CORTISSOZ, With original illustrations by Frank Fowler.	166
DECORATIVE ILLUSTRATOR, A. By PERRITON MAXWELL, With original illustrations by George Wharton Edwards.	37
DELINEATOR OF LIFE, A. By PERRITON MAXWELL, With original illustrations by Albert B. Wenzell.	45
ENGLISH-AMERICAN ARTIST, AN. By CLARENCE COOK, With original illustrations by George Henry Boughton.	185
FIVE WOMEN ARTISTS OF NEW YORK. By FRANCES M. BENSON, With original illustrations by them.	9
FROM FINANCE TO ART. By CHARLOTTE ADAMS, With original illustrations by Stanley Middleton.	213
FROM MANY STUDIOS. By CHARLES M. SKINNER, With original illustrations by twenty-two well-known artists.	95
GLIMPSES OF PICTURESQUE PLACES. By GEORGE PARSONS LATHROP, With original illustrations by Harry Fenn.	135
HALF HOUR WITH STUDIO BORES, A. By CHARLES DE KAY.	153
ILLUSTRATOR OF CHILD LIFE, AN. By WILLIAM MCKENDREE BANGS, With original illustrations by Maud Humphrey.	162
LOVER OF THE SEA, A. By JNO. GILMER SPEED, With original illustrations by E. M. Bicknell.	245
MAKING OF MASTERPIECES, THE. By EDGAR MAYHEW BACON, With original illustrations by prominent American artists of their best pictures.	109
MAN OF ARTISTIC IDEAS, A. By ARTHUR N. JERVIS,	92
MODERN MARINE PAINTER, A. By HENRY MILFORD STEELE, With original illustrations by Carlton T. Chapman.	101
MORAN FAMILY, THE. By FRANCES M. BENSON, With previously unpublished illustrations by most of them.	25
MY FAVORITE MODEL. By GEORGE PARSONS LATHROP, With original illustrations by numerous artists.	169
NATIONAL ACADEMY OF DESIGN, THE. By JNO. GILMER SPEED, With original illustrations by prominent members.	73
NEWSPAPER ART AND ARTISTS. By ALLAN FORMAN, With original illustrations by leading artists of the American press.	126
ORIGINAL MARINE ARTIST, AN. By EDGAR MAYHEW BACON, With original illustrations by Frank de Haven.	231
PAINTER IN BLACK AND WHITE, A. By PERRITON MAXWELL, With original illustrations by Thure de Thulstrup.	21
PAINTER OF MARINE SUBJECTS, A. By JNO. GILMER SPEED, With original illustrations by James G. Tyler.	148
PAINTER OF PRETTY WOMEN, A. By CROMWELL CHILDE, With original illustrations by De Scott Evans.	105
PAINTER OF SUNSETS, A. By CHARLES M. SKINNER, With original illustrations by George H. McCord.	120
PAINTER'S PROGRESS, A. By ALFRED TRUMBLE, With original illustrations by Leonard Ochtman.	155
PEASANT AND PICTURE. By GEORGE WHARTON EDWARDS, With original illustrations by the writer.	200
PENNSYLVANIA ACADEMY OF THE FINE ARTS, THE. By CHARLES MCILVAINE, With original illustrations by prominent members.	137
PICTURES THAT HAVE INFLUENCED ARTISTS. By CHARLES M. SKINNER, With sketches from memory by well-known artists.	187
POET IN LANDSCAPE, A. By ALFRED TRUMBLE, With original illustrations by Bruce Crane.	89
REFORMER AND ICONOCLAST. By WILLIAM J. BAER. With original illustrations by William M. Chase and others.	237
SHADOWS OF THE ARTIST'S IDEAL. By MARGUERITE TRACY, With illustrations selected from our last prize competition.	257
STORY TELLER ON CANVAS, A. By CROMWELL CHILDE, With original illustrations by W. Verplanck Birney.	190
STUDENT OF DRAWING, A. By HENRY PENE DU BOIS, With original illustrations by Alfred Paris.	242
STUDIO AND THE STAGE, THE. By HILLARY BELL, With parallel and contrasting illustrations.	262
VERSATILE ARTIST, A. By ALEXANDER BLACK, With original illustrations by Carle J. Blenner.	159
WILSON DE MZA. By FRANK FOWLER, With representative examples of the deceased artist's work.	60
WOMAN IN ART. By ELIZABETH W. CHAMPNEY, With original illustrations by numerous artists.	201
WOMEN ARTISTS IN CANADA. By ALEXANDER BLACK, With original illustrations by members of the Woman's Art Association of Canada.	195

PORTRAITS OF ARTISTS

ABBATT, AGNES D.
ALLAN, WILLIAM R.
ATTWOOD, F. G.
BARNES, CULMER.
BEAL, H. MARTIN.
BEARD, DAN.
BEEBE, A.
BELL, E. A.
BELLEW, FRANK P.
BERAUD, JEAN.
BICKNELL, E. M.
BIRCH, REGINALD B.
BIRNEY, W. VERPLANCK.
BLASHFIELD, ALBERT D.
BODFISH, W. P.
BOSTON, JOSEPH H.
BOUGHTON, G. H.
BUDD, CHARLES J.
CALVERLY, CHARLES.
CHAPMAN, CARLETON T.
CHAPMAN, MARY BERRI.
COAST, OSCAR R.
COFFIN, WILLIAM R.
COLIN, MAXIMILIAN.

CORSON, KATHERINE LANGDON.
CRAIG, THOMAS B.
CRANE, BRUCE.
CUMMINGS, THOMAS S.
CURRAN, CHARLES C.
DAINGERFIELD, ELLIOTT.
DAVIDSON, JULIAN O.
DAY, FRANCIS.
DE HAAS, M. F. H.
DE HAVEN, FRANK.
DE LONGPRÉ, PAUL.
DIGNAM, M. E.
DIXON, M. R.
DOLPH, J. H.
DRAKE, W. H.
DUBE, L. THEO.
DURAND, E. L.
EATON, HUGH M.
EDWARDS, GEORGE WHARTON.
FENN, HARRY.
FITLER, W. C.
FRASER, MALCOLM.
FREER, FREDERICK.

GUNN, ARCHIE.
HATFIELD, J. H.
HAWLEY, HUGHSON.
HOLMAN, LOUIS H.
HOWARTH, F. M.
HUDSON, C. W.
HULBERT, KATHERINE ALMOND.
JOHNSON, CHARLES HOWARD.
KELLOGG, AMY L.
KEMBLE, E. W.
KOTZ, DANIEL.
LANDER, BENJAMIN.
LANMAN, CHARLES.
LAUBER, JOSEPH.
MIDDLETON, STANLEY.
NEWCOMB, MARIE GUISE.
NICHOLS, H. D.
OCHTMANN, LEONARD.
PALMER, WALTER L.
PENFIELD, EDWARD.
PÉRARD, VICTOR.
PLUMB, H. G.
PRATT, ROSALIND C.

REINHART, CHARLES S.
RELYEA, C. M.
REMINGTON, FREDERIC.
ROSELAND, HARRY.
RUDELL, P. E.
SANDHAM, HENRY.
SCOTT, MRS. M. E.
SHURTLEFF, R. M.
SMALL, FRANK O.
SMITH, C. MOORE.
SONNTAG, WILLIAM L.
STEPHENS, ALICE BARBER.
THOMPSON, WORDSWORTH.
TRAVER, G. A.
UPTON, FLORENCE.
VAN DEN BROECK, CLEMENCE.
WATSON, HARRY S.
WHEATON, FRANCIS.
WHITMORE, CHARLOTTE.
WILES, IRVING R.
WOOD, THOMAS W.
ZEIGLER, LEE WOODWARD.
ZOGBAUM, R. F.

ILLUSTRATIONS

ARRANGED ALPHABETICALLY BY ARTISTS' NAMES.

Abbatt, Agnes D., 171, 187, 188, 204.
Adney, Tappan, 52.
Allen, Thomas, 265.
Anshutz, Thomas P., 227.
Ashe, E. M., 55.
Baker, J. Carleton, 133.
Baker, Martha S., 204.
Bancroft, Milton H., 141, 143, 221.
Barnes, Culmer, 96, 179.
Barritt, Leon, 131.
Beal, H. Martin, 99, 176, 189.
Beal, Reynolds, 241.
Beard, Dan, 92, 93.
Beckwith, J. Carroll, 48, 51, 85, 193, 194, 227, 228.
Bell, E. A., 176.
Bellew, Frank P., 117, 181.
Bensell, F. E B., 223.
Benson, Frank W., 267.
Bicknell, A. H., 275.
Bicknell, E. M., 171, 245, 246, 247.
Birch, R. B., 95, 155.
Birney, W. Verplanck, 111, 190, 191, 192, 193, 194, 227, 228.
Blashfield, Albert D., 175.
Blashfield, Edwin H., 98.
Blenner, Carle J., 116, 159, 160, 161.
Bodfish, W. P., 118, 179.
Boston, Joseph H., 110.
Boughton, George H., 185, 186, 187.
Bradley, Horace, 53.
Breck, George W., 90, 159.
Bristol, J. B., 80, 157.
Brooks, Maria, 12, 15, 20, 113, 179, 210.
Broughton, Charles, 52.
Brown, Ethel Isadore, 224.
Brown, J. G., 233, 234, 235, 236, 237.
Brownell, Matilda A., 241.
Budd, C. J., 175.
Bunner, Rudolph F., 113.
Burlingame, Charles A., 110.
Burr, G. E., 178.
Butles, Mary, 149, 297.
Caliga, I. H., 274.
Cariss, Henry T., 219.

Carlin, Frances, 207.
Carr, Lyell, 158, 170.
Carter, F. A., 173.
Cawein, F. W., 98.
Chapman, Carleton T., 101, 102, 103, 104, 153.
Chapman, Mary Berri, 179, 201.
Chase, William M., 237, 238, 239.
Child, Edwin B., 50, 55, 157.
Christy, Howard Chandler, 239.
Claghorn, J. C., 223.
Clarke, Daisy E., 196.
Coman, Mrs. C. B., 17, 18, 210.
Cook, Josephine M., 211.
Cooper, Colin Campbell, Jr., 139.
Corson, Katherine Langdon, 202, 204.
Coultaus, H. C, 126.
Cox, Walter B., 131.
Craig, Thomas B., 176.
Crane, Bruce, 89, 90, 91, 110, 153.
Cropsey, Jasper F., 110.
Curran, Charles C., 100.
Curtis, Elizabeth, 239.
Decke, Erich, 171.
Davenport, Homer C., 129.
Davidson, J. O., 117.
Davis, Georgina A., 111, 173.
Davis, Warren R., 225.
Day, Joseph R., 225.
DeGrimm, C., 125, 132.
DeHaven, Frank, 112, 116, 231, 232.
DeLipman, M., 131.
DeLuce, Percival, 83.
De Meza, Wilson, 60, 61, 62, 63.
Denslow, W. W., 129.
DeThulstrup, T., 21, 22, 23, 24.
Dignam, Mrs. M. E., 115, 116, 190, 195, 197, 201.
Dixon, Mrs. M. R., 113, 173, 205, 210.
Doggett, Allan B., 95, 98, 153.
Dolph, J. H., 73.
Dougherty, Parke C., 228.
Drake, G. B., 175.
Drake, William H., 109.

DuMond, F. V., 172.
Dunk, Walter M., 223.
Dustin, S. S., 99, 178.
Eaton, C. Harry, 114.
Eaton, Hugh M., 179.
Edwards, George Wharton, 37, 38, 39, 40, 118, 181, 198, 199, 200.
Eisele, Frederick, 225.
Elliott, Benjamin R., 225.
Elliott, Emily Louise, 195.
Emmet, Jane Erin, 241.
Emmet, Lydia Field, 182, 210, 211.
English, F. F., 142, 219, 222.
Enneking, John J., 266.
Essig, George E., 217.
Evans, DeScott, 105, 106, 107, 108.
Fenn, Harry, 135, 136, 180.
Ferris, Jerome L. G., 140.
Ferris, Stephen J., 25, 29.
Field, Edward Loyal, 189.
Fithian, Frank, 139, 219.
Fitler, W. C., 109.
Flagg, Jared B., 75, 177.
Fleming, Thomas. 127.
Fogarty, T. J., 50, 98.
Fowler, Frank, 73, 166, 167, 168.
France, Eurilda, 203.
Fraser, John A., 114, 174.
Fraser, Malcolm, 53, 55, 159.
Freer, Frederick W., 85, 176.
French, Frank, 99.
Gaul, Gilbert, 57, 58, 59, 60.
Getchell, Edith Loring, 220.
Glackens, L. M., 141.
Glackens, William J., 142.
Goist, P. F., 223.
Goodes, William M., 141.
Gordon, F. C., 55, 157.
Gormley, Anna, 198.
Grafly, Charles, 137.
Graves, Abbott, 269, 276, 277, 278.
Greene, Gertrude, 203.
Grisayedoff, V. 133.
Gruelle, Richard B., 97.

Gruger, F. R., 142, 228.
Grutzner, Eduard, 158.
Gunn, Archie, 114, 179.
Halsall, William F., 280.
Harley, Charles, 142.
Harper, W. St. John, 178, 190.
Hart, Mary E., 208.
Hartley, J. Scott, 73.
Haskell, Ida C., 208.
Hassellouseh, Louis, 225.
Hatfield, J. H., 171.
Hays, Frank A., 228.
Heller, Eugenic, 210.
Hedwick, Howard, 95, 101.
Hemming, Edith C. S., 195.
Hemsted, M. J., 196.
Henken, J. Henry, 96.
Henri, Robert, 141.
Henry, E. L., 84, 88, 109.
Herts, H. B., 153.
Hills, Laura, 267.
Hirst, Claude Raguet, 208.
Holacker, William, 127.
Holme, Lucy D., 228.
Hooper, Will Philip, 176, 190.
Houston, Mrs. Francis C., 278.
Hovenden, Helen C., 139.
Hovenden, Thomas, 142.
Howarth, F. M, 96, 189.
Howland, Georgiana, 239.
Hudson, Grace, 203.
Hudson, William L., 80.
Huger, Katherine M., 201, 206, 211.
Humphrey, Maud, 162, 163, 164.
Hurd, Louis F., 94.
Huston, C. A., 217.
Hutchens, F. T., 109.
Jamison, Henriette Lewis, 210.
Jeffrey, Helen, 207.
Johnson, Charles Howard, 98, 131.
Jordan, David Wilson, 219.
Keep, Helen E., 203.
Keller, A. I., 157.
Kellogg, Amy L., 52, 153.

ILLUSTRATIONS (CONTINUED)

Kelly, J. Henderson, 225.
Kelly, James P., 137.
Kemble, E. W., 169.
Kendall, W. Sergeant, 96.
Kerr, George F., 176.
Klepper, Max F., 169.
Knickerbocker, J. H., 99, 126, 133, 134.
Knight, Daniel Ridgway, 141.
Kyko, Theodore, 132.
Lamb, Ella Condie, 48.
Lampert, Emma, 108.
Lauder, Benjamin, 110, 189.
Langley, Charles E., 241.
Lanman, Charles, 83.
Lansdale, W. Moylan, 227, 130.
Lathrop, Clara W., 201.
Lauber, Joseph, 48, 53, 54, 154-250.
Leferre, Charles, 126, 133.
Leighton, Scott, 207, 268, 271, 273.
Lesley, Edith, 201.
Lesley, Ellen F., 179, 201, 207.
Lindsay, A. M., 219.
Linson, Corwin Knapp, 169.
Lippincott, Margarette, 203.
Little, J. Wesley, 87.
Livingston, Roland H., 175.
Lyman, Joseph, 87.
Mackubin, Florence, 201.
Mann, Emily S., 211.
March, Carl, 127.
McCarter, Henry, 137.
McChesney, Clara T., 203.
McConnell, Mary, 198.
McCord, George H., 74, 119, 120.
McDougall, Walter, 131.
McNeill, A., 132.
Meeker, E. J., 169.
Meyr, Ernest, 241.
Middleton, Stanley, 198, 213, 214, 215, 216.
Millar, A. T., 182, 240, 241.
Miller, Charles H., 73, 183, 184.
Minor, Robert C., 87.
Mitchell, Ida, 195.
Modler, Louis, 83.

Moessner, Thomas F., 128.
Moran, Annette, 31.
Moran, Edward, 27, 28, 30, 31, 32, 34.
Moran, Emily, 35.
Moran, Leon, 31, 34, 35.
Moran, Mary Nimmo, 28.
Moran, Paul Nimmo, 29, 30.
Moran, Percy, 34.
Moran, Peter, 25, 26, 29, 34, 137, 138, 176, 217.
Moran, Thomas, 31, 33.
Morgan, George T., 227.
Mortimer, Charles, 126.
Mowbray, H. Siddons, 48.
Neely, J., Jr., 225.
Newcomb, Marie Guise, 14, 15, 16, 201, 212.
Newman, Carl, 142, 217.
Nicholls, Rhoda Holmes, 9, 10, 11, 13, 114.
Ochtman, Leonard, 165, 166.
Ogden, Henry A., 117.
Osler, Clara D., 196.
Paine, B. D., 227.
Palmer, Walter L., 75.
Paris, Alfred, 242, 243, 244.
Parkhurst, Harry L., 175.
Parrish, Clara W., 59, 173, 207.
Parsons, Charles, 80.
Parsons, Orrin S., 95.
Pell, Ella F., 111, 169, 190, 208.
Penfield, Edward, 55.
Pennell, Joseph, 137, 140, 220.
Pérard, Victor, 48, 59, 96, 118, 155.
Pezant, Aymar, 23.
Phillips, Burt G., 75.
Phillips, Mary M., 198.
Pitts, Fred L., 141, 227, 229.
Plumb, H. G., 176.
Poore, H. R., 83, 141, 221, 225.
Pope, Alexander, 273, 279, 280.
Porter, Benjamin C., 73.
Porter, W. A., 220.
Provost, Charles H., 178.
Rado, Ilona, 99, 162, 189, 207.
Randolph, Grace, 204.

Redman, John J., 132.
Redmond, Frieda V., 211.
Redwood, A. C., 51.
Reid, G. A., 155.
Reid, Robert, 52.
Reinhart, Charles S., 41, 42, 43, 44, 77, 87, 155.
Relyea, Charles M., 98, 175.
Remington, Frederic, 178, 181.
Rhees, Morgan, 117, 173.
Richards, F. T., 223.
Richards, T. Addison, 77.
Richards, W. T., 139.
Rix, Julian, 68, 69, 70, 71, 72, 118.
Robbins, Horace Walcott, 75.
Roberts, Howard, 223.
Roseland, Harry, 116, 175.
Rodell, P. E., 116.
Ryder, P. P., 80.
Sandham, Henry, 169, 274, 280.
Sartain, William, 87, 139, 223.
Satterlee, Walter, 27, 113, 155.
Schell, F. B., 220.
Schell, F. Cresson, 141, 217.
Scott, Mrs. E. M., 18, 19, 209.
Seiss, C. Few, 227.
Sellers, Horace W., 225, 226.
Shurtleff, R. M., 77, 86, 117.
Simon, Hermann, 156, 218.
Sniffie, George H., 82.
Smith, C. Moore, 52.
Smith, D. D., 179.
Smith, Gean, 157.
Smith, Harry T., 131, 133.
Smith, Millicent Grayson, 196.
Snell, Henry B., 50.
Sonntag, William L., 78, 83.
Southwick, Jamie Lea, 208.
Steennett, Helen, 195.
Stephens, Alice Barber, 64, 65, 66, 67, 137.
Stephens, Charles H., 219.
Sterner, Albert E., 121, 122, 123, 124.
Stumm, Maud, 51, 99, 210.
Sullivan, Mabel Ansley, 195.

Symington, James, 144, 145, 146, 147, 171.
Tait, Arthur F., 81.
Tarbell, Edmund C., 265.
Tewksbury, Fanny W., 211.
Thompson, W. T., 224, 225.
Thouron, Henry, 141.
Tiffany, Louis C., 80.
Tompkins, Frank H., 278.
Traver, G. A., 55, 56, 96, 157.
Trego, William T., 137.
Trowbridge, J. W., 130.
Tyler, James G., 116, 148, 149, 150, 151, 152.
Underwood, Abby E., 210.
Upton, Florence K., 204.
Van den Broeck, Clemence, 196.
Van Deusen, A. W., 187.
Van Hoisten, Hugo, 120.
Van Sant, J. Franklin, 129.
Varian, George, 173.
Vilhart, G. E., 220.
Vinton, Frederic P., 270.
Waldeck, Nina V., 198.
Walker, Sophia A., 204.
Ward, J. Q. A., 73.
Washburn, C. L., 241.
Watson, Harry S., 66, 117, 178.
Webster, Fred, 159.
Wencell, Albert B., 45, 46, 47.
Wheaton, Francis, 111, 181, 187.
Wheelan, Albertina R., 175, 211.
Whitmore, Charlotte, 207.
Wiles, Irving R., 49, 75, 85, 87, 157.
Wiles, L. M., 49.
Williams, Mary R., 211.
Wilmarth, L. E., 87.
Wirt, Dr. Marvin A., 223.
Wood, George B., 219.
Wood, Thomas W., 76, 83, 85, 155.
Woodbury, Marcia Oakes, 274.
Wray, Henry Russell, 219.
Wright, Charles H., 127, 132.
Yeocel, W. G., 127.
Zeigler, Lee Woodward, 95, 171.

AMERICAN ART AND ARTISTS.

FIVE WOMEN ARTISTS OF NEW YORK.

By Frances M. Benson.

The colony of women artists in New York has established itself wherever there is to be found a good north light among the housetops of the long lane of ambition, just off the high road to success. Its members are mostly young and enthusiastic, working for very love of their art; economizing with tea-pot and cracker jar, teaching and doing odds and ends of designing and decorating to make ends meet, and put by the wherewithal for journeys to the promised land across the sea—the Mecca of all true disciples of Color and Form.

They come from all over the country, attracted by the art atmosphere of certain quarters of the city; the prospect of touching elbows with already famous painters; the frequent exhibitions and noted sales, and the big windows where gems from renowned brushes may be studied without money and without price.

"A STUDY IN PINK."

From Water Color Sketch by Rhoda Holmes Nicholls.

The woman artists have a little world to themselves, partly because society does not know the way to the sky parlors, nor understand the jargon of technique, and partly because the necessity of catching a gleam of light on the instant, demands the improvement of each shining hour and mood. Work means concentration, and concentration means solitude. They depend on the exhibitions and various stores to dispose of their sketches, because among all their friends could not be taken up a collection sufficient to purchase them.

As they get on in the world, their prosperity is marked by the addition of dull old squares of tapestry, pieces of quaintly carved furniture, a jar of marvellous mould, or an extra rug, and on certain days an effective light is turned into the studio and the presiding genius, in picturesque array, places before congenial spirits the tangible results of her inspiration, and maybe a cup of tea.

When a woman steps boldly beyond pretty copying and does work that is strong and imaginative, she is admitted to comparison with and the companionship of brother artists; she may not be elected to active membership in the Water Color Society, but she may hope for honorary membership in that august organization, and more than content herself with being an officer of high degree in the Water Color Club.

"VENETIAN SCENE."

From Water Color Sketch by Rhoda Holmes Nicholls. Copyright, 1891, Houghton, Mifflin & Co.

Such a woman is Rhoda Holmes Nicholls, one of New York's best-known artists, although she has been here but eight years. She is an Englishwoman, who pursued her early studies at the Bloomsbury School of Art, London, where she won the Queen's Scholarship of forty pounds a year for three years, and an additional ten pounds from her Majesty's private purse, so pleased was that lady with the pictures sent for her approval. Mrs. Nicholls had also the advantage of three years in Italy, studying the human figure in the studio of Cammerano and landscape with Vertunni, besides attending the evening classes of the Circolo Artistico, where artists of all nations teach and criticise each other. Here a Spaniard gave her hints of wonderful color, and a vigorous

AMERICAN ART AND ARTISTS.

German taught her tone. She was elected a member of the Roman Water Color Society, being the second woman on whom was conferred so great a distinction, and Queen Margherita personally complimented her on her studies of Venice, exhibited at the Annual Display.

Then she went to Africa for its wonderful lights and sombre grandeur of mountains seen amid cloudless skies; its stretches of parched vegetation, and its flat-roofed dwellings with arched doors and enclosed courtyards. She set up an open-air studio among the Kaffirs and ostriches, and brought back innumerable sketches true to life.

After a honeymoon in ideal Venice, she came to this country with her American artist-husband, and her water colors attracted immediate attention from the brilliancy of their execution. Within a year she received a medal in the Boston exhibition for a small picture of "Venetian Sunlight," and shortly after, the gold medal from the A. A. A. (Associated American Artists) of New York, for "Those Evening Bells."

Mrs. Nicholls has the rare talent of painting with a breadth of observation and a strength of touch almost phenomenal; as one of the judges remarked: "She seems like a woman, and paints like a man." Her Venetian pictures are among her finest bits of work, and she did some exquisite illustrations for W. D. Howells's "Venetian Days," two of which are reproduced on these pages. She seems to get the "scene, sunny moods of the sea city, with its transparent atmosphere and the still heat of its unflinching sun, and the most vivid contrasts are made with a skill that blends without obliterating. Her pictures not only appeal to, but they hold the attention, until some hidden meaning comes out point by point, and the beauty grows with the beholding.

There is bound to be a certain personality of the artist in any picture, and in these you find suggestions of a keen understanding, a close sympathy, and a touch of motherly pride and love; for the bright-faced, sweet voiced little woman is as nearly as devoted to the children of her imagination as to the two babies playing about her studio.

Mrs. Nicholls is still a young woman, notwithstanding the work she has accomplished, and she has all the youthful capacity for viewing the world from its bright side. There is nothing gloomy, nothing cynical in her treatment of subjects. Her pictures are not a daily grind for bread and butter, but the exercise of a great

From Water Color Sketch by Rhoda Holmes Nicholls.

"A WINGED DRAM-BROOM."

gift in connection with her duties as wife and mother. Her studio joins her husband's on the top floor of their cosey home, and the flaxen-haired boy and girl are not the least of the treasures to be found therein.

Maria Brooks is another little English woman recently come to our shores, and the way of her coming was distinctly pointed out by the hand of fate. Some wealthy Canadians, through their London agent, purchased several of her pictures, and were so taken with them that they wished to meet the artist. In their wholesouled fashion they invited her to spend a winter season with them, and suggested that if she felt she could hardly spare the time for a mere visit, she might make it a semi-professional one, and they would leave cards for a private view of such pictures as she would care to dispose of in Montreal. Learning through her solicitor that her unknown friends were people of high standing as well as lovers of art, Miss Brooks accepted their invitation, and has never been back to the other side, except on business. There was a niche in New York waiting for a portrait-painter, and Miss Brooks fitted it perfectly. Her likenesses do not merely represent—they are the people before her. She

From Water Color Sketch by Rhoda Holmes Nicholls.

"A DECORATIVE PANEL."

has the faculty of painting a man at his best—of catching and transferring to canvas the expression friends love to see. "You trust me a hundred faces," she told a subject one day, "and every time you come you bring a different one. Now we will talk awhile until you get around to the one I want;" and there she sat, work in hand, chatting away about her pictures, her glossy green parrot, anything, everything, until the young lady, unaware, lost her self-consciousness, and the desired expression could be deftly introduced into the picture. She says the hands have as much character in them as the face, and are really more difficult to do well, because the sitter is seldom willing to give the same time for them as for the head. Just now she is doing a series of little girl pictures, full-length but very tiny—just a dash of vivid coloring and a suggestion of a childish whim.

It is to a child that she owes the turn her life-work has taken. She had been in the South Kensington school five years, designing, decorating, illuminating; no woman student there had ever stood so well in perspective and anatomy; and she

AMERICAN ART AND ARTISTS.

From a water-color sketch by Elihu Vedder. IN THE CHESTNUT-NUT SEASON.

AMERICAN ART AND ARTISTS.

From Painting by Marcia Brooks.

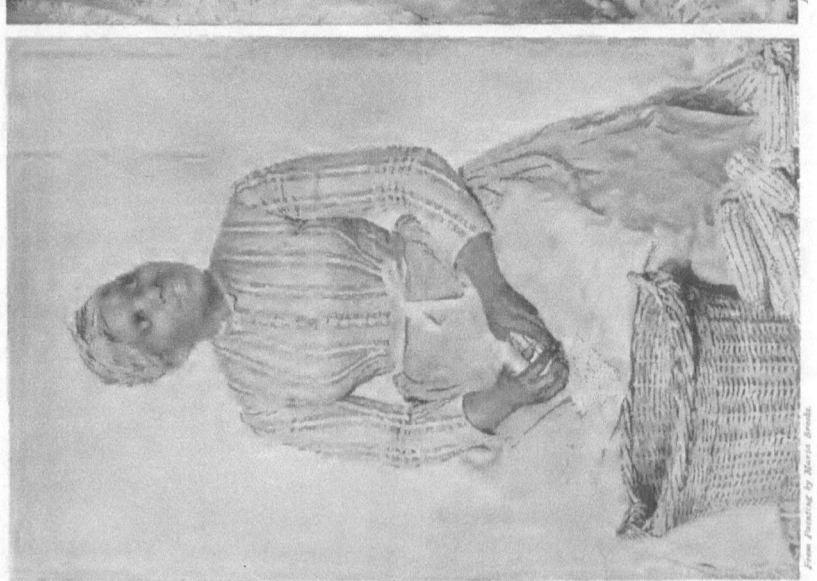

From Painting by Marcia Brooks.

AMERICAN ART AND ARTISTS.

From Water Color Sketch by Rhoda Holmes Nicholls.
"HIS LITTLE SON."

had won gold, silver, bronze, national, and local prizes beyond count, but had no definite line of work. A copy of her "Angel Heads" attracted a lady who wished a picture of a little son, and though Miss Brooks had never painted a portrait, nothing would do the mother but that the small boy should be made to appear as angelic as possible. The result was that the artist was overwhelmed with nine orders at once for portraits, and of these seven were afterward hung in the Royal Academy. Her work was exhibited for fourteen successive years at the Academy, until now she is content to show it in her roomy studio in The Sherwood.

Marie Guise Newcomb is the only woman in this part of the country who makes a specialty of painting animals, and abroad she is known as the Rosa Bonheur of America. She studied horses and dogs under Shenck, the animal painter of Paris, and sheep with Chaedlieu, and does a bit of landscape now and then as a divertisement or a background. She is a great lover of animals, and spends hours at a time among them, familiarizing herself with their moods and habits.

At an up-town riding academy a box-stall was given her for a studio, and wealthy owners gladly tied their high-bred horses to the door-post for her to study. Mrs. Newcomb paints as much as Miss Brooks would do a bishop's, and with as much relish; and as her sisters in art study anatomy of the human form, so did she dissect quadrupeds in her mother's conservatory, a quarter or a half at a time. She was fortunate in having a friend in the lady owner of a stock farm, and together they investigated the secrets of animal construction.

Having become acquainted with the animals subdued by civilization, Mrs. Newcomb decided to go to Arabia and study the wild horses and the perfect Arabian steeds. She spent a winter in Algiers, adding to her collection sketches of Bedouins and camels. It is against the Arab's religion to be pictured, and their fear of it is greater than of the Evil Eye, consequently they distrust the people who pretend to paint merely the picturesque street scenes and interiors. Not knowing this, Mrs. Newcomb one day attempted to copy a corner with an orange stand and a toothless old hag guarding it. The old woman kept her eyes on her, peaceably enough, until she got a glimpse of her scarlet shawl going in the sketch, when, with a lot of unintelligible gabble, presumably Arabic oaths, she tore the canvas from the easel, swung it around her head with imprecations, rent it, and stamped on it in the wildest fury. The innocent artist was frightened half out of her wits, but the gendarmes were attracted by the mob collecting, and rescued her from an unpleasant position.

From Water Color Sketch by Rhoda Holmes Nicholls.
"THE WRITERS."

The Arabs learn to speak some French from the military stationed among them, and in that way they can converse with the ordinary traveller. Mrs. Newcomb finally made friends with them, and was invited to eat kous-kous—a really palatable mutton broth—from the common bowl on the ground, with wooden spoons they carved themselves. The head of the family ordered the oldest of his eight wives to bring from a box in the wall a piece of priceless tapestry, upon which the guest was to sit cross-legged; and, after the kous-kous, was served the delicious Arabian black café, a fine powder with hot water poured over it, nothing the like of which is reported to in our country. They were much interested in our countrywoman's fashion of wearing gold ornaments in her teeth, and explained to her very carefully what their custom was in such matters. They also wanted to stain her fingers from tip to middle joint—a mark of very great distinction—assuring her that it would never wear off. From such inside experiences as these Mrs. Newcomb made a quantity of valuable sketches, such as are seldom secured by the artist traveller. From Algiers she

From Water Color Sketch by Rhoda Holmes Nicholls.
"A SUMMER DAY."

went to the oasis of Biskra, travelling by night in a seven-horse diligence on account of the heat. The nights were as light as day from the white sand and thickly starred sky, and while out in the desert she learned the meaning of the Arab's love for his horse. He watered and fed the animal before seeking his own rest, and he would as soon think of mutilating his own flesh and blood as of beating the faithful companion of his journey, or of "bobbing" the beautiful mane and tail in ugly British fashion.

The first picture Mrs. Newcomb—then Marie Guise—sent to the Paris salon was a golden haying scene, with sturdy farmers and strong Brittany horses, and to her great joy it was accepted and well hung. Her greatest work, as she considers it, is entitled "The Work-Horse's Need," and is of life-size

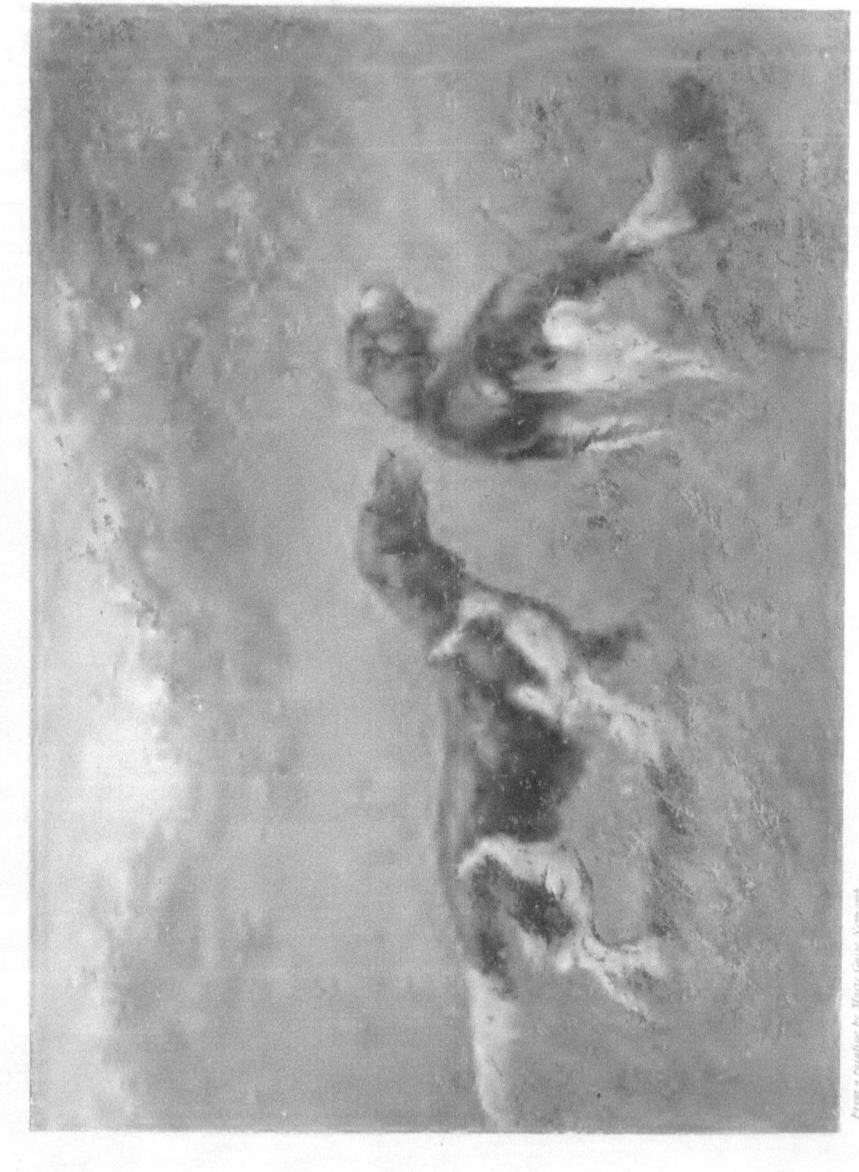

AMERICAN ART AND ARTISTS.

heads of four horses drinking from a street fountain. This picture represents several months' close work, and into it she has put all her love of the animal and knowledge of its nature. The eager, thirsty beast, forgetting the heat and the weight of the load harnessed to it in the craving for water, and the grateful, satisfied animal waiting for the word to toil on again, are shown with almost human

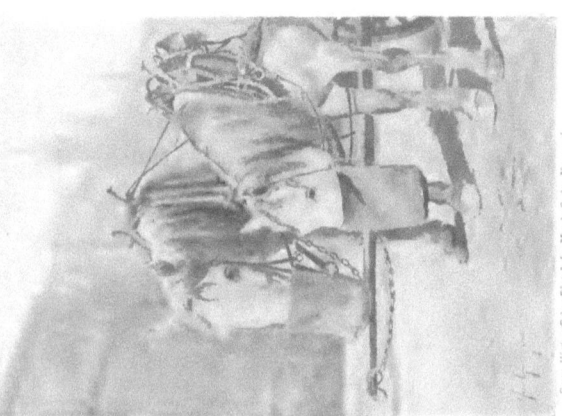

From Painting by Maria Brooks.
"PORTRAIT OF FATHER NONES."

pathos in the dumb faces. This picture is to be sold for the benefit of one or two small drinking fountains, as a special relief for work-horses.

Mrs. Newcomb is a cheery little woman, with an easy, cordial manner and a winning personality—one of the chosen few who gain the confidence of strange animals and children. She understands them, and they trust her.

When Mrs. C. B. Coman began the study of landscape, she supposed that all good work must abound in detail, but an exhibition of French pictures was a reve-

lation to her, and she gradually came to believe that detail was useful only so far as it enhanced the value of the great qualities of light, air, and space. She studied in the French schools, spending her summers in Normandy and Holland, indulging her intense love of nature and outdoor work. She says her idea of perfect happiness is fair weather, some trusty colors, and a quiet spot where none can intrude. Of course the indoor painter does not have to brave the elements nor contend with a constantly changing scene, neither does she have the varied beauty of earth and sky spread before her eyes. The Dutch painters say that half an hour is all one can safely work at the same landscape, while from still life all out has to take in consideration is the waning light.

Mrs. Coman has a sketch that was obtained under special difficulties. It was her last day in Holland, and she walked three miles through rain and wind to a wayside shrine standing between two gnarled old trees. The limbs of the trees had been blown one way by the strong sea winds, and formed a slight protection for the crucifix, where many a poor sailor's wife had knelt imploring safety for the absent one. The sketchers tied their easels to the trees and kept one foot on the palette, while they put in the rough water for the background and outlined the wind-carved crucifix. The stormy day harmonized perfectly with the pathetic subject, but by and by, when the call for home was sounded, the wind caught easels and trappings, wafted them out of sight forever, and literally blew the sketchers home. These interesting experiences are denied the figure-painter.

Shortly after Mrs. Coman's return from abroad, she lost by fire all the products of her six years' labor—studies, notes, etchings, photographs,

From Water Color Sketch by Maria Gatto Newcomb.
"NOONTIDE."

AMERICAN ART AND ARTISTS.

From Painting by Marie Guise Newcomb. "LISTENING."

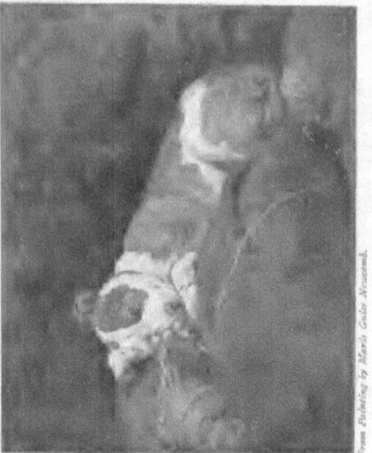

From Painting by Marie Guise Newcomb. "PLAYED OUT."

tapestries, and bric-à-brac from Holland, Italy, and France. This was an irretrievable loss, and she has been obliged to paint entirely from memory all her pictures, such as "A French Village," "Street in Cernay," which have received much favorable comment. Her studio now is in her Adirondack cottage, where she gathers around her friends and pupils, who, like herself, are enthusiastic over the open-air and impressionist schools.

Mrs. E. M. Scott finds her inspiration in flowers, and particularly in roses. One of the best critics has said: "She has a special understanding with roses. They seem to like to have her paint them, and look their loveliest and tenderest for her." At one exhibition she had a spray of Mermets, fresh and dewy, in exquisite tones of pink, placed in a vase that came from a cardinal's collection in sunny Italy, the blueish gray of the pottery melting

IN HOLLAND.

From a painting by Mrs. C. B. Coman.

AMERICAN ART AND ARTISTS.

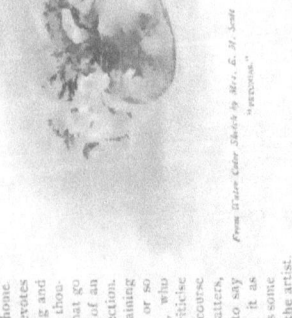

From Water Color Sketch by Mrs. E. M. Scott
"PEONIES."

From Water Color Sketch by Mrs. E. M. Scott
"ROSES."

From Painting by Mrs. C. B. Coman
"ADIRONDACK WOODS."

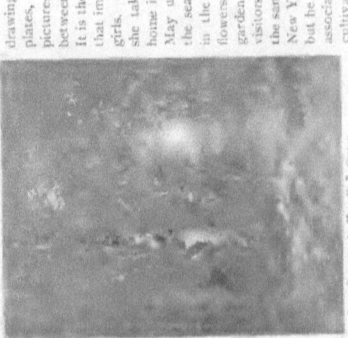

From Painting by Mrs. C. B. Coman
"A FLORIDA ROSE GARDEN."

tures in her summer home. In the winter she devotes the morning to teaching and the afternoon to the thousand and one things that go toward the education of an artist in every direction. They have an entertaining little club of a dozen or so ladies and gentlemen, who meet fortnightly and criticise unsigned work. Of course each piece is torn to tatters, but they are careful to say what they like about it as well, so there is always some crumb of comfort for the artist.

Mrs. Scott has such a pretty studio, with its books, bric-à-brac, and cosy seats built in, with shelves overhead filled with pottery. Of course there are pictures everywhere—on the walls, on easels, on the floor, leaning against anything that will support them—even behind the door. In one corner is a collection of blue delft from Holland; another is devoted to fragile glass in iridescent urns and vases of quaint device, amber jugs and wine bottles from vineyard lands

into the delicate color of the roses. At the Boston exhibition her cluster of stately peonies in a glass pitcher, hung in the centre of the end wall, was observed of all observers for the extreme delicacy of treatment.

Mrs. Scott says her first attempt at drawing was the copying of fashion plates, because, when she was young, pictures in the family were few and far between, and even chromos were scarce. It is the memory of her early struggles that impels her to help ambitious young girls. Having no daughters of her own, she takes her pupils to her summer home in the Fishkill hills, where, from May until October, 1,400 feet above the sea, they work together on views in the surrounding valleys, or from flowers culled from her old-fashioned garden. Max goes, too, and welcomes visitors to the mountain top studio with the same dignified grace that she shows New York friends. Max is only a cat, but he has learned a thing or two from association and travel; he is a very cultivated cat, indeed.

Mrs. Scott does the most of her pic-

Painted by Mrs. E. M. Scott

EARLY ROSES

AMERICAN ART AND ARTISTS.

"MAKING FRIENDS." Drawn by Maria Brooks.

"PINK SLIPPERS." Drawn by Maria Brooks.

A PAINTER IN BLACK AND WHITE.

By Perriton Maxwell.

THURE DE THULSTRUP, a pen draughtsman of positive touch and facile execution, a painter of marked technical ability in the monochromatic mediums, an æsthetic industrian closely identified with American illustrative art, and a man well versed in wars and travel, comes to us from the chilly clime of storied Sweden, where he was born, at Stockholm, in 1848.

Of Mr. de Thulstrup's personal character and career but little need there be said; it is the character and career of his art, rather than that of the artist, which most concerns the writer. It will therefore suffice to remark that the youthful De Thulstrup received one kind of education at the Royal Military Academy of Sweden, from which institution he was in due time graduated with the usual honors expected of men predestined to renown and riches. Soon afterward Mr. de Thulstrup took his first lessons in the larger school of life, and began that broader education which is called experience, and which ends only with death. It was in an eventful period of our artist's life when he went to bed one night an ordinary citizen of Stockholm and awoke the next morning to find himself a soldier entitled to wear the imposing uniform of a Swedish lieutenant of artillery.

Then, tiring of this honor, he left his birthland and journeyed southward. After knocking about the principal cities of the Continent for a time, his military predilections came to the surface again, and asserted themselves so strongly that he joined the French army and went to Algiers with the famous "Legion Etrangères." At this point of his life the future picturist of American periodicals was quite convinced that he had been born a warrior, and with this conviction firmly fixed in his mind, he suffered but slight difficulty in finding an abundance of rare entertainment and congenial employment during the Franco-Prussian conflicts of 1870-71. Perhaps it was because he experienced some sudden revulsion against the grim carnage and prosaic business of European warfare, or perhaps it was merely to gratify a long-cherished desire to become acquainted with the men and things of America, that he set sail for this country in 1873. At all events, the trend of his thoughts changed radically as soon as he touched these shores. War and soldiery completely fled his mind, and very soon after his arrival here the embryo illustrator was installed as a student in the then recently organized Art Students' League of New York. This was the initiatory act in Mr. de Thulstrup's art career. It soon became evident that he would have no more of military life excepting on paper and canvas. He had relinquished his carbine for a stick of charcoal; he had abandoned his bayonet for a brush, and henceforth his only battles were to be fought with the none too easily conquered problems of his new vocation.

Mr. de Thulstrup's life as an illustrator really dates from the publication of his first drawings made for the old Daily Graphic of New York. He remained in the service of this journal for several years, and when he finally severed his connection with the Graphic, it was to become a special staff artist for Frank Leslie's periodicals. There is sufficient evidence in the fact that Mr. de Thulstrup's gifts of versatility and sound workmanship were early displayed and early appreciated. In 1881 he was engaged by Harper & Brothers as a general illustrator for their publications, and by this concern he is still actively employed.

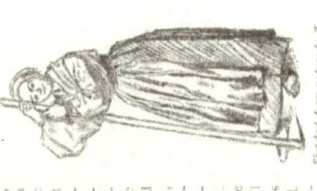

Mr. de Thulstrup's black and white productions are not to be too severely subjected to the critical analysis which may more properly be bestowed upon his work in color. And yet there are but few of his colored canvases that one would willingly exchange for a single bit of brilliant technique from his pen point or one of his spirited and broadly executed paintings in black and white. More than any other illustrator of the day is Mr. de Thulstrup a thorough technician. He is a painter of pictures for the press. His illustrative work, executed for the most part under high pressure, has all of those nice artistic qualities which the cultured eye first looks for in a painting—honest brushwork, good composition, and large suggestiveness—and seldom are those primary painterial virtues wanting. While this holds true, it is also to be noted that the greater public of artless folk, who ask only that their eyes be delighted, find full enjoyment in the contemplation of Mr. de Thulstrup's work.

There is a happy union of suave subject and vigorous execution in all he does. His men, women, and horses are well-groomed and high-bred. There does not seem to be any particular reason for their existence, but you are glad that they are alive, if it

AMERICAN ART AND ARTISTS.

is only because they offered acceptable material for Mr. de Thulstrup's richly-dowered touch. It would at first appear, if one may judge an artist's mental equipment by means of his pictures, that there was a man whose perception of life is as broad as Shakespeare's own. But Mr. de Thulstrup's view of life is all upon one side. He has met many persons whose manners charm. His characters have many faces, and fall in admirably with their surroundings. The people of his pictures are never tragic or morose; they are remarkably well-behaved. They smile and bow and make themselves agreeable to each other all the day, and you long to see the spell of amiability broken. You cannot help wishing at times that something calamitous would happen to disturb their oppressive equanimity. Still, they are such worthy persons, and their characteristics are so well presented, that you dismiss the desire for disturbance as something quite ungenerous, though warranted. It would be a pleasurable experience to find in any drawing or painting of Mr. de Thulstrup's making, some show of honest sentiment. He seems to be either supremely contemptuous or studiously careless of the subtleties of human emotion. It is hardly just to assume that he purposely ignores what may be termed the sub-surface qualities of a picture—the psychical and sensory side. And yet in none of his picturements, charmingly conceived and superbly executed as most of them are, is it possible to find a fleck of poetic feeling.

It may be that Mr. de Thulstrup has no regard for what is called the spiritualité or soulful part of a painting, and he is not to be condemned off-hand for that in these days of numerous artistic dreamers who are without the power to acceptably embody their fine visions on canvas. But be all this as it may, we have the fact unmistakably fixed in pigment that the clever artist under consideration here, elects to present in his own strongly individual way the common scenes of contemporary life in this and other lands; the daily doings of the best persons in these lands, and the whole prescnement made surprisingly real and vivacious as to the externals of things. In the representation of soldiery and horses the story Mr. de Thulstrup has to tell is invariable, engaging, and curiously dissimilar to his renderings of other animated subjects. Especially in the violent action of the horse does he display rare powers of observation and a knowledge of equine peculiarities quite uncommon. His horses trot or gallop, tear or plunge, balk or stand immovable but alert, at the will or whim of his brush; this vital activity is also part and parcel of his pictures of military life, and one cannot refrain from inquiring, when viewing these stirring scenes, why some of the same vivacious movement and asserted feeling is not put into the artist's pictures of ordinary men of health and lively affairs?

Mr. de Thulstrup's talent for recording the bright facts of nature is unsurpassably fine, and it is with a deal of local pride and self-satisfaction that one calls to mind that the talent is a flower native to our soil though sprung from an exotic seed. What Mr. de Thulstrup lacks in divination and emotion he more than liberally repays in profusion of themes and a never-failing cheerfulness. There is a visual delightment in the familiar poses and no less familiar faces of his men and women. Delightful are the grace and light-heartedness of his women, and equally delightful the sturdy build and athletic proportions of his men.

It is beyond the grasp of mediocre skill to obtain such brilliant effects with so small an expenditure of artistic effort as Mr. de Thulstrup is continually doing. His is a consummate artistry, inherent to his nature, as truly of himself as is his hair or his complexion. It is to be expected that the alien who comes to this coast and takes up with the necessarily unfamiliar ways of our life, should always retain a few of his home-acquired habits and betray in one way or another his foreign birth, and that upon the most momentous as well as upon the most insignificant occasions.

But Mr. de Thulstrup has been saved from the common embarrassment because he learned the artistic speech of the place of his adoption before so much as the first principles of his own racial language of the brush and pencil had been taught him. Though somewhat advanced in manhood when he came across the brine, he was sweetly unconscious of the eminence he was one day to attain in the field of American art. That he has fairly won his way to the top and holds at the moment a position among the foremost illustrators of the day, is due altogether to his own unceasing industry married to a singular acuity and vigor of pictorial perception. The firmness of his touch and the charming idiosyncrasies of his method were taught him in no school. His perfect drawing is purely the result of observation and practice. There are no affectations or obtrusive mannerisms in his work. The pictures he puts out of hand in these latter days are accurate, clear, and frank expositions of objects as they appear to normal eyes. He resorts to no cheap subterfuge of art, and seeks to charm more by his rugged sincerity and close adherence to natural truths than by the subtler schemes of pen point and brush.

The best work that Mr. de Thulstrup has done is to be seen in the long gallery of black and white paintings and sketches formed by the recent volumes of the Harper periodicals. Especially in the larger supplementary designs issued with Harper's Weekly do we see him at his best, and are afforded a closer view of his present artistic capacity. To say that he will perform many more brilliant feats of artistry in the limited medium he has chosen to employ, requires no special gift of prophecy. Such a robust talent as that which is the happy possession of Mr. de Thulstrup must of necessity expand and reach out after loftier things. He takes life very seriously now, but his seriousness is that of a conscientious student absorbed

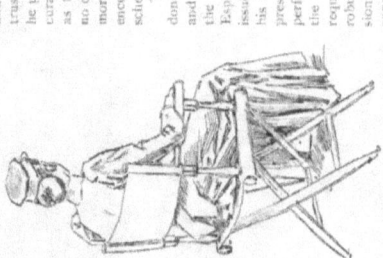

Painted by T. de Thulstrup.
Traced from the original by the artist.
"A SUMMER GIRL."

"SNUG AS A BUG."
From a pencil sketch by T. de Thulstrup.

22

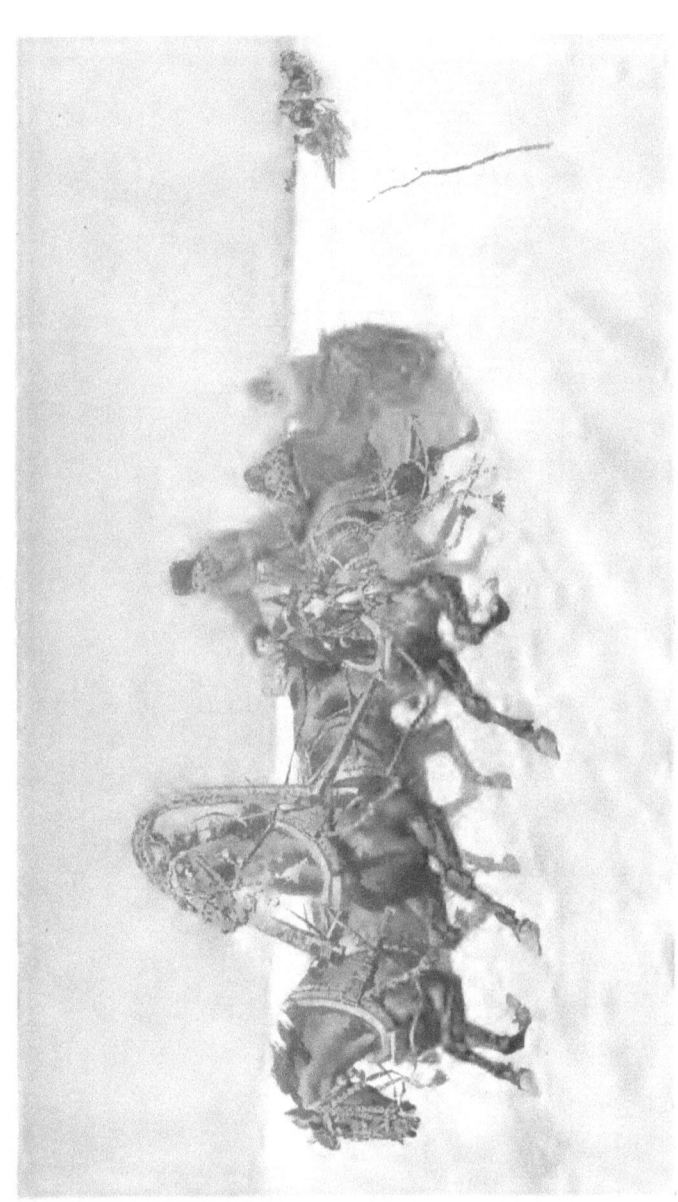

From a painting by Thure de Thulstrup. THE TROIKA, OR RUSSIAN THREE-HORSE SLEIGH.

AMERICAN ART AND ARTISTS.

in his studies. We cannot complain of his indifference to our pictorial inclinations. Though we get from him nothing but the hard realities of life, we get them with a verve and freshness which warrant no dissatisfaction. The most casual examiner of Mr. de Thulstrup's effects must realize that his remarkable precision of handling and assurance of outline does not come to him by a succession of happy accidents; the persistent labor and careful analytical study he puts into the simplest of the drawings would make the tyro at illustration gasp with awe and admiration. To what extent Mr. de Thulstrup carries his care for absolute truth, the sketches and studies which accompany this limited review of his powers will afford some comprehension.

The bold and free outlines of the young woman seated on a camp-chair, with her back toward the spectator, is as good an example of the artist's supple manner of pen-manipulation as could be given. The close studies of draperies in his pencil memoranda, and the spirited action of the mediæval cavalry-man and his fiery mount, display the versatility of the true illustrator, and show what simplicity of style, coupled with soundness of drawing, will do for the depictor of the ordinary. Very much at ease is Mr. de Thulstrup in his pictured environments. Whether he be on the deck of a transatlantic steamer, in the broughham of a Monseigneur, or before the belching cannons of fort or cruiser, the accessories of his illustrations are just what they are in reality, and not composed in the studio for the bare purposes of picturement. You entertain no doubt of his familiarity with the ever-varying backgrounds against which his figures are posed. You soon learn to trust him in the minor parts of a picture as you rely upon the veracity of the camera. But the difference between the realism of the camera and the realism of art is the difference between mechanism and thought—matter and mind—and when individuality stamps fancy and originality upon the thought, comparison ceases absolutely.

The sphere of book and magazine illustration is one which yearly widens and gathers to itself complexity. There are few men engaged professionally in the art of illustration to-day who feel free to wander in every path which offers pictorial posies for the mere plucking. The art is divided into specialties; this man is at his best in character delineations, and that one has shown himself a master in portrayals of marine life and oceanic episode. Still another illustrator is noted for his skill in picturing the gay life of the metropolis, while the man in the studio next to him confines himself to suburban views and people, or perhaps portrays with exquisite delicacy the doings of an imaginative world and its fancied populace. None but the men of widest experience and broadest culture are entrusted to run the entire gamut of modern illustration, and those who are given this liberal privilege are not only the men most worthy in their art, but are the ones who would be most easily ruined by consignment to a solitary spot in the broad domain over which they are wont to wander at will. Absolute masters of all they survey. In this choice company Mr. de Thulstrup holds a prominent and respected place, and very few of his professional compeers are indeed more deeply deserving of the high honors thrust upon them.

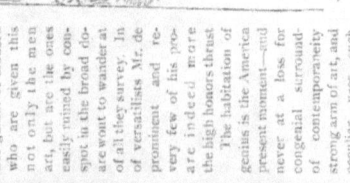

Study for a painting by T. de Thulstrup.
"IN FERAL OARS."

The habitation of genius is the America of the present moment—and never at a loss for congenial surroundings of contemporary strong arm of art, and peculiar uses such pleasing phases of Mr. de Thulstrup's of to-day—of the time domiciled he is amusement amid its ings. From his castle he reaches out a selects for his own strong types and every-day existence as most winsomely appeal to the numberless delvers in current illustrated journalism. He is still a young man, is Mr. de Thulstrup—young as artists go—with a mind constantly engaged in conjuring new ideas and planning new campaigns in the realm of art. Life has a favorable aspect to him now, for to succeed in one's calling and receive the substantial awards which ride with success is more to the aspiring workman than all other pleasures. Happy in his life as in his art—if it be permissible or even necessary to separate the two—Mr. de Thulstrup is most deserving of congratulation. Of his future career as either a monochromatic or multichromatic artist one may forecast many things agreeable. Certain it is that further enlarging his scope of subjects and attaining his art to the deeper and more resonant chords of human nature, he may be sure in the future of holding the affection of the people whose present regard for him is purely one of admiration.

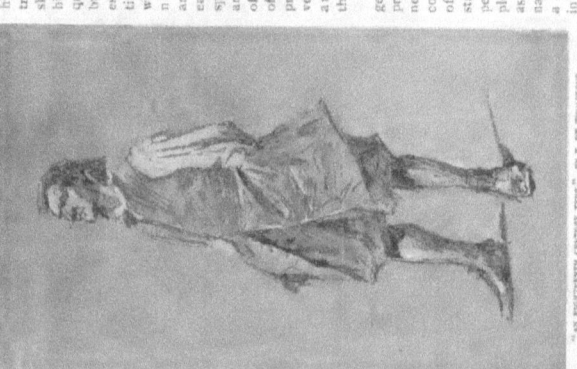

"AN EGYPTIAN CAMEL TYPE." BY T. DE THULSTRUP.

THE MORAN FAMILY

By Frances M. Benson

(With previously unpublished illustrations by most of them.)

"Nobility and genius run in families," it is said; but in this country, where titles point to a man's profession instead of his ancestors, genius marks higher than any mere patent of prefix or possession, and is the real nobility. One man of arts, letters, or sciences will raise a family from obscurity; two may immortalize it. It is rare indeed that any one family can boast of more than two clever members. It sometimes happens that when one member has distinguished himself to such an extent as to make the family name known in the land, a half dozen emulators spring up amongst his kindred, who immediately begin preening themselves in his reflected light, deceiving only themselves and the disinterested. When, however, the several members mark not separate and distinct fires for themselves as individuals, and attain prominence in each particular line, the radiance is no longer the flickering light of a single ray, but the fixed brilliancy of a many pointed star.

The Moran family is the most famous one in this part of the country for the extent and variety of the divine gifts lavished upon it by the custodian of genius. There are sixteen members of scape, animal, portrait, etchers, and illustrators, these are so near the they are known as the

It is pretty generally possible for an artist to drudgery of labor is genius, but the Apostles humblest branches of it is on record that his younger days, was house the customary mings, and that he did dreamer, carried a calm best known out-of-door continent; and Peter, apprenticeship with a

it who are marine, landscape and genre painters, and an even dozen of head of their class that "Twelve Apostles," believed that it is impracticable, that the beneath the dignity of have not disdained the their calling. Indeed, Edward, the elder, is not above giving a three coats and trimit well; that John, the era until he became the photographer on the the etcher, was the lithographer, drawing

on stone the foundations of flaming advertisements. Thomas, the student, was the delicate boy, but his later ambition stimulated his strength to such a degree that for thirty years he has averaged twelve and thirteen hours a day of close work, doing—besides his work in color—as much magazine and book illustrating as any living man except Doré.

These four may be called the original Morans. Their wives and sons have kept up the family traditions and extended its members by taking up painting under the tuition of husband and father, and, with the aid of family criticism, have done wonderfully good work. The severest test for a Moran picture is the family conclave, with its abundance of expert objection, and occasional bit of friendly praise, but in spite of discouragements, there is something in the atmosphere of the Moran studios that inspires success.

The original Morans, being musicians as well as artists, invariably married into musical families. One wife has a magnificent voice, another is a superb pianist, and the children have the genuine Moran touch upon stringed instruments. What reunions this versatile family can have! Besides the common meeting ground of pictures and music, there is among them a rare story-teller, brimming over with reminiscences, they have been the world over and brought back trophies and memories exhaustless, they have an intimate acquaintance with books and the makers of them. Most of them have a close knowledge of stage people and appurtenances, and have played in small parts enough to get the inner life of that form of the representation of nature.

It seems very like a poetic dream-life to go into the studios where velvet-coated genius divides its attention between a palette and a pipe. There are luxurious rugs, priceless tapestries, collections of swords, pipes, and musical instruments, with

AMERICAN ART AND ARTISTS.

here and there a gay bit of color or the glint of gewelled glass. You will notice, however, that there are not many divans or lounging places in these workshops. The occupants are toilers to whom the eight-hour system would be a vacation. They have made their way to the front by no freak of fortune, but by constant application.

The elder Morans possessed the way through discouragements of poverty and environment; the younger generation, though more favored in the selection of helpful surroundings, have had to work for an individuality that would save them from being considered mere copyists. "That is why we boys have cut loose from the marine and landscape of our fathers and gone in for figures," said one of the cleverest of the sons. "We were constantly hearing about 'second editions' and 'chips of the old block.' People criticised us according to what our fathers accomplished before us, and from the start we were handicapped by the great things expected of us. If our names had been Smith instead of Moran, it would have been vastly easier for us to make ourselves known on our own account."

In spite of the artistic trend of the family, Edward Moran, the leader and teacher of them all, does not believe in heredity; he claims it is all due to circumstances. Back of him, so far as anybody knows, there wasn't even a sign painter. The

From painting by Peter Moran. "SUMMER TIME."

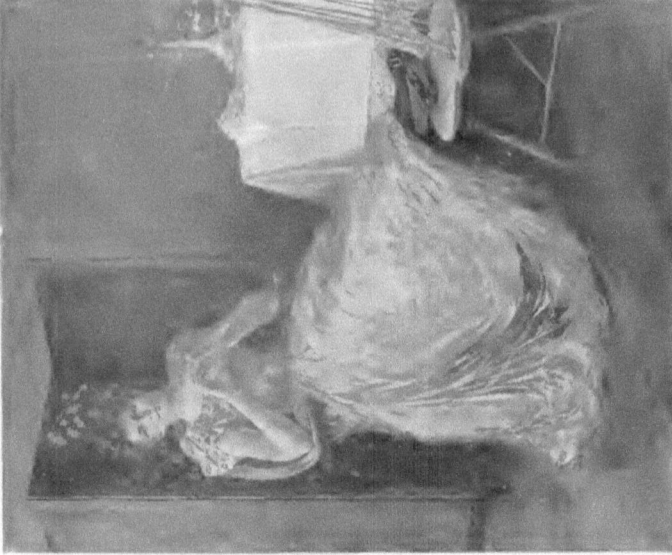

From painting by Paul Nimmo Moran. "A SIESTA."

From painting by Peter Moran. "PANORAMIC."

ancestors were handloom weavers in and about Lancashire, England, and the children of each generation grew up in the factories, with lives woven in and out with the woof of the week's work.

Edward was the eldest of fourteen children, and began to be a wage-earner from the time he could reach the web, as was customary in that district. His first lesson in art was from a French neighbor who was famous the country round for decorating the interiors of the modest homes with animals and sprawling vines, when he

HENDRICK HUDSON. FIRST SHIP ENTERING NEW YORK HARBOR, SEPTEMBER 11, 1609.
From a painting by Edward Moran.

AMERICAN ART AND ARTISTS.

was not wheeling potatoes to support his family. He found time to teach the nine-year-old Edward to cut marvellous figures from paper, and afterward to draw the outlines of them on walls and fences. Boylike, Edward did not stop there, but was guilty of tracing them even on the white cloth in his loom. One day, when his piece of cloth came to the measurement by booking, it was found that fifteen yards had been disfigured with charcoal sketches, and the graceless weaver, instead of being reprimanded as he probably deserved, was dismissed with the advice to drop the shuttle and take up the crayon altogether.

Soon after that the entire family came to America in search of new fortune and less crowded factories. They settled in Maryland, but the prospect of a continual grind was too much for Edward. There would be no opportunity to study, nothing to learn but machinery. He did up his belongings in one big red handkerchief, and, with twenty-five cents in his pocket, walked to Philadelphia, begging food as he could by the way. Then came the tug-of-war, with no money, no friends, no trade except the despised one of a factory hand; it was a prolonged struggle between starvation and the determination never to go back to the loom.

From painting by Edward Moran.
"SEA SHALLOWS."

He went to work with a cabinet-maker and afterward in a bronzing shop, and to this day the skilful artist is quite at home with the tools of those trades. Give him a glue-pot and a piece of string, and he will accomplish wonders. However, there was no painting in that, and he gave up a comfortable berth to take a job of house-painting, believing it to be a step along the line he had marked out for himself. Outdoor work in cold weather with a three-pound brush stiffening in his hands was more than he bargained for, and he finally went back to the factory, where the future painter of some of the grandest ocean scenes of his day was seemingly swallowed up in a superintendent of machinery, at the munificent salary of six dollars a week. It was his business to keep the looms in repair and in action, and if he was smart enough to do that and draw a little besides, he explained to his conscience that he was fulfilling the spirit of the law, if not the letter. One day the proprietor walked in while he was industriously engaged in finishing off a most interesting bit of black and white, and then there was a cool acknowledgment that the artist had been appropriating whole half-hours whenever the superintendent was able to crowd them in, and that he felt perfectly justified in defying man's regulations to make use of the talent the Creator had given him. Strange to say, the proprietor agreed with him, asked permission to call at his little bare room to look over the sketches already made, and finally gave him a letter of introduction to James Hamilton, a Philadelphia artist.

That was really the beginning of the end. Edward opened a studio in an attic room over a cigar store, with an entrance up a back alley, furnished it luxuriously with one chair and a New York Herald to sleep upon, and for three months alternately worked and starved. When he was the hungriest a lithographer asked him if he could draw on stone, and as he would have considered it dying in the face of Providence to acknowledge that he had never seen the stone referred to, he cheerfully accepted the conditions and the position, depending on his mother wit to help him through. He succeeded in earning seventeen dollars before the firm went to pieces, and in the meantime painted two pictures that were purchased by a Philadelphia collector. This gentleman gave him his first commission,

From etching by M. Nimmo Moran. "OPEN THE GATE."

From etching by M. Nimmo Moran. "A LONG LANE."

"THE COUNCILLOR." GOEBOIS.

From etching by Stephen J. Ferris

"AN OLD NEW ENGLAND ORCHARD."

From etching by Peter Moran

agreeing to pay him one hundred dollars for a certain amount of work properly executed.

When the family heard of this turn of fortune, they moved to Philadelphia in order to give the younger boys a chance. One after another they went into Edward's studio, and took their first lessons from the big brother who had been so brave-hearted and persevering, and to this day he is very proud of having started them on careers so successful.

It was in this studio, years after, that the celebrated "Bohemian Council" met once a week. The class was composed of actors, literary men, and musicians, and after rehearsal on Wednesday afternoon such men as Joe Jefferson, Couldock, Louis James, F. F. Mackey, Bishop, and like celebrities visiting Philadelphia, formed a semicircle around the teacher, who for one hour did all the work and all the talking. The first lesson was devoted to putting black and white together in irregular forms, teaching the use of the pigment. Next, each form was turned to accent, as the students close, to show how easily a definite object could be made from indefinite outlines. After that the three primary colors and white were used, then another color added, and so on, until in ten lessons the distinguished gentlemen were turned out full-fledged painters in theory, if not in practice. After each lesson was finished, there was smoking, music, readings, and story-telling until time to adjourn to lunch across the way. Newspaper men reported the witty sayings of the "Bohemian Council," and if the minutes were in existence to-day, they would be eagerly pounced upon by publishers and readers.

There is a very amusing illustration of the grit of the founder of the family, which, it is safe to say, pervades the whole. Edward became a member of the Academy of Fine Arts, which received a charter from the state of Pennsylvania, and was supposed to encourage home talent. Unfortunately for native artists, some of the directors had made a collection of German pictures, and when the exhibition opened, it was found that these importations filled the line to the exclusion of American artists, whether Academicians or not. Edward decided that he had some privileges as a member, and one of them was to show his contempt for cheap foreign pictures and the collectors of them. Varnishing day came, he had been invited to varnish, and as the committee did not specify the kind of var-

AMERICAN ART AND ARTISTS.

From painting by Edward Moran.
"LEIF ERIKSON'S EXPEDITION TO AMERICA IN THE YEAR 1001."

From water color sketch by Paul Sinebier Mersia.
"THE ROYAL COLOR."

From watercolor sketch by Leon Moran.
"THE MATADOR."

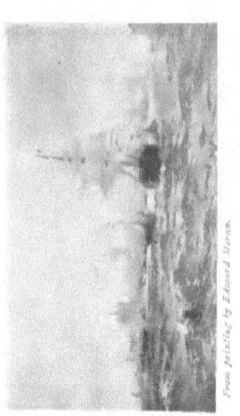

From painting by Edward Moran.
"NEW YORK, FROM THE BAY."

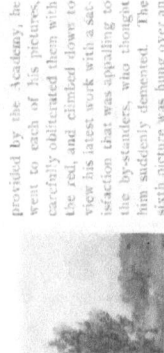

From painting by Juanita Moran.
"A STATEN ISLAND STUDY."

From painting by Edward Moran.
"SHIPS NOT A CALM."

nish to be used, Mr. Moran concluded to varnish his pictures to suit himself. He boiled together beer and bottled porter, adding dry light red until he had two quarts of an opaque liquid that was warranted to tint a canvas a beautiful red, without injuring the colors beneath it. Taking his "varnish" and a ladder provided by the Academy, he went to each of his pictures, carefully obliterated them with the red, and climbed down to view his latest work with a satisfaction that was appalling to the bystanders, who thought him suddenly demented. The sixth picture was hung over an opening where the ladder would not go, so he took a pocketknife and nearly cut the canvas from the frame.

Of course, there was a bedlam of indignation among the directors, but they decided the best way to punish the impudent artist was to let the scarred pictures hang throughout the exhibition, placarding them to the effect that the artist had been deliberately defaced them after hanging. The daily papers took it up, arguing for or against the American pictures that had been skied: people flocked to see the cause of the commotion and to side with foreign or domestic art, and, after all, the red pictures were the feature of the exhibition. The attendance was so large, the directors advertised to keep the exhibition open two weeks longer, but on what was to have been the closing day Edward Moran removed his pictures and let the directors continue the two weeks with the German views. The red canvases were laid on the studio floor, and with a bucket of water and a floor mop their faces were washed clean and bright, apparently none the worse for the unusual treatment. Matthew Baird, an art lover, whose patriotism and sense of justice had been aroused by the controversy, purchased the entire lot, rented prominent windows, and during the two weeks displayed them as " expatriated pictures." It was the best advertisement the artist

AMERICAN ART AND ARTISTS.

ever had, and instead of being crushed by the action of the hanging committee, Moran came out triumphant, richer by far in fame and pocket than when he went into the contest.

He had decided to leave Philadelphia, but before going wanted to show his good will toward the place. The government was asking help for the sufferers of the Franco-Prussian War. Moran gave an exhibition of all his pictures he could get together; got up the first illustrated catalogue printed in this country, drawing the reproductions on stone himself, and gave the proceeds of admission fee and catalogue sale to the fund, besides painting a special picture, called "The Relief

From painting by Thomas Moran. "A LONG ISLAND LANDSCAPE."

Ship entering Havre," which the Union League Club purchased for eight hundred dollars.

Annette, the wife of Edward, was a Southern girl who had merely dabbled with paint tubes in boarding-school fashion before she met her husband. Now she is his severest critic and, he says, his ablest one. Some of her landscapes have been reproduced as studies for others, but of recent years she has been content as a home-keeper rather than an artist.

Perry and Léon, their sons, are the youngest painters of prominence in New York. They work together until it is almost impossible to even pronounce the names separately, and yet there is a striking individuality in the work of each. One delights in figures of modern ladies, and the other in last-century gentlemen.

From painting by Edward Moran. "LIFEBOAT GOING TO THE WRECK."

Both have made a study of early English, French, and American costumes, and are in such demand for historical work that they have little time for anything else. They are conscientious workers, never descending to fantastic catchpenny methods to attract public favor, and with an exquisite use of color combine an unusual grace of motive.

Thomas Moran is the landscape painter of the family, and he is the hardest-working one of the lot. Although not of robust build, his endurance is marvellous, and he may frequently be found in his studio from early morning until midnight. There is not a process of photography, lithographing, or etching, but he is familiar with it, and his experiments since 1860 have been embodied, by request, in a collection of over four hundred pictures, prints, plates, and sketches, which will be exhibited at the Denver Art League as a complete history of the development of an American artist during the last thirty years. For his mastery of the processes, and his exact knowledge of cause and effect in nature, Thomas Moran has been dubbed the "scientist-artist, and his pictures of the Yellowstone are almost authoritative on rock formations and waterways. He does not believe in the merely faithful copying of what the eye sees. For that reason he spends months at a time studying how the hills are builded and the valleys cut away, and then comes home, to paint from memory and the laws of nature, the pictures that have no equal in American landscape.

Mary Nimmo Moran, who is one of the best women etchers in the country, never touched a brush to canvas until she married Thomas; but she found if they were to be congenial she must understand her husband's pursuits. Under his guidance she took up drawing, water-color and oil; and the family, children and all, went off on sketching trips, working out of doors during the long summer months. When Thomas went West for three months' roughing it among the Rockies, he

From a painting by Thomas Moran.

SCENE IN VENICE.

AMERICAN ART AND ARTISTS.

From painting by Edward Moran.
"AN ARAB."

coated six plates and suggested that his wife try her hand at etching while he was gone. It seemed utterly absurd to her to attempt it in the absence of her teacher, but as he had carefully explained the theory of the use of the point, the least she could do was to put it in practice. No indoor copying for her, though; she took her plates right out of doors, made a little preliminary drawing on paper, and went to work. When the husband returned, he pronounced these plates to be funny-looking things, and two of them not worth putting under acid. The other four were bitten, and there was a good deal of Moran amusement over what the perpetrator was frankly informal were "jolly queer etchings." She did not think much of them herself, but, strange to say, the Society of Painter-Etchers of New York decided them to be of great artistic merit, and on the strength of them elected the lady to membership. Then the same four were sent to the exhibition of Painter-Etchers of London, where they were all well hung, and the committee, supposing M. Nimmo Moran to be a man, voted him—or rather her—into membership with that august body—the first woman admitted to the charmed circle. Since then, Mrs. Moran has done about seventy plates, which have put her in the front rank of New York etchers.

Thomas and Mary Nimmo are perhaps the most noted couple of the family, but their two daughters inherit the talent for music and not for art. The son Paul has both gifts to a generous degree, being a remarkably fine violinist, one of the best mandolinists in the city, and an artist as well. He has not had the life-long studio-training given his cousins, because his father was afraid of biasing his career, insisting that he would rather his son should be a good bricklayer from choice than a poor artist from influence. In obedience to the parental wish, Paul went about the world searching for an education and a vocation, but finally returned with the conviction that he would rather be a poverty-stricken artist, if need be, than make money in any other profession, and now father and son are working side by side. Paul is essentially a painter of American subjects, believing there is ample opportunity for the native brush in the varying types of different sections.

Peter Moran is the animal painter and etcher. Being the youngest of the original four, he followed the example of his elders,

From water-color sketch by Percy Moran.
"WAITING FOR BREAKFAST."

learning lithographing and engraving, but the studio of Edward and Thomas had more attraction for him than the store, and he spent every spare moment making experiments with his brothers' paints. He tried marines with Edward and landscapes with Tom, and soon became convinced that he would succeed in neither. Animals were undoubtedly his forte. He began the study of animal anatomy, and in the meantime earned a living as a scene painter and as an actor of small parts with Mrs. John Drew in the Philadelphia theatre. When he had put by sufficient means for a trip to England, he went over to study the works of Landseer and Constable, with an occasional landscape as a background, and when he returned, received a medal at the Centennial Exhibition for his picture, "The Return of the Herd."

In his early etching was an entirely neglected art, and Peter's collection of one on exhibition in fourteen seventy-fourteen was twenty-fourteen was the American department, in all the enthusiasm of the revival of etching, few have been more prolific with the point than he, over two hundred plates going out with his signature, including many views of the extreme West, where he lived for several years among Indians and Mexicans. He is now president of the Philadelphia Society of Etchers, vice-president of the Art Club, and a teacher of painting, etching, and composition in the Woman's Art School, keeping up the family reputation for industry.

Peter Moran's wife was one of his best scholars, but has always been reluctant to enter the public lists. She has done a large number of etchings, noticeable for boldness of line and picturesque effects, but it has been more to keep in touch with her husband than to acquire fame or fortune. Their son Charles, like a true Moran, began making pictures before he was out of his swaddling clothes, and bids fair to become one of the illustrators of the future.

John Moran was the first, and for many years the only artistic landscape photographer in America. He was sent by the government on the expedition to the Isthmus of Darien, and around the globe to Cape Town during the transit of Venus. The family bent was strong in him, however, and he developed into a landscape painter after all. His pictures are rarely seen, because he is

From painting by Edward Moran.
"SUNDOWN."

AMERICAN ART AND ARTISTS.

one of those delightfully impractical geniuses one reads about—he is in the world but not of it. His life is bound between book covers, and when he comes in contact with the outside existence, it is as a leaf torn from the binding, fluttering aimlessly in the wind. Of his two sons, Horace is a designer and Sidney an illustrator.

There is one other member of the Moran family who deserves mention, because as a sister of the original four she brought into the family, by marriage, the best portrait painter and etcher in Philadelphia. Elizabeth Moran Ferris has done little herself with brush or pencil, but, as she once expressed it, she has "held the light for husband and son to work by, standing between them and the petty cares of life, that they might pursue their work unhampered." Stephen J. Ferris, the husband, is equally well known for his portraits in oil or water color, and etchings, both originals and reproductions. Gerome Ferris, the son, is an exceedingly good colorist, with the true artist soul. His figures are the daintiest creations imaginable, and his drawing is strong and free.

Such is a brief outline of the working members of the Moran family.

Known chiefly as manipulators of brush and pigment, they are, almost to an individual, practised and original illustrators. In this difficult and exacting branch of art not a few of the Morans have won their first laurels and earned their first dollars. Of the entire family, however, Thomas Moran is the most widely known and most versatile illustrator. Long years ago—in the fifties, to be definite—Thomas Moran, after a fashion of his own, necessarily crude and unsatisfactory at that time, produced effects with metal plates and printing blocks that are to-day, in a more perfect form, in almost universal employment. Mr. Moran's predilection in the graphic arts was—and, indeed, is now, unless mistake has been made—for etching and plain lithography. With the other members of the Moran clan, reproductive work has been confined for the most part to pen-and-ink drawing.

From painting by Leon Moran.   "THE SACRIFICIAL MEADOW."

Percy and Leon Moran have won great distinction as illustrators, the deftness of their execution and the daintiness of their themes making their work exceptionally attractive to publishers.

What one has to consider in reviewing the achievements of this remarkable family of artists is not so much the vastness of its collective genius as the unceasing industry and enormous production of its individual members. In all the years that the Morans of one branch and another have engaged in artistic performance there has been no discoverable waning of either power or accomplishment on the part of any of them. With the passing of each year the oldest as well as the youngest of this gifted circle of relatives give indications of ripening knowledge and more extended skill. It is as if these Morans were a tribe of hunters who yearly went in quest of precious prey, each of the tribe betaking himself or herself to a section of the land left unexplored, and all returning to a common rendezvous at a given time, tumbling their treasures before the delighted eyes of the public, and seeking for themselves so little credit for their pains, that many are apt to forget the contented explorers in viewing the outcome of their intelligent exploration.

But to cast off metaphor for lucid facts, let it be noted, in summing up the value of the Moran family to contemporary art, that whatever their failures, their shortcomings, or their fruitless ambitions, they were at no time guilty of insincerity or intolerance for the ways of others. To what extent this breadth of mental view has enabled them, one and all, to attain artistic honor and renown it is not for the writer to assert. That each one of them is deserving of whatever part of beneficent fortune has fallen to his or her lot, cannot be denied by those who know the commons geniality, the fresh talent, and the honesty of effort which so strongly characterizes this group of blood-bonded artists. The history of the Moran family is to a great extent the history of American art. That the future aesthetic production of this country will also embrace a long line of Morans is not improbable, and if the Morans of the future are as gifted as those of the present their coming is to be earnestly hoped for.

But, come what may, the work which bears the signature of any of the Morans will unquestionably be worthy of notice and have upon it the thumb-marks of talent. They are a rare company, are these Morans, and what they have done in the past, as well as what they are likely to do in time to come, will at least be individual, if not wholly remarkable. But what commendation could be greater?

From etching by Emily Moran.   "VENETIA."

AMERICAN ART AND ARTISTS.

RETURN FROM THE MEADOW.
From a painting by Peter Moran.

36

AMERICAN ART AND ARTISTS.

A DECORATIVE ILLUSTRATOR.

By PERRITON MAXWELL.

(With original illustrations by George Wharton Edwards.)

Some months less than thirty years ago there lived and frolicked in the little town of Fairhaven, Connecticut, a bright-eyed, brown-haired youngster who developed, along with a remarkably robust appetite and an equally robust love of fun, a richly dowered fancy for decorating local barn-doors, well-curbs, and dog-houses with the aid of chalk or charcoal and in the most approved style of untutored boy art. The boy, careless and happy, no longer exists, but his brisk imagination, his aptitude for limning pleasing pictures, and his wholesome affection for humor still remain and flourish vigorously in the person of the man whom the art world knows to-day as George Wharton Edwards—illustrator, painter, and writer.

About the time that the awful discovery young Edwards made that there were no more dogs and curbstones in the immediate neighborhood of his home which had not at some period offered a smooth and tempting medium for his budding artistry, he tendered to those who would give him ear a complete confession of his innermost desire to wield the artist's brush, live under a roof of glass, and wear a palette on his thumb. It was not very long after this open avowal of his chief ambition that there

began to appear in the magazines odd bits of illustration, sparkling, strengthful, and wholly new. These drawings gave birth to no little comment in circles of art, and speculation was fired by the query as to win this new man brandishing the name of Edwards could be, and from whence he hailed. Curiosity upon this point was soon appeased. The name of the new-comer appeared with pleasing frequency upon charming sketches in all the foremost periodicals of the day, and now—well, it is quite exceptional if one can pick up an important illustrated magazine at random and fail to find between its covers at least one picture done in line or "wash," and signed by George Wharton Edwards.

With the sprouting of his first mustache Mr. Edwards came to New York, bringing with him a shrivelled purse and a generous fund of hope for great artistic success. He made decorative designing his specialty at the outset, believing that in this department of practical æsthetics lay the pleasantest and most immediate monetary rewards. In this special line he displayed at an early day that rare good taste, that refined feeling for form beauty, and the same acute and subtle imagination which have all along distinguished his work. The effect of this early practice in the department of the decorative has been unmistakably exploited in every one of the artist's serious productions. However irksome may have been these early endeavors, the amount of good it has done Mr. Edwards in an artistic way is quite incalculable, and not to be regretted by those who discern and understand the best that is in his pictorial output. To be sure, his style has changed perceptibly with the passing of the years, there is less floridity and fullment now than in by-gone days, but none

"THE STEED."

"THE BALLET GIRL."

"SANS CULOTTE."

AMERICAN ART AND ARTISTS.

"A FIELD OF CORN."

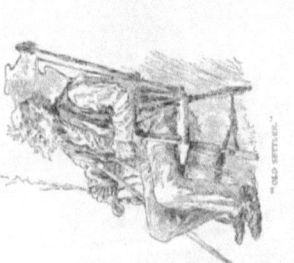

"OLD COTTON."

of his fellow-illustrators—or brushmen, for the matter of this—has surpassed him in the freshness of his fancy or the gracefulness of his execution.

It was the good fortune of Mr. Edwards that he was not compelled to waste the valuable hours of his youth in a foreign art-school. He would have gained but little from the meagre curriculum of the big Parisian or Munich ateliers. His touch might have become more bold, but then the rare quality of delicacy which we most admire in this man's work would be absent. He handled the draughtsman's tools by a sort of instinct, and by instinct learned to draw. He taught himself how to swim in the great and turbulent sea of art by first plunging into the deepest part of it. His courage and industry have enabled him to keep upon the surface almost from the start.

It was a happy day when the youthful Edwards threw off the shackles of one publisher to work for the whole fraternity of book and magazine makers. The

"EARLY MORNING."

Society of American Artists, 1892

later were not slow to appreciate the products of his facile pencil. When assured of the sweets of success, he decided to be something of a painter as well as an illustrator of merit. Though to-day illustrative work is Mr. Edwards' prime vocation, painting is to him something more than a mere matter of recreation. Year after year witnesses the completion of at least one notable canvas, to say nothing of a dozen or more breezy water-colors and an occasional pastel. The most pleasing thing about Mr. Edwards' monochromatic pieces is the dash he gets into them; the deftness of his handling and the cunning of his conception, which tickle the fancy and delight the eye. In these accomplishments he reminds us to a certain extent of Louis Leloir, with something of the frolful fantasy and rich grotesqueries of Doré's earlier period. But in Mr. Edwards' work is that which Leloir never owned, and that which Doré sought but could not attain—the force of feeling in the first; the knack of linear accuracy in the last. Mr. Edwards' pictorial expression is that of the man who has something to say, and understands how to convey his message with the clearness of graphic speech and the precision of artistic statement.

About ten years ago Mr. Edwards made an unconventional journey in search of the picturesque through Belgium, Holland, England, France, and Spain: a journey that inspired many clever illustrations and a score of brilliant short stories; for be it known of those who are not informed in the matter, that Mr. Edwards is quite as ready and refreshing with his writer's pen as with his artist's brush and pencil.

He has since spent three years in Holland and several summers in the less-frequented parts of France, to the vast enrichment of his private portfolios and the pages of the periodicals. Among the good things of life that have fallen within the grasp of Mr. Edwards are a luxurious studio, an intense affection for his work, an amiable temperament, and a boxful of medals won by the merit of as many charming pictures. Though still a comparatively young man, he has turned out of hand much that an older artist might claim with pardonable pride. His art is his own.

It remains for the future to reveal whether or not the indications which now point to an exceptionally brilliant career will be fulfilled in Mr. Edwards. To say that his accomplishments up to the present moment have been as notable as they have been praiseworthy does not carry with it the implication that Mr. Edwards has not in store for us numerous novel and brilliant pictureents. The subjects selected by him are in the main simple in character, though often daring in composition and unique in treatment. But in mentally reviewing all his work I can recall nothing that is not in a cheerful vein; and one owes much to the man who can cast a ray of sunshine from his brush. There is something more definite than mere expectation—something, indeed, that is tantamount to a conviction of greater things to come—springing from an examination of Mr. Edwards' more notable feats in black and white. An illustrator who has the boon of an exuberant imagination and the acquired faculty of abounding artistic skill is lifted much above his professional fellows even in these days of widespread talent and manifold endeavors.

"BRITTANY PEASANTS, BY SEA."

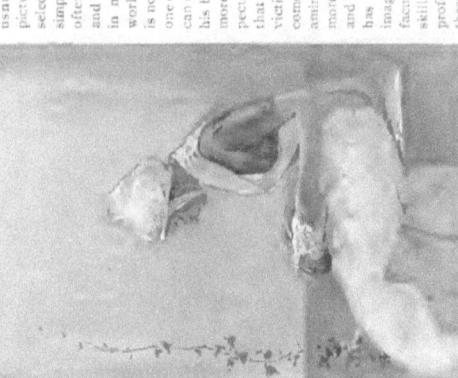

"A DUTCH INTERIOR."

AMERICAN ART AND ARTISTS.

and such is the present status of George Wharton Edwards in the thriving kingdom of native art. To men of his mould one may confidently turn for a clear and concise exposition of the best that exists at the moment in American illustration.

It has often been feared, none the less, by those who are at the pains to closely study and analyze the handicraft of Mr. Edwards, that a talent so diversified as is his may eventually lead him from whatever strength of personality he now possesses, that the very charm of his drawings—this charm being definable as unlikeness and novelty of execution—may prove their ultimate unacceptability. While it might be an easy task for Mr. Edwards to unwittingly demolish himself by his own versatility, such a fate is quite unlikely to befall him now, for he has shown in his work of late a jealous regard for certain peculiarities of style denoting clearly his recognition of a possible calamity. The sketches which form an accompaniment to these remarks very forcibly demonstrate Mr. Edwards' artistry. While obtaining similar results do not look for Mr. Edwards himself that this and that needs look for Mr. Edwards himself that this and that

The perfect case with his effect in the sketch of the pleasing *chic* of the

"DIAMOND FIELDS."

"PANS."

the mobile quality of Mr. Edwards' artistry. While his many methods of obtaining similar results do not in any instance suggest, there is such a wide variance appearance that one must assure a fisher boy on page 85; character notes in his frui-tory peasants on page 90, and the fine decorative quality of his painting "Early Moonrise," reproduced on page 87, declare their maker a man of singular artistic acumen. It would be difficult indeed to get greater expression with slighter effort than Mr. Edwards has done with a few swift pen strokes in his little sketch of "Unc' Remus." In the "Old Settler" the character is much more laboriously obtained, and the whole effect less spontaneous and forceful, but the truth of nature is faithfully recorded. Based on the actualities of nature, Mr. Edwards builds his pictorial themes as Aldrich, Dobson, and Swinburne build their rhymes—fusing with facts that subtle something which, for lack of terms more comprehensive, we call the poetic instinct or a feeling for the finer harmonies of art. No happier union in art can be imagined than that which comes about at long intervals between fancy and fact; it is the

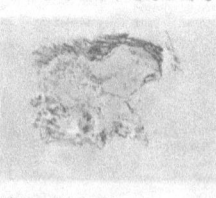

"TOWARDS SAN PEDRO."

marriage of Adonis and the grocer's daughter on the next block.

After all, one can only take what is put forth, and if an artist has done his work with some show of sincerity, he is worthy of the highest praise. A conscientious person is bound to accomplish many creditable things, and when with conscience an artist mixes uncommon natural gifts he bests himself for the most coveted places of his profession. To George Wharton Edwards must be tendered the praise of those who love art for its sake as well as for its utility. He has grasped the lessons, severe and inspiring, taught by art, and has worked to such knowledge the information vouchsafed those only who have battled on the field of commercial affairs. In a phrase, Mr. Edwards has in him those laudable qualities which, rightly cultivated, produce great artists who occasionally are also great men.

The commendable care with which Mr. Edwards turns out of hand his most trying, as well as his most ambitious picture-merits, is a fine lesson to tyros. It is not enough for him to paint an important picture with a lavishment of his greatest skill; he is entirely unsatisfied unless he has put in his minor efforts the same consideration, the same solicitude for the general effect of the finished production. Not by this, however, do I mean that his work is labored and overwrought, for the contrary is true; and in the *chic* and airy execution of both his paintings and illustrations lies his main power.

"AN OLD SETTLER."

AMERICAN ART AND ARTISTS.

AN ALL-AROUND ARTIST.

By F. Hopkinson Smith.

(With original illustrations by Charles S. Reinhart.)

"F. HOPKINSON SMITH."

The successful illustrator of to-day must be a man of pronounced originality of thought. He must not only see clearly, interpret unerringly, and express forcibly the subject matter of the author, but his own personality must be strong enough and pronounced enough to make his work individual, if not wholly unique. This personality may be a disagreeable personality, either upon the ground of good taste, morality, or refinement, but it will never become commonplace.

A coarse-minded man will invariably depict his women with a touch of allurement hidden somewhere beneath the eyelids or corsage. The religious devotee will outline his heroine in serene and lofty pose, and the purely classical, intellectual student will give her the brow of Diana and the poise and coldness of a Greek goddess. Between every touch of each man's brush one will read something of the artist's inner self.

The painter, therefore, who has the purest and best ideals of life is safest to be entrusted with the work of an equally pure and high-minded author: it would be difficult to imagine Ary Scheffer illustrating Zola's "Nana," or Vibert making serious studies of the early martyrs.

In this connection the illustrator is to a certain extent a critic, or, to be more exact, an essayist. One false stroke unsettles the reader's mind, and destroys the writer's conception.

"A STREET IN GRANADA."

The responsibility then becomes a grave one, publisher, and author being interested in a perfect harmony of thought and interpretation between the pen of the writer and the brush of the draughtsman.

Next to the equipment of heart comes the equipment of mind. An all-around illustrator, to be perfect in his art, must be a historian, must know costumes and furniture, arms, implements and interiors, architecture, topography of the several localities, habits of the

"MOORISH WATER-WHEEL, VALENCIA."

"CHARLES S. REINHART."

"A PATIO IN GRANADA."

41

"A POINT BY A CHARMING BEAUTY."

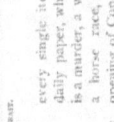

A PORTRAIT.

"LE TRÉPORT."

people and their economies of life. He must, at the same time, be thoroughly conversant with all the forms and requirements of the society immediately about him. He must be a man of the world, know the clubs, the cafés, and counting-rooms as well as he does the boudoir, the afternoon tea, and tennis field. He must keep pace with the fashions, and recognise the difference between a Prince Albert coat worn with a silk hat and high collar, and the enormity of the same garment with a turn down collar and a Derby. He must be able to harness a coach, yoke a pair of oxen, or tuck the pillows in a baby carriage, must hunt, fish, and ride cross country; in short, be thoroughly equipped to express, at a moment's notice, in form and color, every single item in a daily paper, whether it is a murder, a wedding, a horse race, or the opening of Congress.

Of course, if he chooses, he can be a specialist, and only do pretty girls in flowing gowns, without backgrounds or accessories. Or he can be an animal painter, with a limited experience of coaching parades and dog shows, with all the beautiful women and correct fashions left out; or a

AMERICAN ART AND ARTISTS.

"WATCHING FOR THE ENEMY."

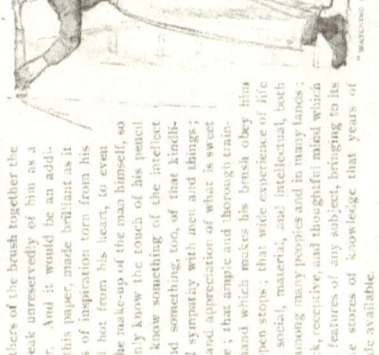

"A COQUETTE OF OTHER DAYS."

"IN REPOSE."

nautical man, and paint yachts and ocean craft; but if he is to aspire to the position of an all around illustrator, he must be as thoroughly equipped as the leading editor of a great metropolitan daily, who in five minutes after the receipt of news from any quarter of the globe, can give you a thoroughly digested, thoughtful commentary, which will carry interest and perhaps convictions the next day to a city full of readers.

It will be admitted at once that however rare such a man may be in journalistic fields, even when only a purely intellectual outfit is required, it is infinitely more rare to find these same qualities in a man with the additional knowledge of the painter's art. A knowledge, too, that is not superficial or half acquired, but as thoroughly mastered as the keyboard of the instrument of a great pianist, or the type on a printed page.

That the world has given us few such men is not to be wondered at when we realize that the art of the illustrator is hardly twenty years old, and that only in the past decade has it taken its place as one of the great progressive arts of the century. It really has only kept step with photography on wood, with the modern school of wood-engravers, and the more recent photo-reproductive processes; and last, and by no means least, with the development of the three or four great magazines which spread broadcast, every year, over the length and breadth of our land literally millions of copies filled with pictures of a quality, finish, and artistic excellence never conceived of a score of years ago.

Among the men of our time who, through this very equipment of heart, mind, and training, have risen to the very first rank in their profession, and who by their strong personality, thorough artistic qualities, and felicity of expression, still hold that position by the side of the foremost illustrators of the day, stands our own Charles Stanley Reinhart.

Were there space, it would be quite within the province of one who has known him intimately from his very earliest art life, and who has during all that time been associated with him in the closest and tenderest ties that bind brothers of the brush together the world over, to speak unreservedly of him as a man and a painter. And it would be an additional delight in this paper, made brilliant as it is by little scraps of inspiration torn from his sketch books and hot from his heart, to even slightly analyze the make-up of the man himself, so that those who only know the touch of his pencil and brush may know something of the kindliness of heart and sympathy with men and things; that innate love and true appreciation of what is sweet and good and true; that ample and thorough training of eye and hand which makes his brush obey him like a flute with open stops; that wide experience of life in all its phases, social, material, and intellectual, both here and abroad, among many peoples and in many lands; and last, that quick, receptive, and thoughtful mind which seizes the salient features of any subject, bringing to its adornment all the stores of knowledge that years of research have made available.

NOTE.—Mr. Reinhart is a native of Pennsylvania, and was born in Pittsburg in 1844. He is related to that very admirable patriot and craftsman, Benjamin Franklin. The particular branch of the Reinhart family from which our illustrator comes has been noted for several generations for its artistic proclivities. The story runs that young Charles' father was wont to hold the future illustrator on the paternal knee and guide the infantile hand through the intricacies of picture-ment. The mother of Charles was not, however, in favor of art as a career. To her it was a pursuit in which the emoluments were out of all proportion to the skill and effort necessitated.

While young Reinhart was debating in his mind whether he should take up the cross of art and drag it to the bitter or vic-

AMERICAN ART AND ARTISTS.

torious end, the War of the Rebellion broke forth, and turned the thoughts of all men into one common channel. In the full flush of his youth Reinhart entered the corps commanded by Col. Tom Scott, which had as its chief duty the transportation of the Union troops. Notwithstanding the severe responsibilities thrown upon him and the strange vicissitudes of war, Reinhart never lost sight of his early ambition, and devoted every moment of his leisure to sketching from nature and mapping out his future career of art. After three years service in the army, with the "late unpleasantness" quite on the wane, Reinhart turned seriously to art, and, though for some time his thoughts wavered by his engagement in a Pittsburg steel factory, he eventually broke loose from all commercial undertakings and sailed for Europe and artistic renown. This was in 1868, and from that time forward he has travelled and studied in various parts of the world, chiefly in the interests of the publishing house of Harper & Brothers, in whose publications the bulk of his work has appeared.

It is interesting to know that the first drawing of any positive merit ever made by Mr. Reinhart was suggested by a question of religion which agitated the country shortly after war times. This ambitious effort of the embryonic illustrator was sent to Harper's Weekly, and the artist sat down in fear and trembling to await the decision of the art editor of that noted journal. A response soon came back, and the substance of it was that, while the nature of the drawing made it impossible to publish it as an illustration to the Weekly, the submitted picture was of such decided artistic value that the unknown draughtsman would be pleased to have the clever but Harpers would enter their establishment and illustrate their several periodicals. This was the stepping-stone to Mr. Reinhart's successful career. From these early days he has climbed upward with unswerving purpose and commendable aims. His work is in the main of a serious, thoughtful character, though no one would think of denying him a fine sense of humor. His women are dainty, well-dressed persons who, you are certain, can engage you in pleasant conversation, and his men are hardly but gentlemanly persons. Indeed, of all the many hundreds of types of men and women that Mr. Reinhart has delineated, there are few whose pencilled presentments do not convince one that they have blood in their bodies and marrow in their bones. There are many illustrators to these days, and skill with the drawing-pen is not a lacking quality in the world of art; are most of our industrious black-and-whites artists, few can claim anything like equality with Mr. Reinhart.

"MORNING SOAP."

"THE WAR CLUB EXHIBITED."
(WILLIAM M. CHASE AND J. R. WEGUELIN.)

"EN BRETAGNE."

In the matter of versatility and general knowledge of the world and its proper reflection through the medium of the pictorial press. He has a ready grasp of needful essentials in monochromatic work. His study of human nature has not been a vain pursuit. He is a prober into the mysteries of human motives and emotions, and frequently he brings to the surface a hidden phase of feeling which he is not slow to exploit pictorially. He appreciates the whimsicalities of the great human play in which most of us have a lively part. He is an artist of many accomplishments, and these, with his genuine and assertive personality, make him artistically eminent, which he is likely to be to the end.—ED.

A DELINEATOR OF LIFE.

By Perriton Maxwell.

(With original illustrations by Albert E. Wenzell.)

CHARACTER and individuality are no common attributes of current illustrative art. The men whose monochromatic productions may be instantly recognized apart from their signatures are few and far removed in thought from one another. Great as is the output of the pictorial press to-day and lofty as is the standard of picturement in black and white, a mere sample of illustrators stand conspicuous among their fellows by reason of decided originality of view and pronounced methods of working. It must be granted that the medium than equal to the genius of the past in the field of illustration. But this being true, the fact but serves to emphasize the talents of those who tion; he has a distinction reaching above the commonmakes no great boast of his fe-

From the level of Albert B. Wenzell and grace. His is fears no competition, quite his own and yet licitous craftsmanship. His competence of hand and eye finds nourishment in the poetry, humor, charm, and grace of existing things and persons. His deepest interest lies in modern men and women and their exhibition manners. The woman of society is his especial joy. In her he has discovered a replete vocabulary of the brush and pen, from which he constructs an engaging reading. He happily records for our pleasure the refinements of her manners and surroundings, and this with an infinite skill. Mr. Wenzell has a keen and appreciative eye for a petite woman, or one who is at least well gowned, and can make a handsome man in funereal evening dress appear positively picturesque. We need no extraneous assurance that prettiness and elegance are inevitably part and parcel of Mr. Wenzell's personage. We can be very certain that his figures are at all times naturally occupied. Their ways are inctured with the expected affectation of consciously beautiful women and consciously clever men; but they do not bring to mind the professional postures of the studio, who are graceful (in their hired robes) at fifty cents per hour.

Mr. Wenzell may be most aptly described as a conscientious historian of American polite society; a chronicler who fixes facts with pigment and draughting pen. He is a redactor of drawing-room episodes, trifling perhaps in the light of intrinsic meaning, but wholly agreeable in their sparkling execution, in their suggestiveness of gayety and good living; in their effect of many colors conjured from a simple palette of black and white. Schooled in Munich, Mr. Wenzell is naturally prone to solid methods of brush manipulation. He has apparently rid himself of the less countenable traits of German art and teaching, and holds to that which may be logically proven good. There is more gladness in his heart over the successful drawing of a woman's back

"A HELLOMISTER FROM STEREALVILLE."

hair, the rigidly creased trousers of a carpet knight, a Renaissance scroll or a Louis XV. screen, than in the making of twenty lofty themes foreign to his accepted sphere of art. It gives Mr. Wenzell an exquisite pleasure to note the sheen of a silken skirt, the curve of a well-proportioned arm, the soft, white shoulders of a healthy woman, and the mirrored blaze of a hundred waxen candles. There is a sort of carelessness for him in gilt-legged chairs and silver ornamented divans; its fondness for the long thin shadows thrown on lightly polished floors asserts itself continually. His drawings are like pictured panels ingeniously inlaid with jewels.

Personally considered, Albert B. Wenzell is frank in manner, courteous, considerate, and broad-minded. He is somewhat above the medium stature, has the bearing of a man of the world, is on the sunny side of thirty, and lives in Flushing, L. I. Mr. Wenzell was born in Detroit, Mich., and left there at an early age to study under various masters in Munich. His most notable work has graced the pages of Life, though many recent and very excellent drawings have appeared in The Century, The Cosmopolitan, and Godey's Magazine.

Interrogating nature at every stroke, recording the brighter realities of easy life, indefatigably courting the true, the bright, and the graceful, it is not to be questioned that his work has vastly influenced the man and formed his thought to a cordial way of viewing things. Despite the fact that Mr. Wenzell works almost entirely in monochrome, his color sense is deeply developed. Of late many of the brilliant pictures of this artist seen in the magazines have been re-

"LOVERS."

produced from colored originals. As an illustrator Mr. Wenzell is highly distinguished, and this distinction has come through painstaking, thoughtful effort. This offers rare encouragement for his future as a painter pure and simple. As it is, Albert B. Wenzell is an artist to whom we may confidently look for the upholdment of the best principles and highest aims of the illustrators' ever-enlarging profession, and one in whom those who recognize art as an essential factor of life find many just reasons for pride.

With a style which, if not absolutely unique, is, however, wholly of himself, and a future prospect in his art that might reasonably be coveted by many of his confrères, Mr. Wenzell is advanced well along that great highway which leads to the city of success.

A COMPOSITION STUDY.

Drawn by Albert E. Wenzell.

AMERICAN ART AND ARTISTS.

THE ART STUDENTS' LEAGUE, OF NEW YORK.

By CHARLES DE KAY.

(With original illustrations by prominent members.)

"FISHWIVES."

Drawn by Joseph Lauber.

"A STUDY IN SEPIA."

Drawn by Walter Oreeb.

Drawn by F. Carroll Beckwith.

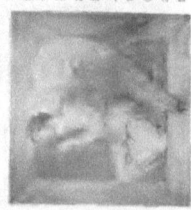

"PRAYING NUNS."

Drawn by Ella Condie Lamb.

THERE are many schools of art in the United States, but when I have done I hope that no one will grudge the Art Students' League of New York the place of honor at the head of all those schools, which it is the purpose of this magazine to chronicle in turn.

Several broad claims may be advanced at once to set at rest any lurking doubt as to the right of this school to carry the banner. *In primis* it has never been beholden to any amateur or outsider for aid, but has always paid its own way. *In secundis* it presents the type of a perfected democracy in which each person does something for the good of the whole, officers are not paid and as few offices as possible exist. *In tertiis* it is already old enough to be the model on which most of the independent art schools of the country have been formed, and to antedate the Society of American Artists of New York. The Art Students' League was called into existence eighteen years ago this June in Mr. Wilmarth's studio, No. 51 West Tenth Street, by thirty persons, who from their point of view saw no hope of reform in the methods of the Academy of Design, and resolved to have complete freedom from interference on the part of the conservative artists who ruled the Academy. It is the general impression, which I confess to have shared, that the League grew from, or was promoted by, the Society of American Artists; but rather was the reverse the case. For not a few of those who started the League aided in establishing the Society two years later. The League began before the Centennial Exhibition in Philadelphia; the Society followed it. And even now, when the Society has become so strong, when the Architectural League has been established, and these two in alliance with the students have so gallantly and cleverly founded the Fine Arts Society,— which of those organizations, I ask the reader to guess, does most to shoulder the burden

AMERICAN ART AND ARTISTS.

AMERICAN ART AND ARTISTS.

of debt and annual expenses? Assuredly, the Art Students' League.

In its present quarters, 215 West Fifty-Seventh Street, the League pays a rent of $9,000, yet has to have rooms outside to accommodate the overflow of scholars. Last year its income was $30,000,

yet, by a peculiar system of fees, an earnest worker gradually reduces the annual cost of his tuition to a nominal sum. At first the charge is eight dollars per month, but if the student becomes a member of the League—quite another matter from being in the schools—the cost is diminished one quarter. At the end of five years the member pays but four dollars a month.

Again, all materials used by sculptors and painters are for sale on the premises by the League's shopkeeper at very near the cost price, a lunch roomer is run on the same principle, and for eight cents that excellent food can be had close at hand at the lowest cost, making it difficult for scholars to run their health by neglecting their meals, as they did once upon a time.

The League has no debts. During the school year to April, 1893, the enrolled pupils numbered 1,124, and the average daily attendance was 450. Artists interested in the League give their time without charge for instruction. There is a monthly meeting of the members for business and relaxation, and once a year the

AMERICAN ART AND ARTISTS.

"AN AMERICAN QUEEN."

Drawn by J. Carroll Beckwith.

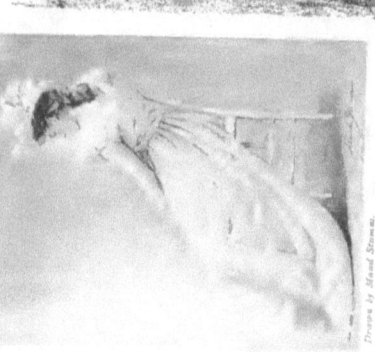

"BABY BROWN."

Drawn by Maud Stumm.

Drawn by A. C. Redwood.

season ends with a ball in fancy dresses. The League has a library and reading-room; during the last year it has saved so much on its various coöperative departments as to permit of a reduction of the fees from pupils, and an increase of wages to models and servants.

A word as to the school day. What are called antique classes, that is, elementary classes in drawing, are in progress morning, afternoon and night. Two painting classes, which are practically for instruction in portraiture, are in session every morning, two every afternoon. At 4.30 p.m. two sketch classes begin work from the draped model. Of life classes working from the nude or draped model there are no less than eleven daily; namely, six in the morning, two in the afternoon, and three at night

These classes vary from fifteen to thirty in number, according to the size of the room. Details like these are necessary in order to understand how so many pupils are able to get instruction in that small portion of the Fine Arts Society, where the League disposes of 12,000 square feet of floor only, and also how it is that the League is so prosperous in its finances. But the sphere of influence of this school has not merely embraced the United States; it has moved with even greater certainty eastward across the Atlantic, and infected Paris and Munich with a communistic, democratic leaven, so far as the students of art are concerned. The philosophic observer may even point to the split in the great artistic army of Paris into the new Salon and the old as a movement which may be traced back through the Society of American Artists to the Art Students' League in New York. Munich and Berlin have caught the infection of independence, while in the immediate American art colony of Paris, coöperation and self-support have been fairly successful. These things being so, what school in America has a better right to lead the van?

The President of the League is Mr. Joe Evans; the Vice-Presidents are Miss Emily Sudo and Mr. George W. Breck. The corresponding secretary is Miss Vir-

AMERICAN ART AND ARTISTS.

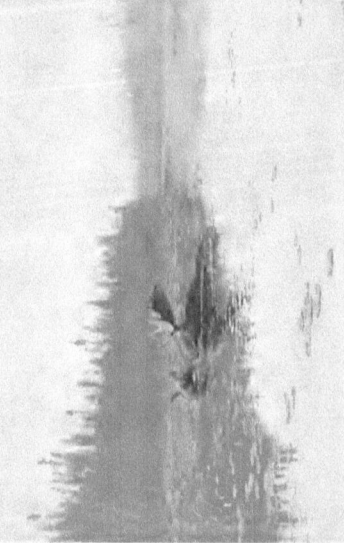

ginia Fitz Randolph. In the government are the Misses Caroline C. Peddle, Wilhelmina Walker and Matilde de Cordova ; Messrs. Charles Miller, Victor Gruff and George Brusle. Note that five of these eleven are women, and that women are in a majority among the pupils. Mr. Evans has made some mark as a painter. Miss Emily Slade

Drawn by Joseph Lauber. "GOSSIPS—ON COSTUME."

Drawn by Hiram Bradley. "AT WORK."

Drawn by Malcolm Fraser.

contributes to most of the current exhibitions, and Miss Teddie is a sculptress with talent. Many of our foremost painters and sculptors of the younger generation have worked in the League classes, either when they were held in Fifth Avenue near Sixteenth Street, or later in East Fourteenth Street, or still later in East Twenty-third Street.

The unfortunate state of sculpture has of late had the President's attention. But the budding sculptors at the League number thirty; Mr. Augustus St. Gaudens visits the sculpture classes at least once a week, and generally oftener; recently Miss Mary Trimble Lawrence has gained the distinction of supplying for Chicago a colossal statue of Columbus, while Mr. Bela

Pratt, another pupil, has been at work at the World's Fair. The sculpture classes of the League are indeed in a flourishing condition at the present time. The League is a buoyant place where young people of both sexes can afford to be merry over their bread and cheese. They are too busy to think of much else

AMERICAN ART AND ARTISTS.

From a painting by Joseph Lieder. RAKING THE SEA-WEED, NEWPORT.

Drawn by F. C. Gordon. "AN ITALIAN TYPE."

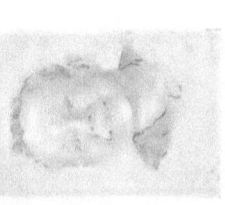

Drawn by Malcolm Fraser. "MADAME."

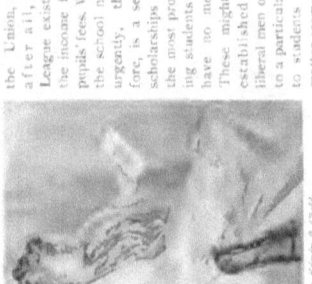

Drawn by Edwin B. Child. "NO PORTRAIT."

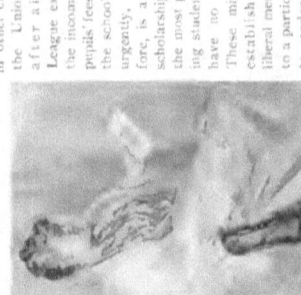

Drawn by G. A. Traver. "RESTING IN THE PASTURE."

Drawn by E. M. Ashe. "IN THE SALON."

Drawn by Edward Penfield. "A NEW SONG."

beside their work, save from time to time when they agree to clear away the easels, turn drawing-boards and canvases to the walls, and enjoy themselves in simple fashion, even as Pepys would say: "and in our mirth I sang and sometimes fiddled (there being a noise of fiddlers there), and at last we fell to dancing, the first time that ever I did in my life, which I did wonder to see myself to do." But though there is a certain disregard for elaborate courtesies in this big school, although in their classes the young men and women meet on terms of comradeship like so many cousins in a huge family, two things are very clear. A student who wishes to live to himself or herself is nowise molested; there are no scenes of riotous fun and horse-play, such as still occasionally break out at the Ecole des Beaux Arts, or at the Julian studios in Paris. And again: there is no instance recorded of anything happening at the League which would tend to disgust the most respectable persons in the profession, and the antecedents of pupils are inquired into before they are accepted. Fortunately the League does not need to take pupils to enlarge the school for an income. On the contrary, it has so large a waiting-list that many competent pupils are debarred through lack of room.

Nevertheless there are certain most desirable things which the League itself can never hope to obtain without the help of liberal givers, and of these the most important for the moment are scholarships, enabling students to live in or near New York while pursuing the course. The League offers free tuition in two cases, one being that of the Art Students League of Buffalo, which is allowed to send a free scholar to the schools of its New York prototype; the other is the Slater Art School of Norwich, Conn. But the parent League can hardly extend this hospitality very far, no matter how many similar clubs are formed in other cities of the Union, for, after all, the League exists on the income from pupils' fees. What the school needs urgently, therefore, is a set of scholarships for the most promising students who have no means. These might be established by liberal men of other cities, and with respect to a particular scholarship a preference given to students from a particular city. The matter seems trivial, but it is not. To speak broadly and candidly, we have hitherto put

AMERICAN ART AND ARTISTS.

the cart before the horse in teaching art in America. We have sent our students to Europe, little or badly prepared, and kept them there too long, trusting to the fallacy that art has no country.

If the usual proportion of time spent in study at home and in Europe were reversed, if an artist gave most of his years of drill to such a school as the League, and used Europe as a means of refreshment, I maintain that we would take a long step toward that goal which the artists of no land reach, namely, the placing of the fine arts definitely in the ranks of arts which express the ideals of a people.

AN AMERICAN MILITARY ARTIST.

By GEORGE PARSONS LATHROP

(With original illustrations by Gilbert Gaul.)

GILBERT GAUL—one of the best known of our American illustrators as well as of painters in oil, who has gained renown in the treatment of two almost distinct classes of figure subjects—must have been born, one would think, with a brush in his hand and a pencil behind his ear, so clever is he in the handling of those artistic implements, and so natural to him seems their use.

He began painting at a very early age; and it was a good while ago that I saw the first of his pictures, which comes back to me as having made an impression that has not since been effaced. He was then already a skilled exhibitor at the Academy. This picture (the title of which I cannot give with certainty, though it may have been something like "The Color Guard") represented an episode of stubborn fighting in some battle of the Civil War. A broken line or group of Union soldiers, evidently hard pressed, was seen facing—if I recollect rightly—the spectator, who thus occupied the position of the supposed attacking force. The attack was not shown in the picture, or at most was barely indicated. The defenders were the whole subject; they only were placed before us, powder-stained, resolute, firing, reloading, or grasping their weapons in expectancy of closer combat, and evidently determined to sell their lives dearly or retreat only when overpowered. From the presentation of this one side of the fight, the other side could be realized easily and with great intensity. The picture, therefore, in addition to its merits of drawing, painting, vividness, and character, was a fine instance of imaginative power and also of the power of exciting imagination in the beholder.

If I refer now to a poem of mine, it is as a connecting link between Mr. Gaul's painting and his black-and-white illustrative work. This poem, "Marthy Virginia's Hand," for which he made a drawing, appeared in The Century Magazine some three years since. It related an actual incident of the war; how a Confederate soldier was found dead in a strip of woods on the battlefield of Antietam, grasping a letter in which his wife had told of the birth of a baby and had made a tracing of the

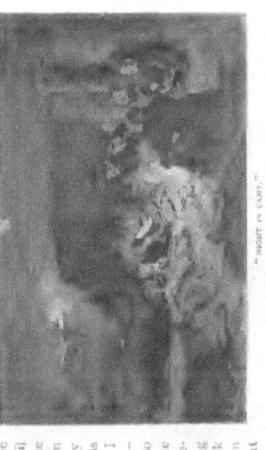
"SIGHT IN CAMP."

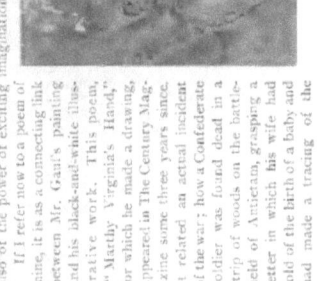
"A RANDOM SHOT."

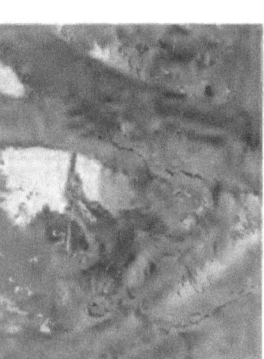
"THE SHARP-SHOOTER."

"YOUNG RECRUIT."

"HOSTILE SHOT."

From a painting by Colbert Cazin. "His Vines in Bloom."

From a painting by Colbert Cazin. "The Captive."

child's hand on the paper. In his illustration Mr. Gaul depicted the soldier lying dead there, neglected, amid the trees, near a mossy rock; the tangled rootlets and thick small branches, the glints of sunlight, the shattered gun, and the leaves and twigs flung down about him by a shell which had burst there, all adding to the grimness and pathos for which his war scenes are remarkable.

But, as has been hinted, Mr. Gaul is by no means confined to this sort of theme, and is, indeed, distinguished in two "lines," as we sometimes call them. It is true, I think, that he has by nature a special *penchant* for these severe and sad yet highly picturesque and stirring realities of armed combat. Yet he is also extremely apt and graphic in the delineation of more peaceful domestic scenes involving both earnestness and humor, brightened by the costume and the romance of a century's antiquity, or belonging to the

"THE WATER BEARER."

vigorous out-door and in-door reality of to-day. Seldom does one find the genius for reproducing military phases united with so versatile a faculty as Mr. Gaul's for picturing, in his illustrations, glimpses of daily human life in a variety of surroundings.

Meissonier prided himself upon his military achievements—on canvas; but his military pieces had not the true war-like quality; they merely multiplied the polished little men of his interior scenes, and transferred them out-of-doors. Nor did his "interiors" contain much diversity of human traits, or genuine feeling and humor,

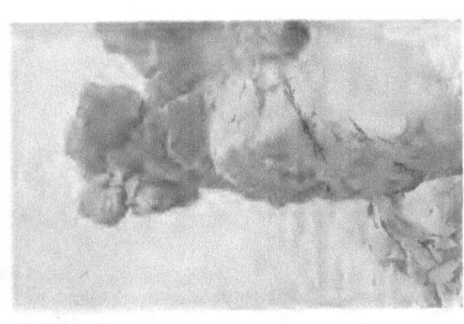

"TOP OF THE CLIFF."

although they often had a spice of tempered wit.

It is the ability of Mr. Gaul to portray things opposite in themselves, and not only to draw the contrast, but also to emphasize it by his treatment, which gives him a mastery of *genre*—that is, of dealing with subjects that may be rated as exemplifying a "species," a "kind," or to take another word, "the characteristic." He knows how to seize a character in many of its bearings at once, and to give it the proper accent.

The manner in which he uses landscape detail in some of his work is also very effective. Evidently the result of careful study, and, like many of his touches in the elaborating of figures, subtile in resources of art, it never loses that energy and solidity which pervade his illustrations. See, for example, his drawings for "Personal Impressions of Nicaragua," where he accompanied himself with the pen, supplying his own text.

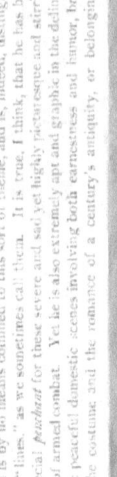

"PAWPAWS."

"THE CONFEDERATE RAID."

AMERICAN ART AND ARTISTS.

"CHEZA."

"A BUSY DRESS MISTRESS."

"THE DOORBELL."

The "Parrot Sellers at Corinto," is that little group of sketches, is very striking in its combination of boats, outspread bird-wings, the weird hooded figure of a woman standing upright, and the swirl and stretch of moving waters. So, too, one may find a good deal of his various skill in his pictorial contributions to Thomas Bailey Aldrich's "Old Portsmouth Foolics."

Mr. Gaul's work, often spirited, is always forcible and interesting. Moreover, while by no means a *poseur* in art or given over to any special fashion or school, he has a happy faculty of posing his subjects from unexpected points of view, bringing out their value at once by a bold stroke, often in a way which at first one would hardly have thought he would venture, yet a way that proves to be natural as well as effective.

WILSON DE MEZA.

BY FRANK FOWLER.

(*With representative examples of the deceased artist's work.*)

AMERICAN illustration as it stands to-day is perhaps the most potent proof of the advance our art has made within the past fifteen years. In technical address, in the skill with which the various mediums of black and white are now employed by our artists of the press, we easily hold our own with the most brilliant craftsmen abroad.

It is not, however, only on the side of execution that we have so greatly progressed. In the more intellectual matter of character, of rescuing from oblivion rapidly disappearing types, and of defining the many phases of our complex civilization, the American illustrator of to-day is accomplishing wonders.

The man with whom this deals, whose untimely death at a period when his talents seemed to have reached their readiest and most delightful play, was one whose temperament revealed a rare distinction. Studying in Paris under Boulanger and Lefèbre, Mr. De Meza's first essay in art was in the branch of portraiture. In the French school he had acquired an effective method which was of the greatest value to him when finally he directed his attention to illustrative draw-

"A PLOW NARRATIVE."

IN THE PARK

Drawn by Wilson de Meza

AMERICAN ART AND ARTISTS.

ing; for mastery of material and readiness of execution are nowhere more needed than in the regularly recurring work of the illustrator.

Before seriously devoting himself to art, Mr. De Meza had studied civil engineering and read law, so that by the time he began to depict life in its various phases he had already touched it, intellectually, at several points. This experience served only as an advantage; for what we find in Mr. De Meza's work in distinction from that of many

"THE ROYAL GERMANS."

other men in the same field is, perhaps, the note of intelligence beyond the merely technical, that is sure to be the property of him who has some knowledge of the learned professions outside of the one he is following.

Mr. De Meza's work also brings one into an atmosphere where good breeding reigns. His charming women, lovely girls, and well-groomed men are not simply people who have donned good clothes in order to figure as the *dramatis personæ* of some social function or incident in romance. His women have about them the charm which comes only from a fine habit of life, his

"A BROWN IN BERMUDA."

men are fellows who have good traditions behind them, and we know that the lovely girls they talk to are safe, even though their chaperons should fail in vigilance. These girls themselves, indeed, are of a sweetness and serenity that inspire chivalry; and it would seem that in their presence nothing unmannerly could quite exist.

Now a quality of this kind in illustrative art is as rare as it is delightful, and De Meza distinctly gave us this. Other illustrators may show greater command of their material,

"IN THE BROAD LIGHT OF THE SUN."

brushwork may be freer, handling in pen and ink more sure; but the indefinable charm that comes from right feeling is too often lacking, while with De Meza it is always there. I am tempted to emphasize the air of refinement and distinction in this artist's work, as there is so constant a call for it from the illustrators of to-day, and with but a few exceptions, it seems so little responded to in kind.

It is not enough to dress a

"MARY WAS ARRAYED WITH GREAT MEAN."

model in fine things and call him fine. If it be necessary to resort to such aids, and it surely is, the artist has a responsibility beyond the graphic reproduction of the person before him. A model in a dress coat is not exactly the type one meets at a reception at the Embassy, or at a diplomatic dinner. The character and bearing of those who go yachting in the Mediterranean appear something different from that which

"NEW GOLDEN TEA."

is paid for at so much an hour for standing or sitting in smart clothes in a studio. Mr. De Meza, in common with other artists, had this hard fact to contend with, but he also appreciated that there was an intellectual as well as a technical side to art. In this case good form is more than clothes, and style more than fine raiment. I have heard laymen protest against

representations of social life, where the work was above reproach, but where the whole tone was bourgeois. Mr. De Meza was fortunately not one to be reproached in the matter of taste. He had also an adequate command of his medium, and has given us sunny and effective studies of out-door life that show with how faithful a reference to nature he always worked. His pencil was employed in such a variety of ways that we are safe in speaking of his artistic talent as versatile, for, beside the society scenes by which he is best known, Mr.

AMERICAN ART AND ARTISTS.

"LOST IN THE WOODS."

such force and interest that it has attracted the attention and received the approbation of one of the foremost of our writers and critics. Throughout this story the alert sensibility of an artist is clearly visible, and the interest of the work itself is enhanced by the graceful drawings with which he has graphically illustrated the text. Of talents like these it would perhaps have not been difficult to predict still finer things. Enough has been said, however, to show how peculiarly fitted this artist was for the work he had chosen. As a tribute to Mr. De Meza's power of will and tenacity of purpose, it may not be out of place to mention the fact that most of the work recorded here be accomplished while handicapped by great bodily infirmity. By taste and breeding he seemed naturally the graphic interpreter of social life, and this side of illustrative art has lost in him a singularly refined and distinguished delineator.

NOTE.—The late Wilson De Meza was born

"BEFORE THE PLAY."

"THE KNIFE WAS MISSING."

De Meza has embellished and illustrated several books for children, where the drawings were made by him on the stone. These books not only show a decorative sense, but, better still for their purpose, a delicate and charming sympathy with the whims and fancies of child life.

Work on the New York Ledger, in most of the leading magazines, in Life, and latterly in The Cosmopolitan, make up the sum of what this spirited young man has left of artistic effort; while quite recently, as though to emphasize the versatility of his gifts, Mr. De Meza published a story of

in Tarrytown, N. Y., in 1857, and after a collegiate course at Lehigh he came to New York. In 1883 Mr. De Meza went to Paris, and in 1885 exhibited his first important picture in the Salon. About five months ago Mr. De Meza was stricken with consumption, and died at Lakewood, N. J., on April 27th. Much of the earliest work of Mr. De Meza was done for Mr. J. A. Mitchell of Life, and several of the characteristic illustrations here reproduced were made for that clever periodical. Later the artist gave his efforts to the enrichment of The Cosmopolitan Magazine, through the courtesy of whose proprietor, Mr. John Brisben Walker, we are enabled to republish a series of recent drawings executed by the dead draughtsman.—ED.

AMERICAN ART AND ARTISTS.

From a painting by Alice Barber Stephens.

A GROUP OF TAILORS.

AMERICAN ART AND ARTISTS.

A CLEVER WOMAN ILLUSTRATOR.

By FREDERICK W. WEBER

(*With original illustrations by Alice Barber Stephens*)

TO be ordinary is as impossible for the illustrator as it is for the chronicler. The clever writer's story is poignant, the clever artist's picture is unique. Novelty is not an absolutely necessary element in the subject, but the treatment derives value from the originality displayed therein. Everyday occurrences acquire interest when described by one whose feelings or imagination can imbue the statement of fact with realistic movement and warmth, and every-day scenes cease to be commonplace when depicted by an artist to whom expression, grouping and color suggest a thought to be embodied in the picture. There are so-called pictures that are lifeless because of their lack of motive; as barren of idea as the "village photographer's" portrait of the country bumpkin in his Sunday suit and "now-look-pleasant" smile. There are many limners who can draw a face or a figure, but it is only the artist who can make the face betray character and the pose become narrative

Alice Barber Stephens is particularly fortunate in this respect. She has achieved pronounced success as an illustrator, and is aided in her art by practical knowledge of the mechanical processes incidental thereto. Her first training in her chosen calling was a thorough course of study in wood engraving, which she pursued at the Philadelphia Academy of Design for women. The fact that for two and a half years she was constantly engaged on Scribner's—now The Century Magazine,—attests the artistic as well as the mechanical excellence of her work as an engraver. She was not satisfied to remain a mere reproducer, however, but essayed the side of an illustrator, for which she prepared herself by the study of drawing at the Pennsylvania Academy of Fine Arts

It is only within a few years that women have been permitted to attain prominence in the ranks of artists and illustrators, although there have been individual women who have compelled recognition by the strong merit of their productions But those who won place were for a long time exceptional instances of whom it is necessary to mention only Rosa Bonheur as a type But in this as in many other things, the close of the century has witnessed a change, and the field of art is as widely open to woman as it is to man There is no reason why this should not be so; on the contrary, there are many reasons why it is really an advance, for woman with her more delicate

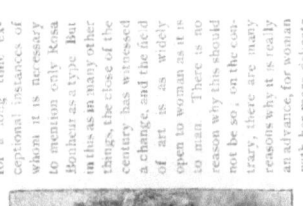

"IN THE STUDIO"

"ALMSHOUSE SHOEMAKERS"

"FOOLING THE BABY"

AMERICAN ART AND ARTISTS.

"A STREET PROPHET."

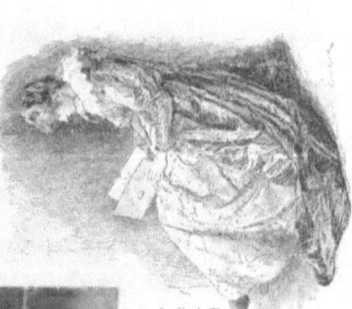

"AN ATTENTIVE SON."

sensibilities and her natural love of the beautiful is apt to have a closer sympathy with nature and life, and a quicker perception of the poetic element which is so strong an inspiration for artistic effort.

Mrs. Stephens has experienced the advantages of changed conditions in the success that has attended her in her new field. Her services were almost monopolized for several years by Harper & Brothers, whose high standard of requirement is universally known. During the past two years she has furnished illustrations for other publishing firms, and her work appears in The Century, The Cosmopolitan, Frank Leslie's, The Ladies' Home Journal of Philadelphia, and various Boston publications. She has been a student as well as a worker, and her studies in American schools of art have been supplemented by instruction obtained in the schools of

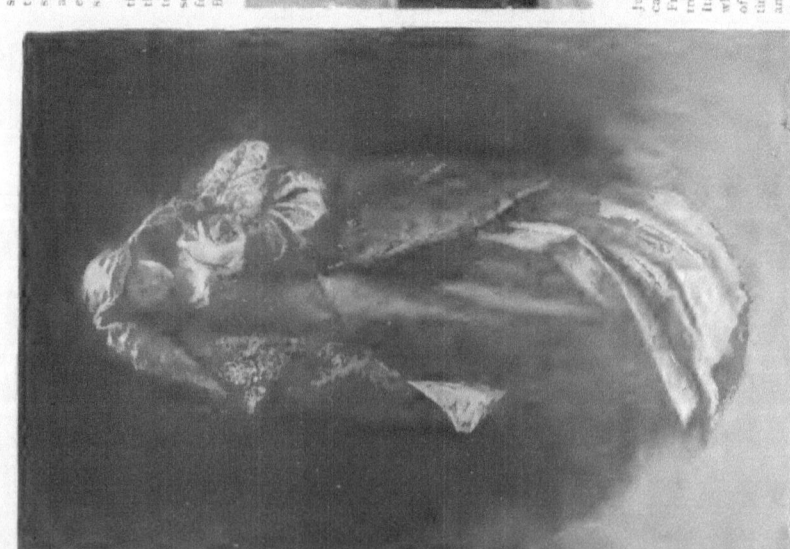

"ROMING CARPET BALLS."

"LADY ELEANOR'S CASTLE."

Julian and Carlo Rossi in Paris, and by careful inspection of galleries in the French capital and the leading art centres of England, Holland, Belgium and Italy. Her work in black and white is strengthened by her study of color, and she has achieved distinction as an artist in both oil and water colors. She is a regular contributor to the annual exhibitions in New York, Philadelphia, and Boston, and her "Portrait of a Boy," exhibited at the Pennsylvania Academy of Fine Arts, won the Mary Smith prize—not so small an honor as the name may suggest.

In her drawing, Mrs. Stephens adheres most closely to nature, and she is always accurate in her delineation of detail. Her faces are expressive, her figures animated, and the surroundings assist materially in the presentation of the subject. So careful is she in every part of her work, that almost invariably her figure pieces are enriched by interesting studies of still-life, and the inanimate combines with the animate to tell the story. She has a delicate mastery of light and shade which enables her to reveal complexion in a countenance, texture in fabrics, and material in surroundings. The finish of her pictures is so elaborate that nothing is left to the imagination except the motive of the work, and that is so artistically suggested that the picture cannot fail to convey the idea embodied in it. She is always sincere. He dealing with the governing motive, and pleasing in the fidelity with which every feature is made to contribute to the naturalness of the general effect.

One cannot forbear the wish, at times, that the artist would be less scrupulous in her care for general minutiæ, but in the light of her thorough knowledge of the subject in hand, and her certainty of touch, her close attention to the small things of nature gives pardon to what often approaches a technical failing. Within the past few years there has appeared a decided strength in the execution, whether of brush or pen point, of the greater mass of Mrs. Stephens' work, and that she has advanced in skill with the digit of time no one can honestly gainsay. She has acquired a facility in the management of her artist's tools that is but seldom displayed among the more serious picture-makers of her sex, and at the present time she stands with the foremost women painters and illustrators of the country. Homely subjects attract Mrs. Stephens most, and her pictures of the old men and women of the Philadelphia almshouse, and the simple minded people of other localities, are among the best works she has executed. She has a liking, too, for subtle effects of sunlight, and her studies of interiors are as accurate in detail as the catalogue of a furniture dealer, and as pleasing artistically as a portrait by Rembrandt. To this combination of painstaking execution and a keen sense of artistic freedom, Mrs. Stephens may safely assign her present prominence. She has individuality and industry, and with such gifts treasure-laden kingdoms have many times been conquered.

A cheery future for artists of the gentler sex is foretold in the successes attained by Alice Barber Stephens. The example she has set by her constant industry and her fortitude in the face of discouragement (for she, with the rest of the world, has had her share of life's unpleasantries) are qualities which any ambitious woman artist would do well to emulate. Art is not a mere accomplishment—and too many women look upon it as such—but a difficult and arduous profession, the learning of which requires the greater part of one's life and an unflagging application. From the days of her obscurity to the present moment Mrs. Stephens has toiled with a real that was certain to bring success, and now that she has become known throughout the land and has acquired a rare skill with brush and pencil she is a worker and enthusiast just the same. Her life amid all her work is a happy one, for she loves her occupation, and the pleasure she finds in making a picture is almost of itself a sufficient compensation for the labor involved. Of such temperament the real artist is born, and Alice Barber Stephens is certainly a genuine artist. She has the fine feeling for color which denotes the real painter. In portraiture Mrs. Stephens has also achieved no small success. She has the unusual faculty of fixing the character as well as the contour of her model's features, and has a way of infusing life and artistic attractiveness into her portrait paintings that make them desirable possessions, even though the person whose face is limned is unknown to one. In short, Mrs. Stephens has the abilities of an experienced portrayer of real things and live people.

"A PORTRAIT STUDY."

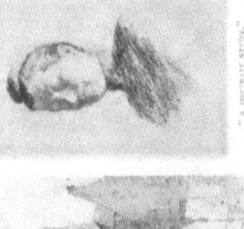

"A BIT OF ANTWERP."

"A COLONIAL DINING-ROOM."

"MY DRAWING."

AMERICAN ART AND ARTISTS.

OLD HAY RACKS IN NEW JERSEY.

From a painting by Julian Rix.

AN AMERICAN LANDSCAPIST

By Alexander Black.

(With original illustrations by Julian Rix.)

THE development of American art within recent years has been marked by no phase more cheering and prophetic than the steady improvement of quality in landscape. We still have artists who go abroad and come home with the blues, or the pale grays, as the case may be—and who seem for a time to have made up their minds to paint Seine boats and Brittany maid puddlers for the rest of their natural lives. But these, happily, are outnumbered by the men who paint American landscape, not because there is really any such thing as patriotism in subject, any geography in sentiment, but because American landscape is the landscape they actually know most about, and because painting Brittany is a temptation to thinking Brittany.

Among the American artists to whom we most naturally turn for an expression of American art ideas and ideals is Julian Rix. If, as I have suggested, there is no such thing as nationality in art, there is such a thing as a national temper—a quality which we can easily understand when we look over groups of pictures as now exhibited at the World's Fair. And I think that the work of Julian Rix might

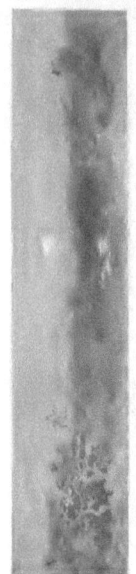

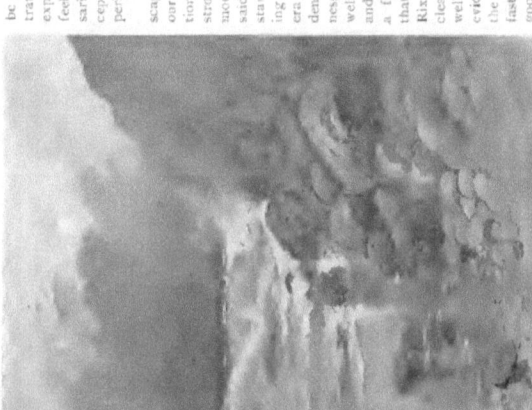

"OLD OCEAN'S WRATH."

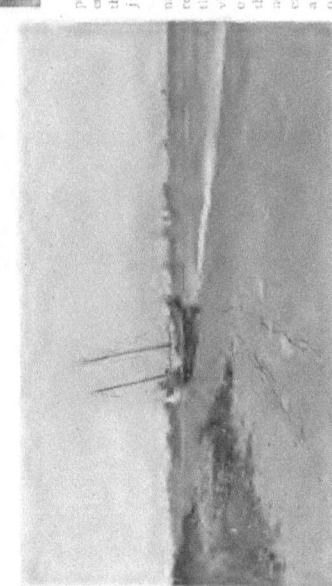

"DOWN THE DEAD FLATS."

be picked out—as illustrating the fact that the expression of a natural feeling does not necessarily involve the acceptance of any hampering conventions.

Mr. Rix is a landscapist who represents our wholesomest traditions modified by a strong personal and modern touch. This is said with a full understanding that it is saying a good deal. In an era when there is a tendency toward freakishness in landscape as well as in figure themes, and when there are not a few inducements to that sort of thing, Mr. Rix has kept his head clear, and his purpose well in hand. He quite evidently appreciates the value of holding fast to that which is good in art expression, while acknowledging and wisely yielding to

"WINTER'S MANTLE."

purely personal impulses toward original methods. It doesn't make much difference whether we class a man as a conservative or a radical in art, if we admit that that which is purely individual governs all; and I think we can say this about Julian Rix.

Two facts are quite apparent in Mr. Rix's work—that he has studied many of nature's moods, and that he has observed closely. His pictures show no tendency to repetition. They each express a distinct idea. This flash of moonlight, this bit of the river, this sand sketch at low tide, this drenched road in the storm, this bleak vista in the pines, each has its own idea, its own story. Each thus declares that the artist is not making the picture the excuse for day-lauding either a jaded decorative sentiment or a narrow theory of natural charm, but rather that, taking

AMERICAN ART AND ARTISTS.

art to be, not the reflection of nature but the expression of ideas about nature, the painter has taken many poises as volcing nature's widely ranging symphony.

I do not mean to say that Mr. Rix has formulated any definite theory of this kind. Most of the strong men in any art are found explaining what they do by a theory, rather than following a preconceived notion of requirements. Theories come lagging along after the impulses. Mr. Rix strikes out in a fresh, energetic, masterful way that is very enjoyable to the onlooker. He always knows what he is after and goes straight to the mark. Moreover, he tells one story at a time. The transcripts accompanying the present article are sufficient to illustrate the presence of this quality in Mr. Rix's work. The brook at the edge of the woodland is a simple story in which our attention is not distracted by any conflicting elements. The moonlight on the beach is firmly and broadly expressed. The

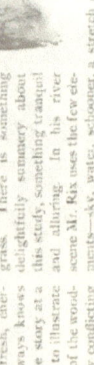

"BROOK."

"WINTER IN THE WOODS."

stream stealing through the valley exhibits a well-centred simplicity that leaves the color to exert its fullest charm. The schooner sleeping at low tide is the central element of a picture admirably terse yet unsensational in its style. Everything in the artist's treatment of the subject tends to emphasize the effect of quietude, of peace. The same feeling is very differently set down in the stretch of water across which the soft sunlight falls until it reaches the old skiff with its nose in the tall grass. There is something delightfully summery about this study, something tranquil and alluring. In his river scene Mr. Rix uses the few elements—sky, water, schooner, a stretch of sand, and an ancient pier head—with highly interesting directness, and with a lively sense of the character in each element. But in addition to all this, in the interpretation of winter moods Mr. Rix shows not less sagacity and feeling. The crisp touch which he knows so well how to use with good effect is here well placed.

In fact, Mr. Rix's pictures remind us that it is the power not merely to observe but to read nature that gives significance to art. It is the power behind the eye that brings us the eloquence. Mr. Rix delights in a storm, in a scene which shows nature aroused. He displays rare dramatic tact in arranging the material of such a scene as comes, for example, with an atmosphere row in the

"MOONLIGHT."

"A SLOOP, BEFORE."

A GATHERING STORM, DARTMOUTH, ENGLAND.

From a painting by Julian Rix.

AMERICAN ART AND ARTISTS.

Rockies, when the old trees are groaning and the bowlders are crashing through the brush and over the cliffs into the valleys below.

It is this keen sense of the dramatic, as well as his feeling for the decorative, that has added materially to Mr. Rix's success as an illustrator. Work in black and white is greatly dependent upon its decorative interest, a circumstance which may explain why every successful artist is not capable of being a successful illustrator. Mr. Rix uses water color with a facility and a felicity that make his wash drawings singularly attractive, and make his success as an illustrator seem easy to him. He accentuates discreetly, and has a versatility that enables him to use a different brush dialect, if we might put it that way, for each theme. Its style is distinctive; no painter escapes, nor wishes to escape, from a manner personal to himself. But he is as free from the suspicion of mere mannerism as any painter with whose

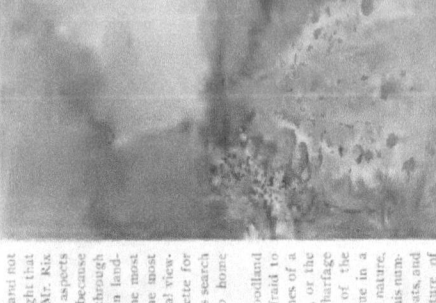
"FOR THE EAST SIDE, NEW YORK."

work I am acquainted. He is always pictorial, and, as even the most casual study of the outward and visible signs may tell us, he is always refreshingly candid. He goes directly at the heart of his subject, and extracts from a collection of general material facts the best elements that compose gracefully on canvas. One cannot remember just how broadly or how thinly any of Mr. Rix's pictures were painted, but then one cannot forget the deep enchantment they exercised over the senses; and this power to excite emotion, it would seem, is after all the final test of art.

NOTE.—The artist whose work is here reviewed is known in the world of art chiefly as a painter of American landscapes, though he has travelled in most foreign lands and found an abundance of rich material for his brush wherever inclination has led him. Nothing in the way of landscape charm, however, bids so strongly for his best effort as the scenery of our own country. Not because he is an ardent patriot, and not because he believes there is nothing that is worthy in other lands, does Mr. Rix persistently present the varied aspects of local scenery. It is rather because he has become convinced through much experience that American landscape is the most diversified, the most luxuriantly strengthful, and the most attractive from a purely pictorial viewpoint, that he has set his palette for native motives, and confines his search for the beautiful in nature to home attractions.

"THE THUNDERSTORM."

Sensitive to the charms of woodland and seashore, Mr. Rix is not afraid to portray the commonplace scenes of a commerce-clogged river front, or the peculiar picturesqueness of wharfage and shipping. An example of the artist's power to infuse art value in a view of but ordinary worth in nature, is well shown on page 186 of this number, where a pier, some heavy boats, and a clouded sky make up a picture of real beauty. From the interior of New Jersey Mr. Rix has obtained many of his choicest effects. He has sketched in the Black Forest of Germany and painted on the dikes of Holland, but nowhere abroad has he found such a wealth of foliage or so many vistas tempting to the true artist as in the lowlands and hills of Jersey. The rugged scenery of California engaged the brush of Mr. Rix for many years, and his early reputation was founded on his stirring delineations of wild Western landscapes. For the greater part of the year Mr. Rix lives in the open, painting direct from nature. His home is in New York, and his studio is one of the cosiest in the big metropolis.—Ed.

"GREEN AND GREEN."

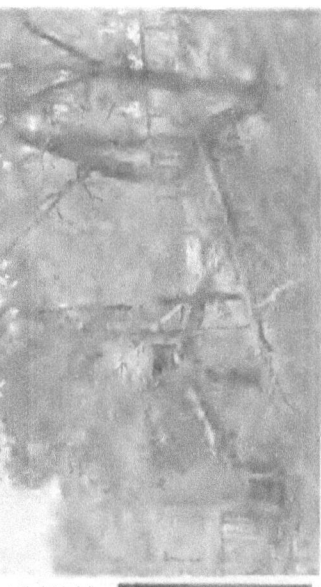

By J. Q. A. Ward. "STATUE OF HENRY WARD BEECHER."

From a painting by Benjamin C. Porter. "MOTHER AND SON."

Drawn by Frank Fowler. "HIDE AND SEEKING."

THE NATIONAL ACADEMY OF DESIGN.

BY JOHN GILMER SPEED.

[*With Original Illustrations by Prominent Members.*]

THE people in America may have had a high regard for abstract art sixty-seven years ago, when the National Academy of Design came into existence as the successor of the New York Drawing Association, but artists themselves were not held in great esteem by the rich merchants who formed the bourgeois society of the metropolis in the earlier years of the century. A chronicler of those times has told how a young artist made love to the daughter of one of those haughty merchants. She listened favorably to his suit, but her father was dreadfully scandalized. Such an alliance—the daughter of a tradesman with a mere artist—was a disgrace to the merchant's family. He could not be reconciled to the union until he was assured by an authority in whom he had confidence that the young man was not very much of

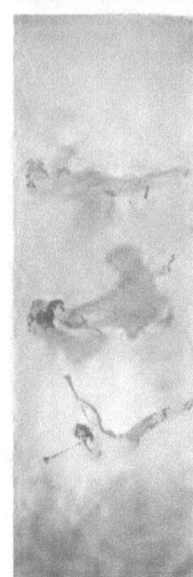

By J. S. Hartley. BUST OF T. W. WOOD.

an artist. This anecdote illustrates the attitude of the rich and influential among the merchants of New York towards art and artists when the National Academy was born. Previous to 1826, the year alluded to, there had been for something like twenty years an American Academy of Fine Arts in New York, but this had not been managed

From a painting by J. H. Dolph. "FIDELIA."

by artists themselves, nor was there in reality much encouragement of art study. The first president of this academy was Chancellor Livingston, the second was DeWitt Clinton, and the third Colonel John Trumbull the painter. But Trumbull appeared to see less reason for placing the casts and pictures in the academy at the disposal of students than his lay associates, and said when appealed to on the subject: "When I commenced the study of painting there were no casts in the

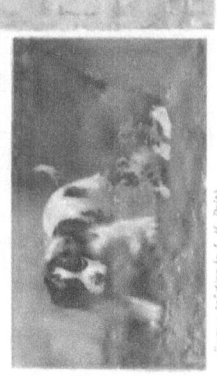

74   AMERICAN ART AND ARTISTS.

ROUNDING THE BUOY.
From a painting by George H. McCord.

AMERICAN ART AND ARTISTS.

country; I was obliged to do as well as I could."

Several students and young artists, rebuffed by the American Academy, appealed to Samuel F. B. Morse, the inventor of the magnetic electric tele-

From a painting by Jared B. Flagg.
"SHE BUTTERFLY."

Drawing by Irving R. Wiles.
"SADNESS."

of 170 works, these being both copies and originals, and comprising oil paintings, water-colors, drawings for machinery, architectural drawings, and engravings. This exhibi-

From a painting by Walter L. Palmer.
"AUTUMN MORNING."

From a painting by Woodward Thompson.
"IN A SNOWY LANE."

graph, but at that time an artist, and he suggested a society "for the Promotion of the Arts and the Assistance of Students." This led to the formation of the New York Drawing Association, of which Mr. Morse was president. Later this association was changed into the National Academy of Design, of which Mr. Morse was president until 1845, and again for one year from 1861 to 1862. The founders of the Academy were twenty-four in number, and consisted of sixteen painters, one sculptor, two architects, and five engravers. A class for the study of the antique was begun, and this was attended not only by students and amateurs, but

From a painting by Horace Wolcott Robbins.
"LACKAWAXEN RIVER."

tion attracted something like 1,200 paying visitors, but it failed to meet expenses, and each of the thirty members was taxed seven dollars to pay the debt incurred. The next year the exhibition was not quite so large, but during fifty-seven days the attendance averaged thirty-eight paying visitors daily. This year the exhibition paid its way, and the exhibitions have continued to do so from then till now. This second exhibition was attacked with great violence by writers in the public press, and probably it deserved nearly all of the uncom-

by academicians themselves. There is a dingy and somewhat battered register of students still in use at the Academy, with a list of the students who held tickets for the year 1826. Mr. Morse's name heads the list, and following his are the names of Henry Inman, Thomas S. Cummings, A. B. Durand, and others who in the beginning and for many years thereafter had a controlling influence in the affairs of the Academy. The first exhibition was opened in May, 1826, and consisted

AMERICAN ART AND ARTISTS.

From a painting by Thomas W. Wood.
"CHECK UP, NEIGHBOR."

From a painting by R. M. Shurtleff. "A WOODLAND PATH."

From a painting by Walter Satterlee. "THE SUN ALMANACH"

From a painting by T. Addison Richards. "GORGE OF TRINS, MARTIGNY, SWITZERLAND."

Drawn by Charles S. Reinhart. "A BIT OF BEING RESIGNED."

was then in advance of general public knowledge and general public taste, and it has continued to be so up to the present time. Some of us, who do not always recognize that art cannot prosper without an appreciative public, have sometimes been indignant at the conservatism of the Academy, and have cried out in anger because our views were not the views of the majority. This has never done any good, and is not likely to do any. The Academy in the future is certain to progress as it has in the past—slowly but surely.

Before the holding of the third exhibition there was a great advance, for it was decided by the council that none but original works should be exhibited. This rule has continued. Speaking of it, General Cummings, the historian of the Academy, has said. "The rule was adopted for the purpose of placing all exhibitors on an equal footing. It had been found that young artists, returning from abroad and exhibiting copies of works of established eminence, had frequently been placed, by the want of discrimination in the public, far in advance of the more meritorious artist at home, exhibiting his own originations; an injustice it was thought the duty of the Academy to remedy. The restriction was a proper one, and ever very justly received favor."

From a very early date in its career the Academy was bothered about a home. It

plimentary things that were said of it. But in considering the history of an institution like the National Academy, the environment of the artists must be considered as well as the works they painted before judgment be passed upon the value of such works. The main purpose of an academy is educational. Educational progress is slow and gradual, not instantaneous. The knowledge and appreciation of art in New York and in America sixty years ago was, as has been intimated, very limited. The academicians did not know much, the public knew less. But the Academy

From a painting by W. L. Sonntag.

SUNSET IN DIXVILLE NOTCH, N. H.

AMERICAN ART AND ARTISTS.

PLACE D'ARMES, GOUVERAC, TUNISIA.
From a painting by Wordsworth Thompson.

AMERICAN ART AND ARTISTS.

changed from place to place many times, and once, through efforts to get a house of its own, became bankrupt. This was the second bankruptcy. The first was caused by the generosity of friends of the Academy traveling in Europe. A New Yorker in Rome would see a cast or a statue and admire it. Forthwith he would think of the Academy and its school of art, purchase the work, and ship it to New York. Rome was a far cry from New York, and the freight charges on these gifts et amassed all the funds of the Academy, and left the institution insolvent. A rule had to be adopted that no presents would be accepted unless the freight charges were paid in advance. In those days the Academy, with thirty-five members, sailed very close to the wind, and the financial sea was often ruffled. But the finances were managed with skill and prudence, and in 1863 the corner-

From a painting by J. B. Bristol. "DOWN THE BOULDERS."

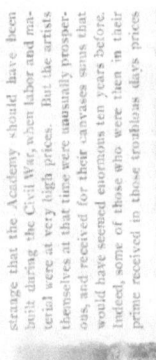

Drawn by Charles Parsons. "ABANDONED."

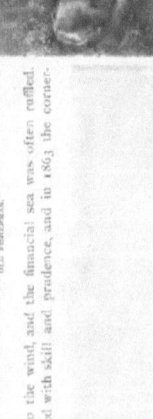

Drawn by Louis C. Tiffany. "THE BURIAL."

Drawn by W. L. Hudson. "OLD FORTUNES."

From a painting by P. P. Ryder. "A FAITHFUL SERVANT."

stone for the Venetian building at Fourth Avenue and Twenty-third Street was laid with imposing ceremonies. The speakers were Parke Godwin, William Cullen Bryant, and George Bancroft; and Mr. Daniel Huntington, who had become president the year before, swung the stone in place, using a silver trowel to spread the mortar.

It seems but a little strange that the Academy should have been built during the Civil War, when labor and material were at very high prices. But the artists themselves at that time were unusually prosperous, and received for their canvases sums that would have seemed enormous ten years before. Indeed, some of those who were then in their prime received in those troublous days prices that they have never since realized. The exaggerated prices incident to disturbed social conditions and an inflated currency have spoiled the future career of more than one member of the Academy. The exigencies of the war were such that even the knights of the brush and palette were called on to do service. Under the facetious head, "the Drawing-Draft," in THE EVENING POST of August 21, 1863, we find this record:

"Among the persons drafted yester-

THE TWINS.
From a painting by Arthur F. Tait.

OUTLET OF LITTLE HARBOR, COHASSET, MASS.

From a painting by George H. Smillie.

day in the Fifteenth Ward were ten artists, as follows: W. P. W. Dana, W. J. Hennessy, Daniel Huntington, William Hart, John O. B. Inman, John Pope, Albert Bierstadt, J. E. Griffith, George H. Hall, and Theodore Pine.

I have found no record as to how many of these sent substitutes, and how many shouldered muskets and went to the front. It would probably make an interesting chapter in the annals of the Academy. General Cummings

From a painting by Ferrand de Lacy.
"THE SOUL'S REALM."

Drawn by J. W. Wood.
"WHEN WE WERE BOYS TOGETHER."

From a painting by Charles Larman.
"TWILIGHT."

From a painting by Lewis Vedder.
"MUSIC."

at that time appears to have been more interested in the financial affairs of the institution, and the merits and advantages of several proposed building sites, than anything else, and so he passed the war period by with only a very few allusions to the great conflict.

Turn we now again to the old register of students. What will first strike any one who looks through this

From a painting by H. R. Poore.
"SOMEBODY'S SIGNAL."

come across many who have become truly distinguished. In the class of 1826 was Thomas Cole; in that of 1827 was William Page, in 1835 Daniel Huntington's name is first entered; and so on and so on. It will be no doubt surprise many to know that Thomas Nast was a student at the Academy in '56, '57, and '58. In the class of '60 were Walter Shirlaw and R. M. Shurtleff, and in that of '63 Elihu Vedder. A number of artists who attained a certain ephemeral distinction, and a few whose work promised well, but waned in worth as the years went by, and who are now unknown, are registered with a fine flourish and boldness

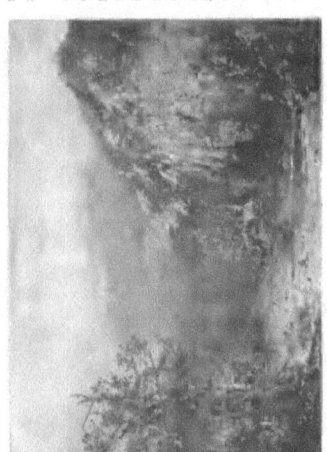

From a painting by H. L. Smeltz.
"[...]"

of writing in the quaint old roster. Singularly enough, many of these early stragglers for artistic fame have become successful business men. In 1865 first appears among the students the name of Augustus St. Gaudens, and the person who kept the register saw so little promise

book is the fact that many men who afterward became conspicuous in other professions and in business spent sometime as students in the schools of the Academy. Probably not ten per cent. of the students in these schools have devoted their lives to art; but surely, as amateurs, they have been of much advantage in spreading a love and a knowledge of art among the people. But among the small minority of names of artists we

From a painting by E. L. Henry.

ON THE TOW PATH.

AMERICAN ART AND ARTISTS.

of genius in this most gifted academician that he did not take the pains to spell the name correctly. It would be interesting to go through the whole list, but the space at my disposal is inadequate.

Among the present members and associates are the best men in the country. All the schools of art are represented, though the conservatives may still be in the majority. This is as it should be. The conservatives in such an institution should always rule, so that by making haste slowly genuine progress will be made year by year. In the last year of his life George William Curtis spoke at the annual banquet of the Academy. He said: "Art is but a form of expression, but in every art the mute Milton of Gray or the Victor Ignatius of Browning

From a painting by T. W. Wood.
"THE DIFFICULT TEXT."

From a painting by Francis C. Jones.

is a pathetic figure of the imagination, not of life. The living Milton, in whatever form of art he may appear, seeks first to sing, but the instinct of song is unsatisfied if his singing be not heard. Mr. Emerson was once asked why his interest had declined in a youth who had seemed to him full of promise. With his wise, kind smile he answered: 'When I found that he did not crave an audience, I doubted his genius.' The Academy does not give the artist genius, but it gives his genius play. It gives him the audience that his genius craves; and all the artists, combining and concentrating their common interests in the Academy, surround themselves with ever accumulating and

Drawn by J. Carroll Beckwith.
"A SCRIBE."

richer tradition, make themselves felt in the community as an aggressive force, and give themselves the splendid advantage of organized power."

NOTE.—The illustrations which accompany this article call for brief mention. The decorative drawing by Frank Fowler is the artist's first drawgin for a large mural painting which was recently

From a painting by Charles C. Curran.
"AT SUNSET."

placed in the ball-room of one of the great New York hotels. The sculptured presentment of T. W. Wood (the venerable president of the Academy) is from the facile chisel of J. Scott Hartley, one of the few sculptors whose work is regularly exhibited in the annual displays of the institution here referred to. The

WINTER WOODS

From a painting by R. M. Shurtleff

AMERICAN ART AND ARTISTS.

"Friends" of J. H. Dolph is an example of that inimitable animal painter in one of his happiest moods. "Mother and Son," a dignified, suave, and careful piece of portraiture, comes from the easel of Benjamin C. Porter, whose name is associated with a long line of paintings (chiefly portraits) of similar character to the one

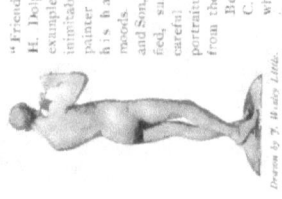
Drawn by T. Henry Little.
"MOTHER STUDY."

From a painting by Joseph Lyman.
"NEW ENGLAND LANE."

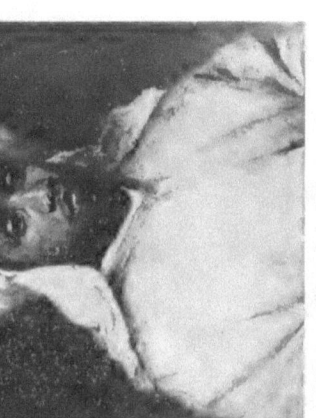
From a painting by William Sartain.
"BEDOUIN CHIEFTAIN."

Drawn by C. S. Reinhart.
"FROM MY STUDIO, TRAFALGAR."

and L. E. Wilmarth. Those students who have studied for a period in the Academy's schools, and whose work reflects honor on its methods of instruction, are ably represented by Will H. Hudson, Burr G. Phillips, and J. Wesley Little, each of whom has contributed to the illustrations here offered. William Sartain's "Bedouin Chieftain" is certainly as good a picture as he has ever produced; Fred. W. Freer's pleasing and studious style was never more fully exemplified than in his painting called "Her Conquests." The drawings from the

here shown. John Quincy Adams Ward is a notable figure in American art history, and the noble statue of Henry Ward Beecher is one of his most dignified and artistic accomplishments. In the "Mill at Bayside, L. I.," Charles H. Miller's versatile hand is cleverly displayed. The landscapes by Walter L.

From a painting by Robert C. Minor.
"LOOKING SEAWARD."

Drawn by L. E. Wilmarth.
"CAPTAIN SATURN HALF OF THE HEROINE OF HIS SEDUCTION."

Palmer, Horace Wolcott Robbins, R. M. Shurtleff, T. Addison Richards, J. B. Bristol, R. C. Minor, Joseph Lyman, and Charles Lanman are each representative and characteristic. In figure work specimens are shown of the trained artistry of T. W. Wood, Wordsworth Thompson, Walter Satterlee, P. P. Ryder, Louis C. Tiffany, Irving R. Wiles, Jared B. Flagg, H. R. Poore, Percival de Luce, Louis Moeller, Charles C. Curran,

gifted pencils of Charles S. Reinhart and J. Carroll Beckwith are graceful and strongly individual of these two artists' methods. In marine art the page reproduction of George H. McCord's "Rounding the Buoy," and the tender, sentimental bit of waterview and drifting hulk by Charles Parsons, are delightful in their conception as they are sound in execution. All in all, a decidedly eclectic array of subjects is presented.—En

AMERICAN ART AND ARTISTS.

From a painting by E. L. Henry. A HALT AT THE TAVERN.

AMERICAN ART AND ARTISTS.

A POET IN LANDSCAPE.

By ALFRED TRUMBLE.

(With original illustrations by Bruce Crane.)

THE painting of landscape is subject to perhaps the greatest abuse of any department of art. There is certainly no other in which the hand of incompetency so boldly displays itself. To paint the figure requires a serious knowledge of form and of the most exquisite niceties of color, light, and shade. The same rule applies to the painting of cattle, and all forms of still life demand accuracy of observation, skill of draughtsmanship, and a mastery of the rendition of colors and textures. In landscape, the tyro who can neither draw nor paint, but who has been schooled to a few tricks of brush and palette by an instructor, himself frequently, if not contumaciously, incompetent, produces what passes for an effect, and is supposed to constitute a picture. Who that attends our exhibitions, or visits the dealers' galleries, is not familiar with the weary waste of libels on the great art of Claude and Ruysdael, of Turner, Constable, Rousseau, Corot, Diaz, and the masters whose genius has caricatured the brow of nature with gems of art, which pass the criticism of juries and tradesmen and are given contemptible publicity?

The true landscape painter, however, remains as great an artist as the painter of history. Indeed, what is his vocation but the chronicling of the history of nature, so infinite in its varieties, so endless in its alternations of the lightest gayety and tragic gloom? To him nature is as living a thing as humanity itself.

"A NEW ENGLAND MEADOW."

He knows and loves the organic vitality which burns in the mighty bosom of the earth, and sends the life blood pulsing through tree and grass and flower. He reads the romance of summer showers, sweeping over parched fields and meadow lands, and of the time of the snow, which blankets and protects the incessantly progressive life of nature against the fangs of the frost. The true landscape painter is, in short, a poet as well as an artist.

"THE GRAY VEIL."

He might be a painter of the figure if he chose, but he turns to nature in the form in which she appeals to him most eloquently. He reaches forth for his ideal according to his intellectual bent, and whether he paints his poems in the Homeric or the Horatian mood, he is always the poet above all.

It is among the gentler poets of American landscape painting that Bruce Crane is to be ranked. Predisposed by his own nature to idyllic rather than heroic themes, this inclination was no doubt confirmed in him by his early association with the late A. H. Wyant, under whom he worked as a pupil, and whose own art was distinguished by its poetic tenderness of thought and feeling.

Born in New York in 1857, Mr. Crane made his first exhibit at the National Academy of Design in 1878, in a shape which demonstrated that the influence of the veteran artist who had been his guide had not been exercised in vain. Immediately thereafter he went to Europe, where he remained several

"BROWN AND GRAY."

90 AMERICAN ART AND ARTISTS.

WINTER.
From a painting by Bruce Crane.

years, painting principally in France, and with surroundings and associations favorable to the development and rounding off of his art. Thus the earlier works which attracted public attention to him were mainly of French subjects. They were characterized by picturesqueness of selection and excellent local color, were executed with boldness and spirit, and secured for the artist prompt recognition as one of the strong men of the advanced school, which found expression in the formation of the Society of American Artists, of which Mr. Crane was an early member.

In 1882, upon his return to America and the establishment of his studio in New York, Mr. Crane gradually turned his attention to native subjects, always in the simpler field of pastoral landscape, and generally drawn from New Jersey or Long Island. And now he began the series of charming pictures of whose highest expressiveness the accompanying illustrations will serve to convey an idea. Summer meadows dappled with wild flowers; winter pastures sheeted in snow; denuded naters, shivering in the chill breath of autumn, or awakening at the reviving caress of spring; the vaporous glimmer of dawn, the tender glory of sunrise, the broad, bold glare of moonday, the splendor of sunset, and the mystery of moonlight and the scintillant flash of

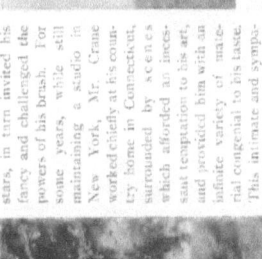

"LANDSCAPE STUDY."

"WHITE BIRCH."

stars, in turn invited his fancy and challenged the powers of his brush. For some years, while still maintaining a studio in New York, Mr. Crane worked chiefly at his country home in Connecticut, surrounded by scenes which afforded an incessant temptation to his art, and provided him with an infinite variety of material congenial to his taste. This intimate and sympathetic communion between the artist and his vocation has resulted in giving us one of the most original, sensitive, and characteristic painters of American landscape to whom our art can lay claim. He is a strong and spirited draughtsman and painter in black and white, and has contributed many illustrations to our great magazines. His impressions of nature are not merely visual. What he sees he feels, and he paints it as he feels it, without either excess or neglect of detail, and without that affectation of technical dexterity which demands that surface shall do duty for soul.

"A BLACK CLOUD."

AMERICAN ART AND ARTISTS.

A MAN OF ARTISTIC IDEAS.

By ARTHUR N. JERVIS.

(With original illustrations by Dan. Beard.)

NO connoisseur or bumpkin, pictorial art holds nothing more affecting than the thought and feeling it stimulates in the beholder. In illustrative art it is peculiarly true that the spirit and significance of a fact in its relation to human life and sentiment are everything, while the fact of itself is nothing. Embodiment of the spirit and development of the meaning of the thing portrayed is a result invariably attained in the drawings of Dan Beard, artist and author. When looking at any piece of his work, the conviction is impressed that it was done by a man who was thinking of something. It is evident that some distinct and positive conception preceded and accompanied the execution. He is one of the most ideal of American illustrators. He brims with ideas. One is refreshed by his drawings as by a new thought. Oftentimes it may be easy, and just also, to point to faults of technique, but if he was any less untrammelled by formula he probably would be less forceful in expression. The popularity of his drawing is his vindication. In his personality Dan Beard is truly an all-around man, and much of his character is shadowed in his work. His drawings carries always an impression of the executor's earnestness. Sometimes it is an earnestness that is almost fierce, but usually it is lightened by the play of fancy, and the result is poignantly suggestive. He works while the idea has mastery over him, and in subjects of especial interest to him his touch yields a thrill. If chance had not led him into the aisles of art he might have been a naturalist. His love of nature and familiarity with it are expressed in many of his sketches, especially on sketch-book pages, those diaries where artists confide their truest and most secret affinities. Another feature of Beard's work is the intense action that hangs in every line; even his

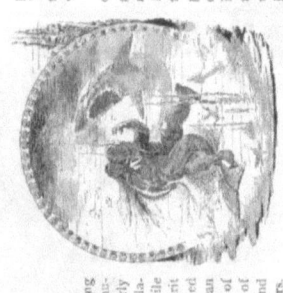

"DED-SEA FASHION."

plant life seems to suggest its own growth. The dash and vim of his execution reminds those who know the man of his ragged, vigorous nature.

He has a strong featured and frank countenance, and it is framed by a straggling beard. His every tone and gesture manifest a native sincerity and earnestness. From his early camp-life he has preserved the off-hand *bonhomie* of the woods and plains, while with it is coupled the courtesy of the natural gentleman. In his character is combined the virility of a Viking with the gentleness and quick sympathy of a woman. Of all the gifted Beard family, Dan was the tardiest in coming to the fore as an artist. After passing his school days

"JAMES RIDING GAME TO TOWN."

in Cincinnati, where he was born on June 21, 1850, he went with his parents across the Ohio River to Covington, Ky. During the troublous times of the Morgan raids, when General Kirby Smith was besieging Covington, Dan was at home as the only man of the house. His father, the late J. H. Beard, N.A., the animal painter, was serving on the staff of General Lew Wallace; Harry Beard was south with the Thirtieth Missouri Regiment; Frank Beard was in West Virginia acting as special artist for Harper's, and J. Carter Beard, whose middle name is the maiden name of his mother, was in camp on the Ohio with the one-hundred-day men. Exact sciences give excellent discipline to the imagination, for the poet must be an analyst, and Dan with his lively fancy and quaint conceits took a thor-

AMERICAN ART AND ARTISTS.

"TYPES OF EICHSTRAUM."

"LOVE'S GRACING."

ough course in mathematics. After his studies ended he obtained employment in an engineer's office, and subsequently was given an opportunity to set out upon insurance surveys in different parts of the country. This chance for travel he eagerly grasped, and the succeeding five years were spent by him in acquiring much of the resources which he has since drawn upon in his art work. His sympathies broadened rapidly, and his independence of thought led him into the fertile fields of new ideas in which he has since revelled. It was during his life as surveyor, also, that he studied the ways of insects, of birds, beasts and fishes. He is essentially a sensitive to the facts of life, and his pieces are inspired by the impressions made upon him. He has, when he chooses, a way of showing the implications of facts which others are too phlegmatic to perceive. All sights and sounds of nature woo and charm him; problems of human life and conduct have in him an enthusiastic student. Miseries and injustices bite him to the quick. With pen and pencil he reports his deductions, and the spirit of much of his work is due to the sting of his feeling.

He has a strong leaning toward allegorical and symbolical drawing, and toward delicate caricaturing. His subtle perception of the humorous and sharp sense of the ridiculous unite with a fertile fancy in yielding odd concepts. The travesty of the fact upon the

"A WINDFALL."

principle affects him keenly; such situations he intuitively analyzes and represents vividly. As an illustrator he explores the subject thoroughly, and reaches subtle meanings. The idea behind the subject is always his model. Much of his best work was done in Mark Twain's book, "A Connecticut Yankee in King Arthur's Court," and probably no better appreciation of his power could be induced than by reading the book without illustration first, and then note how much his work illumines the text, and brings out sharply the points which otherwise might be missed, or at least not fully relished. The circumstance which made Dan Beard a devotee of the Bristol-board was his meeting, in the summer of 1879, with the art manager of The Century Magazine. Beard had some studies of fish which had been drawn for his own edification, and to his surprise they were eagerly taken and paid for. Since then drawing and writing have occupied his time. The "American Boy's Handy Book," his first literary production, is still having a steady sale. He wrote the Tom, Dick, and Harry stories for St. Nicholas, and has contributed to the Youth's Companion and the Scientific American. "Six Feet of Romance," originally printed in The Cosmopolitan, has been included in one volume with "Moonblight," his latest literary effort, which is

illustrated by himself. In his writing are dominant the same characteristics as in his drawing; sharp, decisive strokes, which make you recognize the rugged, virile earnestness of the man, set before you the thought which moved the writer. No misinterpretation is possible; there is no equivocation in the expression; it is bold, keen, and clear. Whether or not you agree with what he says, you are impressed by the clarity and the emphasis with which it is told, and you remember it. The town studio of Dan Beard is a delightful place to spend an hour or so. It is overflowing with old books, old armor, old guns, old swords, and a hundred and one quaint and artistic relics picked up in his travels and unearthed in odd places; his summer studio is in a rugged mountain nook in Pike County, Pa. He resides at Flushing, L. I., where, after many unsuccessful efforts, his fellow townsmen eventually succeeded in persuading him to serve as a school trustee.

94 AMERICAN ART AND ARTISTS.

From a painting by Louis F. Hurd.
SOUTHERN CROSS, GRAND MANAN, NEW BRUNSWICK.

AMERICAN ART AND ARTISTS.

FROM MANY STUDIOS.

By Charles M. Skinner.

(With original illustrations by twenty-two well-known artists.)

"It isn't writing as good poetry since he had his hair cut," was the allegation as to a certain versifier; but, per contra, we may say that the artists are painting better pictures since they snipped their locks. Long hair looks well on some people, but the world no longer accepts it as a sign of genius. This fact has an ultra-tonsorial significance; namely, that a man must win by achievements rather than by claims. Our American artist has always been a good fellow,

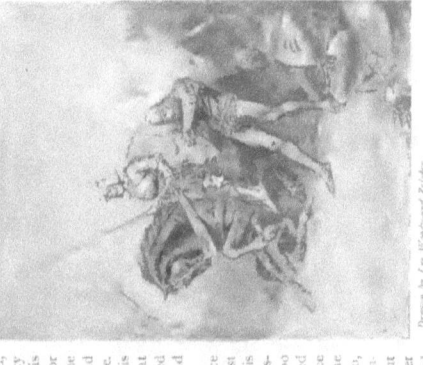

usually a smart fellow, and always a gentle fellow, but there have been times when he did not work. He waited for inspiration. Those times are no more. Every studio is a workshop now, and the man who occupies it toils as hard as a mechanic and as conscientiously as a preacher. He does not write his art with a capital A, but he paints it with one.

cord. Nor, it is to be feared, does he realize that the quality of work now done in America is as high as that of any nation, for he talks now and then about the lack of "art atmosphere," and about European precedence. Gammon! Most of Europe is bragging over pictures that were painted three hundred years ago, and precious bad ones many of them are.

The American artist, since he has "lined up" with the rest of the working world, paid his bills, and dropped his class distinctions—he was always too honest for cant—has produced work of technical excellence and high motive. Where he has found room, as in Chicago, to spread himself, he has astonished not only the natives, but the nations. He is daily a better American and is more individual stylist. The breadth and mag-

The outsider does not comprehend the amount of energy that goes into the making of pictures, the lives that are given to it, the miles of canvas and paper that are annually covered, because the layman sees only fragmentary results. He does not realize that an artist who is fairly well on in years has painted enough to supply every family in a small town with a picture, and that his studies and sketches might be measured by the

AMERICAN ART AND ARTISTS.

nificence of this country, its higher aims and destiny, are getting into his subjects. The period of the blue peasant with wooden shoes is passing. Every exhibition in our cities offers a surprising variety of matter, and imagination is taking higher rank American art is not only conscientious as to technique, but it is art that expresses the mental sanity and independence and the sound morals of the people. It is wholesome art, and clean. Let the American citizen cease his complaining and buy American pictures. If he has no confidence in his own judgment, he has friends who will judge for him, and their verdict must be for the art of America.

NOTE.—It is not enough to see the product of a clever artist's hand and brain. One longs to know something of the personality of the painter or illustrator who has

masses, the episodes of youth—its playhours and its mild passions—which is clearly indicative of the artist's sympathy with his wee models. His chief work has been in the line of illustration for juvenile journals. His specialty is a broad one and admits of endless study—and amusement H Martin Beal is best known in the Eastern sections of the land. He is a familiar exhibitor in the Boston art shows and an industrious contributor to the illustrated periodicals of the "Hub" and thereabouts. His work is marked by refinement of manner and conscientiousness of execution. A portrait of Mr. Beal appears elsewhere in this number, and one can read in his reflected features the distinguishing traits of the man and artist.

Reginald B. Birch has the rare gift of a creative

"A THRILLING CASE OF TOOTHACHE."

"A THRILLING IN STEEL."

Drawn by Culmer Barnes.

Drawn by Harry A. Watson.

"DRAW TO START."

Drawn by J. H. Birch.

"THE EQUESTRIENNE."

Drawn by G. A. Traver.

"HOUSE HUNTING."

pleased by his workmanship and delighted by his play of fancy. We are better satisfied when we know what the man or woman is like who has captured our notice and won our approbation, though any achievement of worth, in a brief way, the commonia which follow are intended to supply this want. That the commentary is not elaborate is more the fault of limited space than any studied intention to curtail the remarks passed upon the artists whose accomplishments in many mediums are here reproduced. Culmer Barnes has a way of putting on paper, with a few direct lines and well-placed

MOONRISE.

From a painting by Richard B. Gruelle.

AMERICAN ART AND ARTISTS.

mind, and a sensitive hand that is quick to realize in substantial form the imagery of his fertile brain. Birch is an Englishman by birth, an American by training, and a Frenchman in his ready grace and his aptness with the pencil. He regards the result as a greater thing than the method, though he is a man with a decided style of his own and a deep feeling for all that is genuinely artistic. As a monochromatic portrayer of children he is quite alone. Edwin Howland Blashfield puts forth in his biggest achievements a stateliness of style and a certain old-world feeling. His manner and thought are of a distinctly mediæval flavor. His tendency is toward idealism in all things. He has a fresh-

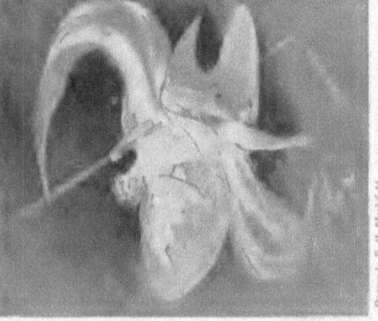

Drawn by E. H. Blashfield. "TWO HANDS OF ART."

Drawn by Charles Howard Johnson. "AN ELIZABETHAN."

ness of fancy that is somewhat reminiscent of Doré, though the difference between Blashfield and Doré is the difference between the trained draughtsman and the unskilled delineator. F. W. Cawein is a Southern artist whose principal work has been in the line of illustration. He draws with decision and has predilections for out-of-doors scenes. He has studied

character in the South until he has familiarized himself with its peculiarities, but, like a good illustrator, he has not confined himself to any one class of subjects. Warren B. Davis is one of our young illustrators to whom the future must have a promising aspect, if present honors count for anything. His best work has been done with the pen, and many of the leading periodicals have given place to his illustrations. Mr. Davis is not alone a worker in black and white, for he has executed and exhibited many pictures, in oil and water colors, which have found genuine favor in critical eyes. A. B. Doggett is an illustrator who is not afraid of multiple themes; he would as soon be versatile as not.

Drawn by A. B. Doggett. "CONTRASTS."

His method of drawing is unhackneyed, and his humor is neither vulgar nor super-refined. If one may read a man by his work, Mr. Doggett believes in the liveliness of life and the picturesqueness of the present period and the people who make it. S. S. Dustin is given to picture-making in which the element of loneliness is very pronounced. Mr. Dustin would in all probability make as clever a newspaper editor as he is an artist, had chance and inclination moulded his life differently. His drawings have a serious, business-like air about them that cannot fail to impress itself, but which

Drawn by F. W. Cawein. "ROVING."

Drawn by T. J. Fogarty. "THE ARCHWAY."

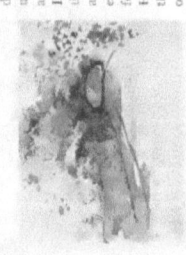

Drawn by C. M. Relyea. "ALONG THE RIVER."

does not in any degree destroy their artistic force. Thomas J. Fogarty is a name frequently met with in the corners of eye-tickling illustrations. He is a sincere worker and is something of a stylist. His drawings generally fit the text which they accompany, which cannot be said of all work one finds in the pictured pages of the day. Frank French is trebly gifted : he can draw a clever picture, engrave it on wood in most exquisite style, and write an article to accompany the engraving with a literary grace that betokens the born writer. Mr. French holds forth for the dainty, the pure, and the picturesque in each of the sister arts to which he gives his time. It is an achievement to master three arts in one life-time—an achievement which many have endeavored to reach and but few have succeeded. Howard Helmick made his reputation by the cleverest character studies of the Irish peasantry ever given to public view. His paintings have been exhibited in the

AMERICAN ART AND ARTISTS.

Drawn by S. S. Beattie. "MY LORDSHIP."

Drawn by J. H. Knickerbocker. "IN THE GARDEN."

Drawn by Maud Stumm. "THE WATER-COLORIST."

Drawn by H. Maerten Bank. "THE BOOKWORM."

Drawn by Ilona Rado. "GREEN MADRAS."

Royal Academy of London and the Salon of Paris. He is now doing for the negroes of the South what he has done for the west coast peasant-folk of the Emerald Isle. Mr. Helmick is a graduate of the Ecole des Beaux Arts and a pupil of Cabanel. J. Henry Henken is skilled in figure work, though he is not unskilful in his picturing of landscape. To a natural talent for careful observation he has added the acquired gift of sound draughtsmanship and ready imagination. The picture from his hand which is printed with these comments is a characteristic bit of illustration. F. M. Howarth has a style as firmly rooted to his name as the mountains are rooted to the earth. He works entirely on the humorous phase of humanity, and his fun is irresistible. While he disclaims any distinction as a true artist, he is as certainly an art maker as any profession-proud painter, for he has pleased a world of people; and, after all is said, the true end of art is the pleasure to be got from it. His fun is clear-cut, original, wholesome, and good tempered. Mr. Howarth attained renown through his "serial comic pictures." He is identified with Puck at the present time, and the examples of his facile pen here given are as good as anything of their kind that has yet appeared. Charles Howard Johnson is a versatilist of nothing. He is equal to any subject, and essays every phase of illustration. It is not often, however, that we see him in so thoughtful a mood as in the drawing which is here published. J. H. Knickerbocker has accomplished more in the department of newspaper illustration than in the more exalted but not more exacting spheres of painting and magazine picturement. Many of the skilfully rendered transcripts from nature, animate and inanimate, which have come into light in the ephemeral newspaper would easily do credit to the better magazines. Orrin S. Parsons is a painter of attractive women and social pastimes. He delights in out-of-door effects, and takes more pleasure in painting a fleck of sunlight as it falls on the face of a pretty girl than most artists can extract from an elaborate and long-studied historical or episodal composition. One of the best things yet achieved by Mr. Parsons is the charming painting here reproduced. Ilona Rado is one of New York's clever women painters who have examined their artistic education abroad, and combine this with their native culture to the end of making their accomplishments take rank with the work of the sterner sex. In pictures of the kind here reproduced Miss Rado excels. C. M. Relyea has made his best drawings for Life. He is a studious illustrator. His penchant is society episodes, in which well-dressed men and semi-dressed women largely figure. Mr. Relyea's talent may be analyzed in the accompanying drawing, which is somewhat out of his ordinary vein. Miss Maud Stumm is a painter of portraits and

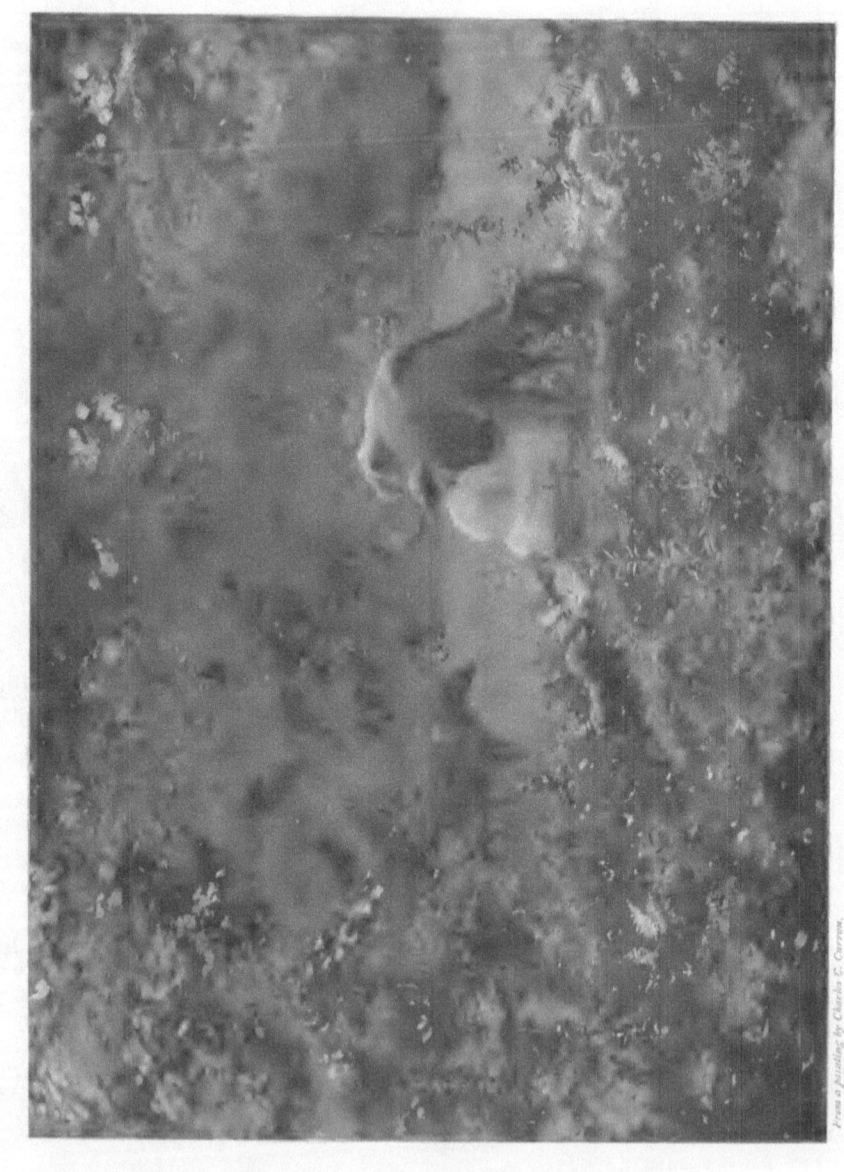

From a painting by Charles C. Curran.
SHIRKING TIME.

A MODERN MARINE PAINTER.

BY HENRY MELFORD STEELE

(With original illustrations by Carlton T. Chapman.)

It has been estimated that at the present time fully one-half of all those who use the artist's brush have worked, to a greater or less extent, in the field of illustration, and, it may be added, not a few have made in it reputations in no sense inferior to those gained in painting pictures.

There are many illustrators who never work in color—capable artists who are not painters; but illustration has become of late years so important a means for reaching the public, as well as a means for providing an income, that every year sees a constantly increasing number of painters represented in the magazines.

Among those painters who draw more or less for reproduction is Carlton T. Chapman. There can be no question but that Mr. Chapman is a painter of a high order. He long ago received the recognition as a delineator of marine subjects to which his merits fully entitle him. His pictures, familiar to those who attend the exhibitions, bear ample witness to his powers. His fine perceptions, his deep sympathy with his subjects, and his vigorous

"OUT OF THE NORTH ATLANTIC."

"THE PRODIGAL'S RETURN."

Drawn by Howard Helmick.

figures, mostly in idyllic style, and her work is noticeable chiefly for its refinement of color and delicacy of drawing. Her pictures are frequently found in the exhibition halls, and her name is yearly becoming more familiar to art followers. G. A. Traver is an illustrator whose liking for rural characters is strongly asserted whenever opportunity offers, and in no other class of subjects does he appear so much at case. The old fellow in the picture here given from Mr. Traver's hand is a capital study, capitally made. Harry S. Watson, the bulk of whose illustrative work has been published in Outing, is fast becoming one of the strong personalities of current monochromatic art. His style is certain, and his information accurate. The old lady of his picture here produced is a swift and clever bit of pen-work, and is one of his most charming line sketches as yet given to the public. Lee Woodward Zeigler is as industrious as he is talented. He is, to judge from his picture in this issue, a delver in books as well as a student of the human countenance. The output of many studios is so fully illustrated by the reproductions which accompany these words that no farther comment is requisite.—ED.

AMERICAN ART AND ARTISTS.

"FISHING BOATS."

"ON THE WORK."

methods of handling them, no less than his thorough understanding of the sea and ships, and his keen and sensitive feeling for color, give to his work a strength and individuality that is admirable.

Although Mr. Chapman is a true sailor and knows thoroughly the open sea, the wilder and rougher moods of the ocean do not appeal to him so strongly as do the picturesque aspects of coasts and harbors, where is the confusion of docks and ships and the tangle of ropes and spars he finds himself completely at home.

The American navy of earlier days appeals powerfully to his imagination, and perhaps the very best picture he has ever painted is a recently completed work representing the famous battle between the Constitution and Java — a remarkable composition, full of spirit and action, and beautifully painted; certainly in strong contrast to his quiet and restful harbor scenes.

While it is true that Mr. Chapman is known chiefly as a painter of marine subjects, it is equally true that as a painter of street scenes, architecture, and landscapes he is bold, original, and successful. The water-colors representing a long summer's work at St. Ives are among the best things that he has ever done. The quaint architecture and the various aspects of the old town are expressed with a freshness, grace, and delicacy

As an illustrator Mr. Chapman is perhaps not so widely known, for his work in this field is of recent date; but what he has done has been so surprisingly good that he has immediately taken his place in the front rank. His work in connection with a series of articles on ocean steamships, which appeared in one of the magazines a year or two ago, was a revelation to many people who had previously considered him purely as a painter. These were almost the first drawings he had made for reproduction, but they were so successful that he soon found himself in demand by the publishers of other magazines, and since then his work in black and white has come to occupy a conspicuous place in modern American illustration. His cleverness in the handling of his subjects, the delicacy and precision of his methods, and his beautiful feeling for what is called the artistic quality, have made a deep and lasting impression.

It may be said also that Mr. Chapman possesses in no small degree one quality which gives him great advantage as an illustrator, a quality which it is to be feared is sometimes overlooked by certain of his contemporaries — he knows how

"ON THE BEACH AT ST. IVES."

"THE BUOY."

that is charming. His picture of Somersby Rectory, the birthplace of Tennyson, presented to the Players' Club of New York, and now in the club's gallery, displays a tenderness of feeling, a breadth of view, and a certainty of treatment that is remarkable. It is a striking example of his skill as a painter in a different vein from that in which we are accustomed to look for him.

ENGAGEMENT BETWEEN THE CONSTITUTION AND THE JAVA.
From a painting by Carlton T. Chapman.

to draw. A painter, by a clever manipulation of his color, may to a certain extent cover up deficiencies in drawing, or, at least, succeed in directing attention away from them. But the man who works in black and white has no such resource; his drawing must stand for what it is, good or bad; and as a strong and certain draughtsman Mr. Chapman is especially noteworthy.

As an etcher Mr. Chapman occupies fully as high a place as that which he holds as a painter.

Some years ago he etched a number of marine subjects, on rather a large scale, which were very well received; but at the last exhibition of the New York Etching Club, held in connection with the annual show of water-colors, he displayed a half-dozen or more small etchings of such excellence as to command the admiration of the critics and the public. The subjects were both marine and landscape, and the execution was so skilful as to justify the opinion that he might profitably devote more time to this branch of art.

Finally let it be noted that Carlton T. Chapman has thus far sedulously avoided the pitfalls that abound in the path of the figure painter, and in this he has shown his wisdom. The field that he has chosen is certainly broad enough, and he is working in it with a rare amount of intelligence and skill.

NOTE.—No better material was ever obtained by Mr. Chapman than that which he gathered during a recent visit to many of the picturesque coast towns and fishing villages of England. The quaint, unassumingly, yet colorful and paintable craft of the English fisherman, and his humble ways of living and unpretentious surroundings, offered to Mr. Chapman's ready brush a veritable mine of interesting material, and kept him in a state of exultation most of the time.—ED.

"A COUNTRY COTTAGE."

"FISHING SMACK."

"AROUND THE SHERMAN'S HEARTH."

A PAINTER OF PRETTY WOMEN.

By CROMWELL CHILDE.

(With original illustrations by De Scott Evans.)

"MY DREAM."

THE East, and the country at large, are indebted to the wide-spreading West in art as well as in literature. That important characteristic, virility, is not seldom prairie-and-plain trained, so to speak. Oftentimes it flourishes best because it has been nursed far away from gas-lit drawing-rooms. It gains its freshness and its strength from the absence of conventional things. Such surroundings made possible the poetry of Eugene Field—exquisite in delicacy as well as perfect in fire—and gave birth to the romances of Edward Eggleston. The plains of the Southwest gave Frederic Remington his point of view, and sharpened his unerring pencil.

Nevertheless, the Scottish ballad tradition of the brave "young Lochinvar" coming out of the West is not so very often repeated here. The palette-and-brush Lochinvar of the Middle and Mississippi States more frequently slays where he is. He fears- and wisely, too-to enter the push and crowd of the art mart of Manhattan Island. The saying is right, he thinks: "Better be the first man in a country town than the second in Rome."

And yet the Western talent has made a broad mark in New York. To the dash of the "open-air cities" is added the delicacy that comes from a daily contact with purple and fine linen. The blending of these two qualities produces, more than all else, the *fin de siècle* man of art.

Such a type of painter is the subject of this sketch—De Scott Evans. Forty-one years ago he was born in Boston, Indiana. The whole of his earlier manhood was spent in Cincinnati and Cleveland, with the exception of one year, late in the seventies, devoted to work in the ateliers of Paris. In these Western cities he painted and studied, teaching art and music meanwhile in the academies. It was not until 1887, when he had reached his thirty-fifth year, that he gathered together his Lares and Penates, his studio furnishings and canvases, and traveled East.

The characteristics of his work assert themselves at once in broad lines. One particular task he has set himself, and made it his great aim. That is the depiction of femininity—the femininity of our day as one sees it a thousand times a year, femininity in its prettiest and daintiest form, the beauty of young girlhood. And here an important distinction arises. The girl that is generally shown by the art world, in color or in black and white, is the Miss of the "Avenue," exquisitely modish, beautifully robed, ever with tip-tilted nose.

Quite another girl looks out of the canvases of Mr. Evans. She is none the less dainty and fair, none the less attractive, but the girl rather of the "upper middle class," a maid more familiar, but without a Van to her name, an ancestry, or the hope of a famous bridal.

"PUZZLED."

It might fairly be said that De Scott Evans has mirrored the truly American girl exactly as she is, and as we like her best.

He sets her, always, in the midst of dainty surroundings, most frequently in a corner of a studio. He robes her in delicately toned fabrics, and prettily poses her. It follows without saying that he who can successfully portray the maid of our times must be a consummate master of "stuffs." The painting of fabrics, one is tempted to declare without fear of contradiction, is Mr. Evans' chief hold as a man of art. His canvases show that he has studied textures thoroughly and well. The sheen of silk, the soft folds of *crêpe du Chine*, the cool of the challie, dear to the heart of woman nowadays, are all shown with something better than photographic accuracy; one *feels* the texture as if it was under his hand.

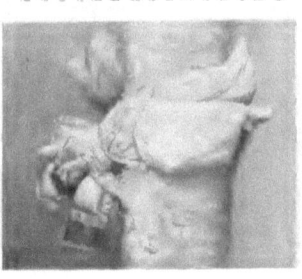

"THE LAST GIRL."

"SPRING SUNSHINE."

His modeling may

106 AMERICAN ART AND ARTISTS.

From a painting by De Scott Evans.

GREEN COCOANUT SELLER, JAMAICA.

at times be at fault, but the fault is seldom glaring. All this is swallowed up, when it does occur, in the charm of the blending of colors, those pale, tranquilizing tones that seem to belong especially to girlhood. In one of his canvases I recall a filmy window-curtain of a pale hue of yellow, through which the houses across the way were distinctly visible. It needed, it seemed, but a breath of air to set it a-swaying.

And all his pictures, modern though they are, seem to call back a memory — that ever-present one to most men—of "the girl I used to know."

They are painted very simply, with little attempt at "composition," in the full sense of that term. No story is attempted, except that deeper one that comes by inference. In nearly all, the single girlish figure is alone. In at least one picture Mr. Evans has gone from girlhood to old age. This painting shows the artist in a different and unaccustomed vein. It is his mother, done with scrupulous fidelity but the charm is simply the rendering of the black dress; the balance admits of not nearly so much praise. It is the "eternal womanhood," as Goethe says, that leads us on, and one cannot but be grateful at the setting of that, realistically, before our eyes.

NOTE.—The range of De Scott Evans' art is not held within the limits of boudoir scenes and portraits of young women. He is a landscapist of no mean ability, an animal painter with much merit in this class of work, and as a portrayer of distinctly dramatic effects he has more than once scored unusual success. In this latter character he is best represented by his touching picture "The Last Kiss," which is reproduced on page 279. There is true dramatic spirit in this painting, and a sentiment which is subdued though not subordinated. Mr. Evans is a contributor to most of the important art exhibitions, and has attained popularity chiefly through his delicate and sympathetic studies of girlhood.—ED.

"GOING FROM TOWN."

"THE EVENING TOILET."

AMERICAN ART AND ARTISTS.

From a painting by Dr. Scott Evans. THE BOTANISTS.

AMERICAN ART AND ARTISTS.

THE MAKING OF MASTERPIECES.

By Frank Mayhew Bacon.

(With original illustrations by prominent American artists of their best pictures.)

Down the banks of the Dove, or by some rushing Norway river or placid Adirondack lake, Izaak Walton or one of his gentle disciples goes a-fishing. Many are the salmon, grayling, trout, and pickerel displayed when the anglers meet to compare and discuss. But the biggest fish?

"Let me see. That fellow that I landed in the riffle was a beauty, but he was nothing to the one that I hooked just below the fall. You should have seen him! What did I do with him? Why, don't you understand, he got away."

The biggest fish always does get away; and so does everything else that is absolutely worthy and perfect and inestimable. The best thought (let it be said for our comfort and encouragement) has never been uttered. We expect a messenger through the ivory gates, and lo! he comes through the gate of horn. That does not mean that something nearly approximating mechanical perfection may not be attained. Technique is mastery of material, and if the artist could merely be a mechanic, as the watch maker is, or the cabinetmaker, he could calmly erase the *non fit* from his crest and sell his birthright for the first mess of pottage that offered. The watchmaker makes a hundred watches, each perfect, each like every other, and he is satisfied. The artist makes a hundred pictures, each different from every other, each imperfect, and he is vastly and forever dissatisfied. If he could execute one which he and the world agreed in considering perfect he would not be willing to duplicate it. Rather, like Thorwaldsen, he would throw down his hands and weep because there was nothing left to strive for. There is the deep and impassable gulf which is forever fixed between the mechanic and the artist. But the fisherman brings to the meeting of his peers not only the story of the fish which he failed to land, but the actual body of the best and largest

that he did succeed in capturing. So the artist brings not only the description of that vision which has eluded him, but the best actual accomplishment of which he has been capable so far, his high-water mark of success. Nor let any one suppose that he offers that which in his innermost heart he thinks the worthiest. Be sure that, if closely questioned, the contributor would own at last, in confidence, that somewhere—of some sweet correspondent who occasionally looks up and remembers him—that in his studio, or perhaps, better still, hanging on the wall beneath which is the desk somewhere there is a picture, "a little thing but his own," in which he has more nearly expressed his highest thought. But he will say, also in strictest confidence, that the critics would have none of it.

His modesty forbids that he shall rely upon his own judgment, which friends and critics conspire to convince him is absolutely worthless—as though a man could see to create and then suddenly be too blind to compare. He offers his most successful work, that which in the scales has tipped the greatest number of ounces of public approbation—or of dollars, which is only another way of saying

AMERICAN ART AND ARTISTS.

the same thing. It is more than interesting to hear what an artist, conscious that his best cannot be exhibited, has to say about that which the world calls his best, and concerning which he himself is only conscious that it is not his worst. In the following pages these imaginative, sensitive artists meet and tell us what they know about that which they best know (and know best), and concerning which we cannot do better than know. And we may listen and learn, and be conscious still that back of all that they have said there is vastly more that they know, unsaid, and that cannot be said, or that they might say and we could never comprehend.

NOTE.—The finest are most generally excellent piece of monochrome art turned from the brush or quill-point of an accomplished illustrator must needs give the latter at full a measure of self-satisfaction as does the most

Drawn by Jacob H. Becker. "CLARA."

praiseworthy canvas give its ambitious

Drawn by Jasper F. Cropsey. "VIEW ON THE HUDSON."

maker. It is a difficult task for the illustrator to pick out from the mass of his black and white productions that drawing which, from every point of attainment, may be said to be his best pictorial attainment.

This difficulty has so stoutly confronted Frank P. Bellew ("Chip") that he cries in his confusion, "Here are two or three sketches of which I can only say they are not quite so condemnably bad as most of my other pictures." But theory is that of healthy modesty, for "Chip" has lam-hed many a fit of indigo demons from the fun-famished souls of comic-paper readers. W. P. Bodfish, versatile with pencil and pen-point, has accomplished at least

two satisfactory pieces of art work— one an illustration drawn for the New York Ledger, the other a painting exhibited some nine years ago in the National Academy of Design. The painting is called "After the Haying," and is prized by its maker chiefly for its tonal qualities and its excellently rendered twilight effect. The artist's interest in his model passed in this picture has much to do with his liking for it. "As one's best painting does not sell," says Mr. Bodfish, "and this one did not, it is perhaps the best thing I have yet done."

Drawn by Bruce Crane. "AN EVENING TRAIL."

William Verplanck Birney, popularly known as a painter of charming household episodes, and pretty women prettily posed within old English rooms and amid the most picturesque furnishings, believes that his finest canvas is the one which shows him in his most unique mood—that of sorrow and tragedy. In the large painting, "Deserted," there is as much dramatic force as can be seen upon the stage, and as a work of art pure and simple it is *par excellence*. Some idea of the principal characters in this pictured drama may be gleaned from Mr. Birney's pencil sketch, which is printed with this.

Carle J. Blenner, though young in years, is an artist whose careful work has brought him into notice and popularity. His best picture is the one he has here portrayed, and in it one may find the true reason of his art advancement and his ever increasing scope.

The most important work of Joseph H. Boston is his portrait of a child—"Gladys." The painting is now in the World's Fair art exhibition. The little girl, rosy-cheeked and large-eyed, dressed in some dark brown stuff, stands before a dark green background. The picture is of the size of life, and is an admirable piece of brush work.

Says Maria Brooks, whose special line of art is the portraiture of children, referring to her best picture: "It is a difficult matter for me to say anything about my masterpiece—the picture which I think the best of all I have painted—for my finest picture, my masterpiece, is as yet unpainted. I did once hope to paint such an one, and at the time 'Wayfarers' (which

Drawn by Benjamin Lander. "THE NEW MOON."

Drawn by C. A. Burlingame. "BY THE SEVERN."

AMERICAN ART AND ARTISTS.

is my best up to date) was finished, what might have been my masterpiece was planned and some sketches made for it.

"The subject was a grand biblical procession, and one which, as far as I know, has never been put on canvas. But circumstances over which I had no control obliged me, though with reluctance, to abandon the idea." Miss Brooks' "Wayfarers" is by all odds the cleverest and most soundly artistic canvas she has yet finished, and too much can scarcely be said in its praise.

C. A. Burlingame is not what one would call a prolific painter, though the pictures which leave his easel are full of that fine feeling for composition and color that denotes the born artist in the striving man. The accompanying sketch is from a water color drawing, and Mr. Burlingame believes it is his best bit of picture-making, though he declares his liking for the thing as wholly undefinable.

A little picture, low in tone and aglow with a quiet charm of color, is Rudolph F. Bunner's "In Ibsen," exhibited at the Academy some years ago. Mr. Bunner says it is his best production up to the moment. It belongs in the class of subjects which particularly appeal to this painter, and in the fixing of which he has more than once achieved a most satisfying result.

Drawn by W. Verplanck Birney.   "Gaucho."

That master landscapist, Bruce Crane, when the query was put to him, "Of all your canvases, which do you consider the very finest?" replied in a somewhat evasive vein, but with perfect candor. "My best picture? Sometimes I give my best picture a coat of white. What is the best is always an open question, and I am not prepared to decide on my own case. But I can speak positively of the picture that brought me much reward. In 1878 I painted some green canvases, with apple blossoms and geese. Real green pictures were something of a novelty then, and the public took kindly to them, in fact, they would look at nothing else from my brush, and the belief was well grounded that I could only paint ' green pictures.' Mr. Richard H. Halsted, a generous amateur and a good friend to many young artists, gave me a commission for a very large November landscape, after having seen some fall studies that I had just made. The result was ' The Waning Year,' exhibited in the Spring Academy of 1882. This was considered my first serious production. Anyway, it brought me considerable praise and some emoluments. The production of this November landscape put an end to 'green pictures.'

Drawn by Ella F. Pell.

Concerning 'The Waning Year,' I can only say that it is one of my best efforts, and thank the good fortune that came to me through the faith of the generous amateur who helped me out of my peagreen predicament."

Jasper F. Cropsey is one of the pioneers of art in this part of the country, and he has been painting since 1844—a long time to be handling a brush. In all these years he has covered many canvases, and the best thing he has done is the Hudson River scene, a sketch of which accompanies these lines. Mr. Cropsey has a charming home at Hastings-on-the-Hudson, and the country round about offers many an inspiration for his persistent brush

AT TWILIGHT.
From a painting by Frank de Haven.

AMERICAN ART AND ARTISTS.

One of the pleasant surprises of illustrated journalism was the publication, in Frank Leslie's Weekly, some months ago, of the first and only portrait ever published of Ruth Cleveland, the much talked about daughter of President Cleveland. This portrait was sketched from the life, and was published at a time when every illustrated newspaper and magazine in the land was striving, by some means, to secure the counterfeit presentment of the youthful Miss Cleveland. The portrait referred to was drawn by Georgina A. Davis, and was made at the President's summer home at Buzzard's Bay. The popularity which this piece of work brought to the artist was undoubtedly pleasing to her, but the picture which has given her most self-satisfaction, and won for her greatest applause among her fellow-artists, is the painting of a man in armor, a sketch of which is printed with this. The "Battle between the Constitution and Guerriere" has often been referred to by competent critics as the masterpiece of Julian O. Davidson, the marine painter. Curiously enough, this painting forms a part of the drop curtain in the Macdonough Theatre, at Oakland, California, which does not alter the fact, however, that it is a superbly executed picture. The canvas which Mr. Davidson believes to be his most successful bit of brush-work also depicts an American sea-fight, and is rich in the finer qualities of color and composition, though there is less of vim in it than is displayed in the artist's certain painting.

Anent the prime artistic effort of Frank De Haven's life, he feels that it was exhibited at the famous Prize Fund Exhibition held in the American Art Galleries of New York in 1889. "The picture," says Mr. De Haven, "attracted more attention than has any other work of mine before or after this event. The scene is a sunset view looking eastward across great sand dunes, the tops of which are bathed in golden light, while the base of each creamy hummock and the marshes thereabout are in cool shadows. The whole effect is reflected in a broad pond separated from the indigo sea just beyond by the pyramidal sand dunes. The sky is filled with thin, vaporous clouds, blue-tinged at the horizon by the on-creeping night, but blending into warm reddish grays at the zenith." The picture differs radically from any other work produced by this artist's fellow-brushmen, and commendation from such a source is full of meaning. The picture is called "Evening at Manomet," and reveals the character of certain portions of the wild Maine coast with pleasing fidelity. The sketch of the painting that Mr. De Haven has made but inadequately suggests the attractiveness of the original.

A representative Canadian woman artist is Mrs. M. F. Dignam. She has accomplished much that is good in the way of artistic portraiture. Speaking of her work, she remarks:

"No picture has given me any sudden acquisition of fame. My first work as an amateur was well received, and my reputation has kept gaining with each year's work. My first essay was in portraiture, which brought me only a local reputation. While studying at the Art League in New York, I painted flowers in the studio of Mrs. Julia Dillon, merely for recreation. During the last ten years, my pictures of native flowers and garden scenes have won for me wide recognition. I paint no studio pictures, for all my work is done out-of-doors, and painted from direct contact with nature. I am much too fond of landscape to sacrifice it to the figures which go with it. Whatever they may be, my pictures must be characteristic of the landscape environment. As the result of out-of-door study in simple landscape painting, the picture 'Clouds and Sunshine.'

"THE SHIPWRECK."
Drawn by Walter Satterlee.

"IN PROGRESS."
Drawn by Rudolph F. Bunner.

"THE WAYFARERS."
Drawn by Marcia Brooks.

AMERICAN ART AND ARTISTS.

is, according to public judgment, my most ambitious and most successful effort." Mrs. Dignam's pictures have in them a breadth and vigor that make them exceptionably grateful to connoisseurs.

A sweet, poetic theme, delicately but straightforwardly executed, is the painting by Miss M. R. Dixon which bears the title, "Into Each Life Some Rain Must Fall." The picture was shown in the Spring exhibit of the National Academy of Design, and elicited favorable comment from many lips and pens. A sketch of this charming composition is published with this. That acute picture judge, Thomas B. Clarke, is the pleased possessor of the canvas, and when recently he was offered double the price he had paid for it, he stoutly refused to sell.

Will H. Drake is chiefly noted by his illustrative work, but his main professional occupation does not prevent him from painting, now and again, some choice landscape theme or interesting group of figures. The drawing reproduced with this article is from his master effort, and it is unfortunate the exquisite coloring cannot be shown. Mr. Drake is most at home in water-color work, the beautiful medium in which his best picture was painted.

A landscape limner of great utility and keenly sensitive perceptions is C. Harry Eaton. His careful essays in the interpretation of nature have found appreciation in many art displays, and it is safe to remark that few painters of American scenery are so thoroughly familiar with local out-of-door life as this artist. He is a student of weather moods, and to him the woods and meadows are open books, whose contents are of absorbing interest. Even the little sketch of his mas-terpiece which is given with these notes reveals that fact.

George Wharton Edwards, who writes as charmingly as he

Drawn by Archie Gunn.
"An evening smoke."

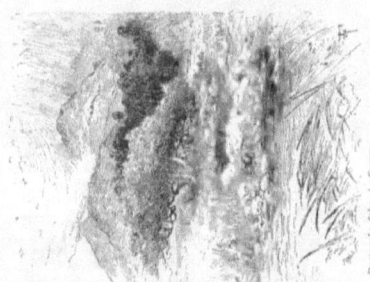

Drawn by John J. Fraser.
"In the heart of Scotland."

Drawn by C. Harry Eaton.
"A marsh meadow."

paints, and pursues both arts with more than ordinary results, describes a well-known work from his brush in the following entertaining manner: "The story of the inception of the writer's best picture and its reception at the Palais d'Industrie at Paris may be interesting to the layman as well as to the artist. The writer reached Belgium early in the summer of 1882, and at once sought the sea-coast, where he was persuaded he would find the class of subject in which he was most interested. He finally found himself at a small town, Blankenberghe, a few miles north of Ostende. Imagine a collection of small, yellow-stuccoed, one-story houses situated behind the dunes, and clustering like a flock of chickens about a venerable gray-towered church. A flat stretch of sandy beach, upon which, arranged in orderly rows, were nearly forty of the most picturesque, blunt-bowed, lee-boarded fishing-boats, which for an artist's purposes were unequalled. The tide was washing up about them, and here and there the fisherwomen were slowly walking shoreward, basket laden, waist deep in the pale green surf. These women were brawny, bronzed, and costumed in white caps and sombre, low-toned bodices and skirts, the latter held well up toward the

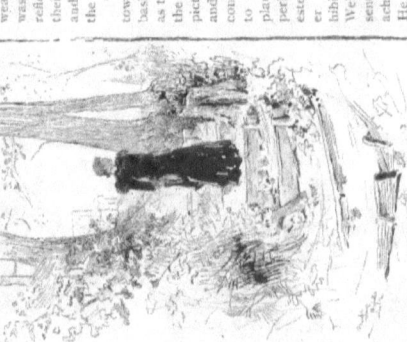

Drawn by Elmer Holmes Nichols.
"Evening spells."

waist, so as not to impede the wearer's movements. The sky was gray and stormy, and the reflections of the boats, with their velvety tanned brown and yellow sails, were deep in the wash of the beach.

"Two women were coming towards him, laden with huge baskets of glistening fish, and as they got in line with some of the boats the writer saw his picture. For weeks he painted, and finally his picture was completed—out of doors—and to the wonderment and applause of the townspeople, who, perhaps, were as much interested in the work as the painter. It was his ambition to exhibit it at the Salon in Paris. Well he knew that thousands sent their pictures in, only to achieve the success of refusal. He journeyed to Paris with the precious picture securely rolled and packed in a coffin-shaped box. In Paris he knew

From a painting by M. E. Pegram.

ALONG A COUNTRY LANE.

few of the painters, and these encouraged him in his resolve to exhibit it. In company with his friend, the late Arthur Quartley, who was also making his pilgrimage to the Mecca of art, he obtained a blank application from an artist color man on the Seine, and to the latter the precious first picture was intrusted. The writer called the picture 'Le Retour de la Pêche.' Then it was sent to the Salon, and then—then he waited in a fever of impatience with intervals of blank despair. He learned that more than five thousand pictures were sent in every year, and of these five thousand some nine hundred only were hung, and that the pictures were simply carried before the seated members of the jury, who eyed them coldly, and if they attracted

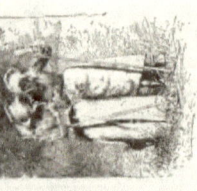

Drawn by Jas. G. Tyler.
"THE TURKEY CARAVAN."

them not, uttered no word. The weeks passed. The ambitious artist could not sleep or eat, such was his anxiety. One morning he returned to his hotel; there in the rack containing his key and candle he saw a long envelope—a pale yellow envelope. It lay upon his table for hours, with the recipient seated beside it, fearful to open it.

"With an energy born of despair the envelope was torn open at last; a pale greenish-white ticket dropped out and a paper whereon was printed, informing you that your picture, 'Le Retour de la Pêche,' is registered under the number 887,' etc. His picture was accepted! That day all the world was in a rosy glow to the writer. His picture was hung on the line, and M. Albert Wolff, the celebrated critic of the Figaro, was pleased to commend it in the columns of that journal.

"The writer received commissions for other pictures, and the following year he achieved a medal. All this was eleven years ago, but he will never forget the sensation of standing in the Salon, oblivious to all surroundings, before his first Salon picture—picture No. 887, which hung on the line—Eheu fugaces!'

Just what this important painting was like is easily seen by referring to Mr. Edwards' sketch. It is a bold and breezy work, and well deserved the honor put upon it by the Salon jury.

W. C. Fitler is a landscape painter who loves the tender aspects of nature, and woos the wild life of the air when the weather is balmy and the breeze is asleep. His pictures are in great demand, for art followers are more enamoured of the calmly picturesque than of the noisy in natural transcripts. Mr. Fitler's best picture is forcibly characteristic of all that went before its execution or have followed after.

John A. Fraser is one of the very few of our older artists who have kept themselves in touch with the later days of their lives—a truly refreshing thing to see. Says Mr. Fraser by way of comment upon an artist's best picture and its evolution:

"It is difficult for one who is always in earnest to say which work he considers his best, but there are reasons why I may consider 'The Heart of Scotland' my most successful painting. First, it is a majestic motive, and failure to convey its full spirit would be absolute. It is unusually large for a work in pure water-color without a trace of 'body' color or pastel; but I used the knife freely and fearlessly, especially in the sky, and secured that luminosity which only transparent water-color on white paper can give. In spite of the serious individuality of its style, and consequent non-conformity to the frivolous and formulated mannerism of the landscape à la mode, the highest jury in the world, at the most select and conservative exhibition held for years at the Salon in the Champs Elysées in Paris, gave it the very best place among the aquarelles. The French journals were unanimous as to its possessing the man's eyes—originality and strength. Such recognition proves that it is still possible to command intelligent respect and admiration by honestly and independently expressing the thought that is one's own. But then I have yet to paint my best picture, and you know, ars longa, vita brevis."

"Archie" Gunn is an illustrator whose name has been associated for two years past with Truth, the New York illustrated weekly. His fancy turns most strongly to pretty women and the average" man about town, of whom much is written and pictured, and but little seen. Mr. Gunn has an airy imagination and a decisive way of drawing, which gives his illustrative

AMERICAN ART AND ARTISTS.

work a more than casual interest.

The most important painting produced by E. L. Henry, whose specialty is quaint figures of quiet people quaintly depicted, is the large nine-foot canvas illustrating the initial excursion of the first railway ever constructed in New York State. The picture contains fifty figures, and abounds in historical details, carefully painted. Another picture, not quite so important as the railway subject, but more characteristic of the artist, is the "Vacation Time," here reproduced.

The simple title "Study of a Guitar" conveys but little sense of the beauty of Frank T. Hutchens' best picture. The original is a large water-color painting, and represents the tuneful instrument so dear to the Spanish heart, surrounded by colorful draperies. The picture was shown in a recent exhibition of the National Academy of Design, and brought forth much praise.

Benjamin Lander's drawing of "The New Moon" is considerably the most interesting of his numerous fine productions. Of the picture he says: "It is my most influential landscape, as the success of the large etching I made from it led me to lay down other art tools for those of an etcher. I should be sorry to say, however, that it is my greatest achievement, since it was one of my early efforts. The scene is laid at Flatlands, L. I. The original picture is owned in Brooklyn, and the etching was published in 1885. A selection of my works was exhibited at the International Exhibition of the Vienna Graphic Arts Society in 1886, and 'The New Moon' was selected for representation in the illustrated catalogue, for which I made a small etching."

Rhoda Holmes Nicholls' greatest picture is "Evening Bells," a sketch of which she has made from her notable painting. The picture was first shown in the American Art Galleries of New York, and received a gold medal at the Prize Fund Exhibition there given in 1886. Mrs. Nicholls' masterpiece has been etched, and the reproduction in

"AFTER REVIEW THE CONSTITUTION AND THE CHILDREN."

Drawn by J. O. Davidson.

"THE YOUTH OF KANDOR."

Drawn by J. Morgan Eden.

New York, and the following year showed it at the Spring Academy Exhibition. Since then it has been displayed in Western cities. The picture represents Salome at the moment when she first discovers the head of John the Baptist. The purely physical nature of Salome revolts against the ugliness of the decapitated head. She is unable to perceive the spiritual light emanating from it, a light which illuminates herself, and by which alone she is visible in history. My other important works are 'Adam,' painted for and exhibited in the Salon of 1889, and afterward in the New York Academy of Design, and a new picture, recently completed, and entitled 'The Storm Gods of the Rig-Veda.'"

The most satisfactory drawing which Victor Perard has made up to date is a view of the great naval parade last April. The drawing made a large four-page supplement to Harper's

this form became immensely popular all over the country. The "Salome" of Miss Ella F. Pell's creation is an admirable picture and may well be considered her finest general achievement. Of this picture the artist says: "Although not the greatest, I consider it one of my important works. It was painted in Paris and exhibited in the Salon of 1890. I brought it to

"WRESTLING."

Drawn by Harry S. Watson.

"THE SILENT WORLD."

Drawn by E. M. Shawliff.

Weekly. Next to this drawing, the scene in Printing House Square, New York, on the eve of the last Presidential election, is Mr. Perard's cleverest bit of black-and-white work. Julian Rix has painted many subjects in many ways, but never has he succeeded in excelling himself since he completed his beautiful canvas, "A Misty Morning." The poetry and soothing silence

AMERICAN ART AND ARTISTS.

Drawn by Victor Perard.

"FISHING BOATS SQUARE."

Drawn by Jeffrey Eily.

"A SUNNY MORNING."

of an early morning effect is realized with marvellous fidelity and artistic feeling. In the original painting one feels the reality of the pictured scene, and forgets for a while that the effect is only the result of a clever artistry.

The two pretty country girls in Harry Roseland's picture, "Confidential Correspondence," have caused him as much visual satisfaction on canvas as they must have caused him in the life. The picture is much the best thing that Mr. Roseland has yet completed, and it has all the niceties of his style and handling without any of the painter's occasional faults.

P. F. Rudell, writing of his best picture, "A Devonshire Forest," says: "It is a reminiscence of a spot in the forest near Chagford, Devonshire, England, and was painted purely from memory. I was wont to sketch near the banks of the source of the river Teigne, and one afternoon, on my way back from sketching, walking along this old path, I was particularly attracted by the beautiful play of this afternoon sunlight. I was so strongly impressed that the scene became a part of myself. It was not until one afternoon the following winter, while idling away my time in my Paris studio, that my thoughts wandered back to Devonshire. Then this scene came upon me so vividly that the desire to paint it became very strong. Late as it was, I seized my brushes and palette, and painted until compelled by the gathering darkness to stop; my picture, however, was nearly completed.

"The following day I felt about to put on the finishing touches, but somehow there was something disappointing. It failed in that fine stereoscopic quality I so strongly felt and desired. In the keenness of my disappointment I became desperate, and deliberately went to work to paint out the picture. It was while doing this that the beauty and strength of the scene came upon me. I stopped the work of destruction, wiped out some of the paint, and ere dark finished the picture, not touching it again, as I felt I had accomplished my desire, though I painted only about seven hours on the canvas. I felt it was my best picture, because it so truthfully conveyed the beauty of the scene."

The best picture that Walter Satterlee has thus far painted is his Brittany subject, "The Lightened Load." He has striven to convey in the picture that strange mixture of hard toil and pure sentiment frequently found among the peasantry of France. The old man in Mr. Satterlee's painting is a type of the Breton grandparent, a type not frequently encountered nowadays.

"The Silent Woods" is the expressive title bestowed upon the masterpiece of R. M. Shurtleff, one of the best painters of wood interiors that we have to-day in this country. Concerning this picture, Mr. Shurtleff writes: "In this painting I felt that I had got atmosphere and light—light that pervaded even the darkest parts; that the anatomy of the ground was well felt; that the picture was more of a unit than any I had done before. The picture is certainly the finest of a long line of similar subjects dealt with by Mr. Shurtleff.

James G. Tyler, painter and lover of the sea, has at least one great picture which satisfies his self-imposed criticism. This is the popular canvas, "The Dream of the New World," his largest and most important work. Harry S. Watson is forging to the front as an illustrator of the magazines. He is a young man of great promise, and the best picture he has produced is the one sketched for this article and published herewith. Francis Wheaton touched the high-water mark of his achievement when he put forth the landscape here reproduced. Thus runs the tale of how a few of the notable "best pictures" were conceived and executed. There is a wealth of instruction, both inferential and direct, to be gleaned from such a symposium as is here arranged.

—ED.

From a painting by George H. McCord.

OLD SAW MILL, CLUNY, SCOTLAND.

A PAINTER OF SUNSETS

By CHARLES M. SKINNER

With original illustrations by George H. McCord.

SUNSET MCCORD, his studio neighbors used to call him, but that was in the days before he had begun to give them a surprise every year. In private life his name is not "Sunset," but George Herbert McCord. He got his nickname because he so gloated over color and light that nothing less than the western glories enabled him to express himself. There are natures that vibrate to certain colors and effects just as the strings of an instrument respond to the tones of a voice or a bell, and this painter was particularly susceptible to the charm of sunset. He broadened away from this agreeable, if restricted, theme after a trip or two abroad and some earnest study of Nature in New Jersey, for he began to find pleasure in the quieter effects and softer tones of the landscape. Those who have watched his course are still sensible, however, of a continuity of the same sentiment that he showed in his work of fifteen years ago, and even in these black and white copies of some of his pictures it will be suggested—the sadness, the mystery, the atmospheric glow and tenderness.

SWEET WATER.

ON THE BEACH.

Do you not feel it? Richness and solidity you are sure to feel in that view of the hay barges drifting down the river toward that world of cloud which hangs above the horizon. Earth and sky contrasts, too, are obvious

COMMONPLACE CORNER.

IN OLD MEADOWS.

BOATS CARRYING HAY.

in the castle, planted like an Alp above the town and the foaming river. The very composition in this work,—the repetition of aspiring lines,—instances a loftiness that is symbolic of its history and meaning. We drop down to humbler themes and methods in the shore views; and the rainy day, but, let us praise humility all we will, we turn again to that glowing picture where

> The splendor falls on castle walls,
> And hoary summits, old in story.

and thank the artist for that rare luxury in this commonplace century— a thrill. The painter of sunsets has moved us as by a drama.

Especially are these qualities shown in McCord's winter-scenes, taken often just after sunset when night is closing down but the snow gives back what brightness remains in the sky. A shudder as from creeping cold comes over sensitive people when looking at these mournful yet fascinating scenes. They form a pleasing contrast of emotion when they hang in some cozy library, warm with a log-fire, softly bright with lamps. It is like witnessing in a comfortable theatre the woes of King Lear, or like sitting, not on the ground but on soft rugs, "to tell sad stories of the death of kings." The melancholy note so common in English poetry reappears in the American painter of sunsets.

THE CASTLE TOWER.

AMERICAN ART AND ARTISTS.

AMERICAN ART AND FOREIGN INFLUENCE.

By W. Lewis Fraser.

(With original illustrations by Albert E. Sterner.)

It is as difficult to define our individual art creeds as it would be, without the aid of the theologians, to define are religious one. I suppose in art, as in religion, our "oight to be able to give a reason for the hope that is within", but art has not had its colleges, its assemblies of doctors to dogmatize, to settle just what one ought or ought not to believe in. This is fortunate or unfortunate according to one's individual temperament.

It is an axiom that he who thinks deeply thinks well. This does not always apply, for Art is a fickle goddess, who smiles upon whom she will — the "banal" sometimes more sweetly than the serious, the untaught boy oftentimes more willingly than the advanced student.

Are there, then, no canons in art in which we may trust? No exponents of its true principles to whom we may look? Plenty, if we accept the "fads," the fashions of the passing moment. I am sure the Byzantine painters had them, and I doubt not that the cognoscenti of their time bowed down before them and worshipped them. But away off in central Italy there lived a shepherd boy, who drew pictures of his sheep on stones and fences, and with Giotto the canons of the Byzantines were forgotten, and later, with his new methods, there came new canons. So it has been since. The heretic of to-day becomes the canonized saint of to-morrow, to be set aside by new heretics and new saints.

We are fortunate in our country in having in art no past, and therefore few traditions, or traditions so recent that they have not had time to crystallize. They are still in the waters of crystallization, and are therefore apt, by the addition of a strange substance, to crystallize into a new, a strange shape. Our Copleys, Stuarts, Alstons, Turnbulls, and what has been seemingly characterized as "the Hudson River school," were all waters of crystallization. They had

Unfortunately, in matters of art,

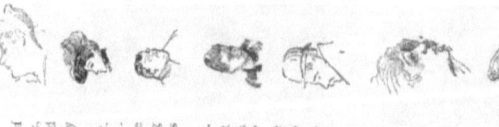

their half-formed canons based on English models; but the soil of a new world introduced the new substance, for it is not favorable, by dint of its indigenous growth, to the propagation of old world plants in old world forms. And before these had time to properly root, the indigenous had, happily for us, choked them.

It is the fashion to bewail the lack of Americanism in our art. I wonder what is meant by this. American art is intensely American. Our nation has grown by assimilating the best that the whole world afforded—the making of it our own, the pruning and trimming of it, and then incorporating it into our system—and our art has grown on these lines.

It would be an insult to those who bewail the non-national character of our art, to suppose that because our artists have not yet painted Jersey Liniment," or barns with "Use Brown's South Salvation Oil," are not American. The truth is, that where our painters have to be found (a matter is not the case, then of personal equation), painted it. If this muses, our Davises, what of our Inscape, our Homars, our Tryons in landin figure? Surely Kappes, and others dividual as it is these are as imthis age of steam possible to be in that we are apt to and electricity seriously in our es-Paris, the tentative efforts take too student just from ibitions, and, because they echo the master under whom he has studied, raise of the the cry, that American art is un-American?

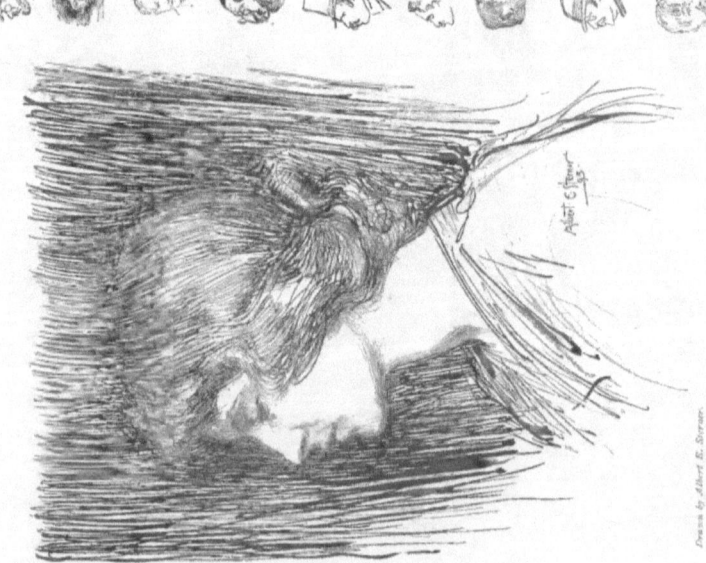

"THROUGH THE WINDOW."

Our country is a large one, cosmopolitan in its population and customs. When Albert E. Sterner made the charming pictures which accompany the Balcony Stories, lately published in The Century, he drew types of Americans—the Americans of New Orleans. These are as untrue to New England as they would be to Timbuctoo; but yet New Orleans and New England are both American. In "Free and I," types which would have been utterly false for New Orleans. But it may be said that in the handling of these drawings he is not American. This is equivalent to saying that Sterner has learned his trade—that he can handle his medium without the restraint of imperfect knowledge, without that imperfection which characterized much of the American art of thirty years ago.

Sterner is a type, and an excellent one, of the American artist—not

Drawn by Albert E. Sterner. "HEAD OF A YOUNG GIRL."

AMERICAN ART AND ARTISTS.

fashioned by France—but properly directed by French precept and example. He had secured a footing in our art ranks before he went abroad, and while his place in those ranks was but that of a private, we knew that he was certain of promotion. He came back wearing the epaulettes and with the brevet of the Salon. The artist had been awakened in him. He saw things with wide-open eyes—eyes not dazzled by the glitter of the yellow and the blue of impressionism, yet profoundly impressed by the spirit of modernity. He was a stronger draughtsman, a better colorist, a more artistic artist, a conservative radical in art. His later visits to Paris have but strengthened these qualities.

Artists do not, save with rare exceptions, arrive at the maturity of their powers at Sterner's age, thirty. He at present thinks better than he does; his works are sometimes faulty in drawing, occasionally show impatience of their subject, and now and then are worried and teased in execution, but, whatever their faults, the artist is apparent, and possessing this quality, they are always valuable.

Sterner is a keen observer of character, as is well shown in the note-book sketches which accompany this article. What could be more admirable than the thumb-nail sketches which surround page 5, or the head of the French *ouvrier* on page 7. Unfortunately his quality in composition is suggested rather than shown in the unused sketch for "Père and I," one of the most charmingly illustrated books ever issued from the American press. He is an admirable painter,

Drawn by Albert E. Sterner

AMERICAN ART AND ARTISTS.

is a Londoner born, with a Parisian temperament and an American curiousness of character. He first saw the sun on March 8, 1863, and came to America when he was eighteen years of age. He lived in New York for a while, studying in the line of picture-making—mostly by himself—until one fine day he pulled up his tent stakes and sailed for Paris. There he studied under Lefebvre and Boulanger. Since this time he has forged to the top of his studious vocation. Mr. Sterner is a member of the New York Water Color Society, and has frequently exhibited at the American Fine Arts Society.

His picture of "The Bachelor" received honorable mention at the Salon in 1891. Mr Sterner's draughtsmanship is distinguished by a nervousness of handling and an economic directness of touch. He goes to his subject clear-headed and free-handed, and tells his story simply. He is a vigorous objector to the catch-penny frills of "popular" picture-making, and even in his earlier days tried to be conscientious in his simplest work.

a soft, rich, and brilliant colorist. This quality of color finds its way into his black and white but slow; he is it this characterized, it yet remains to be said, that his chief quality is his artisticness, a quality which cannot be defined or formulated, but without which no great art work was ever accomplished.

NOTE.—Albert E. Sterner, whose work is reviewed so gracefully in the foregoing paper,

THE SURRENDER.

AMERICAN ART AND ARTISTS.

NEWSPAPER ART AND ARTISTS.

By ALLAN FORMAN.

(With original illustrations by leading artists of the American press.)

SAID Goethe: "We should look on a picture every day." But it is hardly probable that the German poet anticipated the achievements of latter-day American journalism. We are surfeited with pictures, many of them pretty bad pictures, but a good many of them far better than the enemies of illustrated daily journalism are willing to admit. There have been vast strides in this line of illustrative art within the past few years (years of productiveness), and our modern newspaper artist often manages to get a good deal of real art in the few pen scratches he is obliged to make pass for a picture. When one considers the limitations under which they work, the productions of the better class of newspaper artists are surprisingly good. Everything must, in the first place, be done in a hurry. Rapid work is the prerequisite in the modern newspaper office. Then the sketches must be open. If they are closely drawn, the lines will fill and the picture be a smudge, owing to the spongy paper, poor ink, and rapid press work used in producing our newspapers. For these reasons newspaper illustrating has come to be a separate branch of art.

Occasionally, in illustrated critiques of art matters and the like which appear in the daily papers, the clever work of men whose brush and pencil products make the carefully prepared pages of the magazines eloquent with beauty, lose every charm of style and subject when given to the world through the blurred and uncertain medium of the hurriedly printed newspaper.

James Gordon Bennett, Sr., with The New York Herald, led in the matter of newspaper illustrating, as he led in every sagacious advance step in American journalism. The first cut he published was in 1837, just after the great Wall Street panic. It represented Satan playing at ten pins in Wall Street. This was followed from time to time by others, and when General Taylor won the battle of Buena Vista, Mr. Bennett scored a signal beat over his contemporaries by printing a first-class portrait of the victorious general. The Herald's war maps have always been a famous feature and have added much to the prestige of the paper.

Horace Greeley, who always knew a good thing when he saw it, began to enliven the pages of the old New Yorker with occasional portraits. In The Tribune, which he founded later, he published the first political cartoon ever seen in a New York daily. It was after a Whig victory, and showed an old coon fiddling while the young ones were dancing.

With a few spasmodic exceptions, newspaper illustrating fell into desuetude with the larger papers until one Sunday morning in February, 1884, Mr. Pulitzer's rejuvenated World burst upon an astonished public as a veritable picture paper. Pretty bad pictures some of them were, too, but they sent the circulation sky-rocketing toward the zenith of pecuniary affluence. I happen to know, personally, that at that time it was Mr. Pulitzer's design to use the pictures as a "sensation" to attract public attention, and then to quietly weed them out until The World should be brought back to the terra firma of newspaper dignity.

Mr. Pulitzer departed for Europe one day, and left orders for the weeding process to begin. It was a bit of proprietorial finesse characteristic not alone of Mr. Pulitzer. If the circulation of The World dropped under the picture elimination process, it was because of the absence of the great editor; if it kept steady or grew, the great editor was making a great paper. The circulation fell. In those days Business Manager George W. Turner used to revel in a series of charts of circulation which closely resembled the government weather maps. As the pictures were taken out the circulation line went lower, until it looked as if Turner would have to put a sub-cellar on his

AMERICAN ART AND ARTISTS.

"A FIN DE SIÈCLE DAME."
Drawn by Thomas Fleming.

chart, so to speak. Finally he and Colonel Cockerill grew desperate, and they determined to reverse the old seaman's maxim, and disobey orders rather than break owners. They illustrated everything and everybody, from Mrs. Astor's diamonds to the tail of the Lady Flashes, and the circulation shot up again in an almost straight line.

There has never been a second attempt to make The World an unillustrated paper. One after another, the other dailies were compelled to follow The World's example. The Sun sneered and scoffed, and then came out with a series of illustrated watering-place letters, and pictures of new fancies in ladies' hosiery and underwear which excited the envy of Town Topics and sent the office cat into the sub-cellar, where that devoted animal howled a beautiful and permanent scarlet. The Telegram, with the skilful pencils of De Grimm and Grihayedoff, had long been doing the best art work in town, and Mr. Bennett, quick to see the drift of public taste, set them at work on The Herald.

To-day I do not think there is a daily paper in New York or in any of the larger cities, with one or two exceptions, which has not its own engraving plant and staff of artists. The Recorder, The Chicago Inter-Ocean, and The World have successfully put in rapid presses which will print in several colors at one impression. The efforts of The Recorder and The World have, so far, been hideous in the extreme. Mr. Kohlsaat, of The Inter-Ocean, has evidently secured a man trained in the French school, for by careful drawing and the use of tints instead of splotches of vivid color, he has produced some very pleasing effects.

The question has often been asked, "Will illustrations in the daily papers last?" and I reply unhesitatingly, "Yes." Newspaper illustrations have come to stay, and they will keep on improving in the future as in the past. Even the wild color pages of The Recorder and The World will prove the starting point for great progress in newspaper art. So long as the human brain can grasp the details of form more readily through the medium of a drawing than through a printed description, so long will newspaper illustration continue and increase. So long as the cartoon and caricature are the most potent weapons in political warfare, so long will they be used in the daily press. Where there were a dozen competent newspaper artists in the country five years ago, there are a hundred to-day. The limitations of paper, press-work, and time will prevent the daily from ever encroaching on the field of the illustrated weekly, but it will compel the weekly and the monthly to keep well in advance. This sounds like an absurd statement when one compares the illustrated daily newspaper and the monthly of to-day. But compare the pictures in the daily with those in the monthly of thirty years ago.

Mechanical improvements?

Yes; but the world is still moving.

NOTE.—A truly remarkable change has come over newspaper illustration within the brief period of a half decade. It may be true or not, as you like it, that this vast business of picture-making for the press is being carried to a ridiculous extreme, but the fact still remains that the intelligent demand of the hour is for newspaper illustrations and many of them—so that they be well made. We crave a picture-reading people, and we crave the constant and profuse pictorial elucidation of current events; but, let it not be forgotten, we are much beyond that stage in the evolution of newspaper art where an inverted cut of a war map may be printed without fear of criticism in illustration of a ball-room scene, or a coarsely engraved shoe advertisement used in lieu of the President's portrait. Such impudent practices, once countenanced, if not commended, in highly civilized parts, have long since been left to the enlightening press of struggling Western villages. The newspaper illustrations of to-day are, in the main, worthy of careful scrutiny, and in a few notable instances are of positive artistic merit. The men whose facile draughting pens are responsible for the best of these

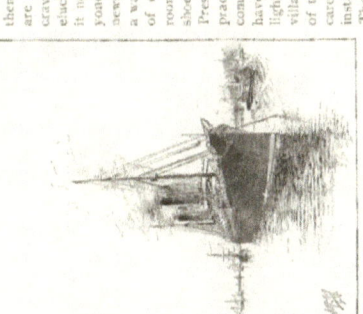

"SUNDAY MORNING AT QUARANTINE."
Drawn by William P. Hofacker.

AMERICAN ART AND ARTISTS.

press pictures occupy a position in the world of art that is not, perhaps, an exalted one, but one which is certainly as estimable and influential as that held by the majority of our art industries. The newspaper artist must of necessity be a man of many resources and an apt pencil. His ability to draw anything or everything at a moment's notice must be coupled with that prime qualification of a thorough journalist—the newspaper instinct. Of the men whose accomplishments in newspaper art have awakened comment and given them high position in the sphere of illustrative journalism, any piece of personal history or professional experience must be of general interest, and to this end the following notes, arranged for the most part from data furnished by the artists themselves, are given in the alphabetical order of the latter's names.

John Carleton Baker is one of the artistic lights of the New York World. He stepped into existence at Knoxville, Tenn., in 1867. He has had many experiences. Under the able direction of Lloyd Branson, this learned the essential principles of art, which knowledge fired his ambition to be at work in his chosen field. In 1887 Mr Baker went to Memphis, Tenn., and accepted a position as reporter and artist on the Appeal-Avalanche. The illustrations of that paper were made by the tedious and soul-trying chalk-plate process, which process Mr. Baker thinks, is an excellent developer of industrious habits and profanity. In 1888 Mr Baker found himself assistant editor of that brisk little weekly, the Sunny South, of Atlanta, Ga. In the early part of 1889 Mr Baker returned to his native town, Knoxville, and associated himself with the Journal of that place. In the fore part of 1891 Mr Baker came to New York, and for a time was a journalistic free-lance, writing special articles for various papers, and illustrating his own writings. Before he was in Gotham many weeks Mr. Baker joined the staff of artists employed by the New York World, and is to-day one of the cleverest cartoonists connected with Joseph Pulitzer's very enterprising journal.

Circumstances have peculiarly fitted Leon Barritt for the work of a cartoonist, as he has had a life-long association with newspaper work. He was a news-boy during the latter part of the civil war, and later a reporter, business manager, and proprietor of a newspaper. Such knowledge as

he has of art matters has been acquired in leisure time from newspaper work, and for ten years or more past he has happily combined his art and literary labor. Mr Barritt was born at Saugerties-on-the-Hudson, November 5, 1852. He early displayed a taste for art, and served a brief apprenticeship with a jewelry engraver in New York, acquiring such a knowledge of this art industry that he has (at such times as circumstances demanded it) made it a source of lucrative return. Mr. Barritt came to New York in 1880, from Middletown, N.Y., where he had been engaged in the publication of the Middletown Daily Argus. During the first year of his stay in New York Mr. Barritt did a general line of newspaper work, but finding an increasing demand for his cartoons, he opened a studio in the business quarter of New York, and now devotes his time entirely to the making of cartoons. For two years past this artist has been under contract to give the sprightly New York Daily Press all of his political cartoons, furnishing them with one large drawing every day. His work on social and other topics has appeared in Truth, and also in the Herald, Telegram, Mail and Express, Commercial Advertiser, and the Brooklyn Eagle and Standard-Union.

As clever as any kind of newspaper draughtsmanship now being done for the big dailies are the expressive and wholly artistic outline sketches of Henry Coultaus, the "H C" of the New York Herald. Mr. Coultaus is a Gothamite of purest water, being born (in 1861) in the natal or "old blue-blood" ward of New York City

Drawn by W. W. Denslow.

Drawn by H. Van Hofsten.

Drawn by Homer C. Davenport.

A SUMMER DAY'S SPORT.

Drawn by J. W. Trowbridge.

AMERICAN ART AND ARTISTS.

At the outset of his career he was a cash-boy in the famous dry-goods house of A. T. Stewart, but was sufficiently skilful with his pencil at the age of nineteen to become a special artist on the staff of The Daily Graphic—at that time the pace regulator of American illustrated journalism. When Mr. Coultaus left The Graphic it was to join forces with W. F. C. Shanks and his newspaper syndicate bureau. When Mr. Shanks became manager of the ill-fated New York Star, "H.C." was his chief art adviser. During the notorious Flack trial Mr. Coultaus furnished some startling court-room scenes and a series of striking portraits of every one directly interested in the case. These drawings were purely outline sketches, and were the first of their kind published in any New York newspaper. A deal of favorable criticism was passed upon these unique illustrations, and "H.C." was immediately placed in a higher class among newspaper artists. Not long after this "hit," the New York Herald made a bid for Mr. Coultaus's services, and he has been with that paper ever since. His style is a perfectly simple one, and his method is direct. In all, "H. C." is a strong individuality in the busy world of newspaper art.

One of the youngest of successful newspaper artists employed on a large journal is Walter B. Cox, whose drawings, reproduced in the New York Tribune, are always brimming with spirit and show the touch of a sensitive hand. Mr. Cox is but twenty-two years old, and the story of his life, as naïvely related by himself, runs like this: "I was born November 26, 1871, in Pascagoula, Miss., and spent the first few years of my childhood in Mississippi. Then my parents moved to Louisville, Ky., where we lived about three years. We then moved back to Mississippi, on the gulf shore. While we were staying there my father died, and our family went to New Orleans, La. It was while in New Orleans that my art education began. After attending an art school for about four months, working two hours a day and attending a sketch class on Saturdays, I came northward and settled in Northampton, Mass. Realizing the difficulty of making a living as an artist in Northampton, I took a trip to

Drawn by W¹th. McDougall.
"THE COUNTRYMAN."

Drawn by Walter B. Cox.
"SARTORIAL TYPES."

Drawn by M. de Lipman.
"BAITING BETS IN THE TRAMWAY."

Drawn by Charles Howard Johnson.
"THE FLIGHT OF TIME."

the metropolis. With specimens of my best work I tramped around the city for two months, getting nothing permanent in the way of employment. While I was hunting work a friend came to me and brought me to the Tribune office, where I was regularly installed. This was the first newspaper work that I had ever done; accordingly I had everything to learn, but under proper guidance I soon learned the method required in making newspaper illustrations." It would appear that this is the sort of perseverance which makes success yield to its desire. It is hardly disputable, at all events, that the sketches made by Walter B. Cox and printed in the Tribune rank with work of similar intention found in any of the illustrated sheets of the metropolis.

In the evergreen valley of the Willamette, Homer C. Davenport, whose work in the Chicago Herald is attractive and artistic, was born in 1867. On the Waldo Hills, covered with verdure and watered by cool springs, his boyhood days were spent. Almost from his cradle days the house walls suffered from his baby caricatures. The father, having some knowledge of the earlier American artists and the narrow margin between most of them and starvation, tried to turn his son's energies into what he considered a more lucrative channel. But the paternal persuasion was not yielded to by the would-be artist. A brief course in a commercial college resulted in a set of books highly ornamented with pen pictures of animated nature, but which the principal of the school declared were hopelessly unbalanced. In a fit of despair, the father sent the boy to the San Francisco Art School, at which date, 1889, his credited tuition began. A few months there, and he began drawing for the Portland (Ore.) Sunday Mercury. Six months in that employ, and a transition to the San Francisco Examiner came about. A short experience as one of the artists of the San Francisco Chronicle, and up to the present moment an engagement with the Chicago Herald, completes to date the brief but rich career of one talented newspaper artist.

Drawn by Wm. Bartlett.
"A SOCIAL RACE."

131

Everyone who has scanned an illustrated newspaper must know the name and artistry of Constantin de Grimm. There are few newspaper artists more prolific, and none more original in thought and execution. He was born in the Winter Palace at St. Petersburg, December 30, 1845, when his father was chief instructor to the children of the Czar Nicholas; the Czar Alexander II. was one of his pupils. The father removing to Berlin in 1860, Constantin's further education was had there at the College Français and at the Dresden Gymnasium. He incurred his father's displeasure by refusing an opportunity to enter the diplomatic service, and went to Leipsic to furnish articles and illustrations for the magazine Daheim. In 1867 he entered the army, and in 1868 was made a lieutenant to Emperor William's own regiment, the First Regiment of Guards. In the Franco-Prussian war he received the Iron Cross for bravery on the field of battle. At Sedan, on September 1, 1871, in command of two companies of the First Regiment, he captured an entire battalion of the French rank and file. He resigned from the army in 1873 to become assistant editor of the Kladderadatsch, the leading comic German paper. A year later he founded Puck at Leipsic. In 1879 he removed to Paris and was for a year a student of the École des Beaux Arts. In 1881 he resumed journalism as a society reporter and dramatic critic, founded in 1883 the sumptuous Club Almanac, and for a year was the Paris correspondent of four London papers. Baron de Grimm was transplanted from Paris to New York in 1884 by James Gordon Bennett, and did his best work for The Evening Telegram. He quit Mr. Bennett's employ after three years, but six years later—October, 1893—was voted, by New York Herald readers, that paper's prize of $2,000 for the most popular cartoonist. He is the art director of Hallo, the popular German comic illustrated weekly, an English edition of which begins publication this autumn. He has in press at the moment the De Grimm Portrait Souvenir, which contains some one thousand portraits of noted personages, all drawn by his own hand. Baron de Grimm is an indefatigable worker. In the nine years of his residence in New York he has not taken a formal vacation of even one day.

Another press artist who was born beyond the Atlantic is M. de Lipman. He comes from Heiligenstadt, a suburb of Vienna, Austria, where he first saw light on the 4th of July, 1865. In speaking of his career M. de Lipman says: "My first artistic efforts date away back to the fourth year of my existence, when I began making, to no highly satisfactory, attempts at drawing portraits of my brothers and sisters, especially of the latter, inasmuch as they were patient enough to pose for more than half a minute at a time. Later on, when I had demonstrated to the satisfaction, or rather dissatisfaction, of my parents, who wanted to make a business man of me, that art was the only profession in which I was at all likely to get along, I was permitted to take a course of instruction at the Academy of the Fine Arts in Vienna. Occasionally I contributed drawings to the local newspapers, but just where my maiden effort in that line was published has slipped my memory." A talented special artist, whose reputation is more extended in the West than elsewhere, is W. W. Denslow of the Chicago Herald. Mr. Denslow's work is marked with a certain enthusiasm of touch which makes it sufficiently dissimilar to the ordinary efforts of the newspaper artist to call forth praise. His personal history is that of the busy newspaper worker the region round. Thomas Fleming of The Commercial Advertiser is well known in New York newspaper circles. Born in Philadelphia thirty-nine years ago, he was originally a lithographic artist, but achieved so much success as a pen portrait artist that he studied newspaper illustration for the purpose of making it a life vocation. When Col. John A. Cockerill left The New York World to buy out the ancient Commercial Advertiser and establish The Morning Advertiser, Mr. Fleming was with him at the start. For many reasons Valerian Gribayedoff is hailed as the father of

AMERICAN ART AND ARTISTS.

Drawn by N. T. Smith. "A GAME OF CHESS."

Drawn by J. H. Knickerbocker. A COUNTRY ROAD.

daily newspaper illustrations. In a broad way it is the truth, and to no other man in newspaperdom is honor so richly due. "V. G.," as he signs himself, is a busy man, for his work is that of pictorial reporter, he can talk as he works, however, and he always finds time to offer his friends a cup of Russian tea or a glass of naliwki, a delicious Russian cordial. In addition to his newspaper labors, he does a large amount of work for Harper's, Scribner's, The Cosmopolitan Magazine, and other large publications. As a portraitist with pen and ink he is unexcelled. A great number of carefully considered and spiritedly executed illustrations have come from the hand of W. F. Hofacker within the past four years. Mr. Hofacker's experience as a newspaper artist began with his engagement on The New York World. After two years' service with this newspaper he joined the staff of The New York Recorder, and has signed drawings which the best of American newspaper illustrators might claim with pride. Hugo Von Hofsten is a newspaper illustrator who comes from Sweden, but whose ideas are quite American, and therefore breezy and original. In 1885 we came to America, hoping to find a wider field for his profession as illustrator, and has since then been connected with various publications in Chicago.

Charles Howard Johnson is now, strictly speaking, a newspaper artist, though many of his finest illustrations have been given publicity in The New York Herald. But twenty-six years of age, Mr. Johnson is widely known as a professional illustrator. Perhaps the very best drawings by Mr. Johnson are those published in Life.

Thirty-three years ago in Rochester, N. Y., J. H. Knickerbocker was born. In 1879 became to New York City and went to work on The Graphic. He remained with The Graphic nine years. He has since drawn for Frank Leslie's Weekly, The New York Herald, and the American Press Association. T. Kytko is not very widely known as a newspaper artist, though he is a man of high artistic talents. Charles Lederer is The Chicago Herald's satirist. He not only makes pictures of all sorts—pictures serious, sad, satirical, humorous, illustrative—but he leads and inspires writers. Carl Mauch is one of the successful foreign artists who have made the United States their permanent home. Mr. Mauch has lived here ever since the Franco-Prussian War. A very busy man is Wilt. Nickougall. What he calls his speckled career began at Newark, N. J., in 1858. He was reared in luxury until he was fifteen years old, when he was thrust out into the cold and became an engraver. In 1883 Mr. Nickougall tells us he made the first cartoon ever printed in a daily paper. He was the first artist to make army sketches (or a daily sheet. He has been on the stage, has written two books, and has drawn about seventeen thousand newspaper illustrations. Charles Nortimes is a World artist whose achievements are among the good things of current newspaper illustration. J. Franklin Van Sant is a newspaper caricaturist. J. Redman's range is wide and his method finished. C. H. Wright is an artist who can handle any subject with the pencil. H. T. Smith hails from the land of the Briton. W. J. Yocell is an expert newsillustrator. With careful presswork, and the use of fine paper, the illustrated news-sheet may some day rise to the dignity of a public art teacher.—ED.

AMERICAN ART AND ARTISTS.

THE VILLAGE BLACKSMITH SHOP.

Drawn by J. H. Knickerbocker

134

GLIMPSES OF PICTURESQUE PLACES

By GEORGE PARSONS LATHROP

With original Illustrations by Harry Fenn.

Many of our readers will recall Helen Hunt Jackson's delightful little book, years ago, named "Bits of Travel," which gave in literature what this handful of Harry Fenn's sketches conveys to us in graphic art. These, like these, open some long covered hoop-hole or little casement of memory, disclosing briefly, yet fresh as they were the first day, glimpses from old loiterings in foreign lands.

Mr. Fenn is as well known to the world as some considerable portions of it are known to him; which is saying a great deal. Although born in Richmond, Surrey, England, in 1841, he must decidedly be counted as an American artist; since all his career has been made here and his works have been brought out and published here. All of which resulted from a sketching tour that brought him hither in 1861, with the intention of remaining six years. The land won him and he, meanwhile, won an American wife. After two

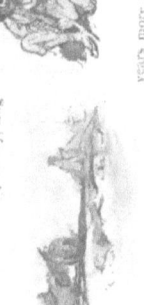

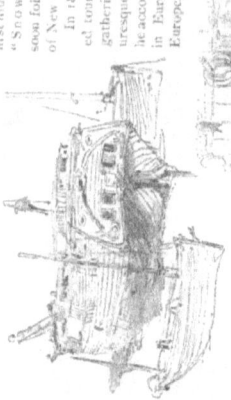

years more in Europe—half of that time being spent in Italy in the practice of water-color painting—he returned to the country of his choice and produced his first illustrated book, Whittier's "Snow Bound," which was soon followed by the "Ballads of New England."

In 1870 he made an extended tour of the United States, gathering material for "Picturesque America." In 1873 he accomplished a similar tour in Europe for "Picturesque Europe," and later went to the Orient with J. D. Woodward, making a long stay there in preparation for "Picturesque Palestine, Syria and Egypt." During some fourteen months of this long trip he never once slept under a roof.

The faithful "Lookout" dog

AMERICAN ART AND ARTISTS.

WEE GOAT.

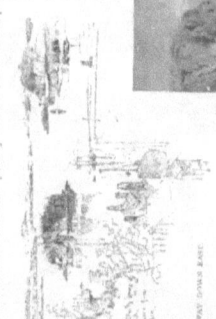

WEE DONEGAL BARN.

WAITING FOR THE MASTER.

OLD-FASHIONED KITCHEN.

seems still to be awaiting the wanderer's return. But this is all in recollection now, for Mr. Fenn long since came home, leaving seductive regions like the Golden Shell—as the bay and city of Palermo are called—where Monte Pelegrino towers like a massive dream—gone the drawing here.

So, too, like living mile-stones half dozen Oriental figures stand for the Lazy Men of the East, apparently divided as to taste and occupation between militarism and music.

The humdrum and the purely useful have their picturesqueness to the artistic tourist's eye; and so we pass on the traveller's track, these fixed, not the Wise but rather from the Orient to England's shore, and note with new surprise the interest attaching to a broad-beamed old hulk in Margate harbor, or visit the barrel-makers, who busily "hoop her up" at the rate of fifty a day. Among the easiest impressions of foreign journeys, also, are those solid, roomy kitchen interiors with wide fire-places and portly bake-ovens, such as we here behold again. American Eastport traces itself in lightery, sketcher lines, but how suggestive of English rivers is the old boat with fish-wet baskets, and how strong the lovely sea-washed Donegal headland!

Mr. Fenn was one of the founders of the Water Color Society, and still, though busily engaged in illustrating, gives about one quarter of his time to water-color painting.

AMERICAN ART AND ARTISTS.

THE PENNSYLVANIA ACADEMY OF THE FINE ARTS.

By Charles McIlvaine

(With original illustrations by prominent members)

There is a veritable savor of 1776 about the Pennsylvania Academy of Fine Arts. Founded in 1805, but little over a century's quarter after the State House bell rang out its immortal peal of American Independence, the first meetings of its founders were held under the same roof sheltering the Congress of Patriots that gave the bell its special tongue.

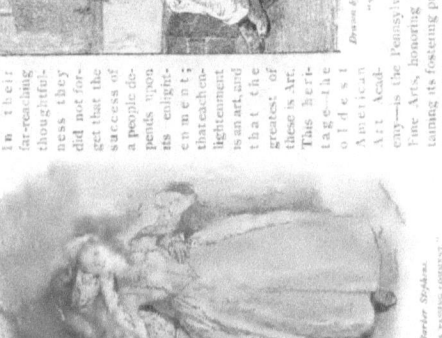

Drawn by Henry McCarter
"THE TOBOGGAN."

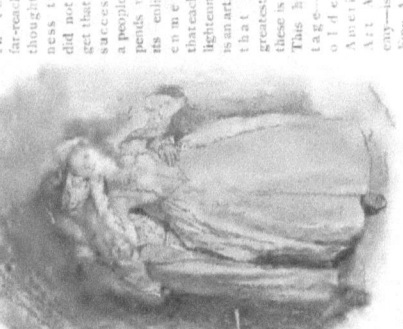

Drawn by Alice Barber Stephens.
"A PASSING CONTRAST."

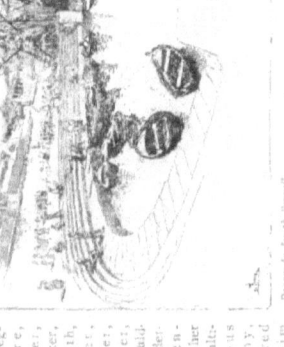

Drawn by Jacob Pennell

Drawn by Peter Moran

From a painting by William T. Trego

From a painting by James F. Kelly
"OLD AND KNOWING."

By Charles Grafly

One of the signers of the Declaration of Independence, George Clymer, was its first president.

Of those who fathered a nation were the parents of the first American Academy. In their far-reaching thoughtfulness they did not forget that the success of a people depends upon its enlightenment; that each enlightenment is an art, and that the greatest of these is Art. This heritage—the oldest American Art Academy—is the Pennsylvania Academy of Fine Arts, honoring its parentage, retaining its fostering protection, and projecting a future for American Art in which shall give it first place among the nations of the earth.

As early as 1791, Charles Wilson Peale, "captain of volunteers," member of the legislature, saddler, clockmaker, silversmith, painter, modeller, engraver, glass moulder, taxidermist, dentist, father of a multitudinous progeny, gathered about him those inter-

DRIVING THE CATTLE HOME.
From a painting by Peter Moran.

AMERICAN ART AND ARTISTS.

ested in giving to the sparsely feathered nation, by the impetus of organization, a school for American Art.

This organization, named the Columbianum, was successfully competed in 1794. The walls of Independence Hall were hung

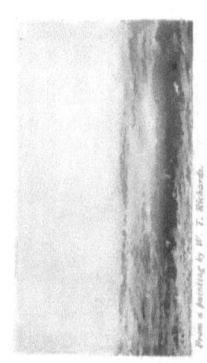

Drawn by W. Sartain.

Drawn by Frank Fowler. "A FAUN."

they would buy, and what they would build, and what they would do, for love of that gracious Genie—Art.

The facts of history are seven-leagued. The strides reach 1805. The building of 1807 has been carted away. On Philadelphia's broadest street, the name,—The Pennsylvania Academy of the Fine Arts, is carved on stone over

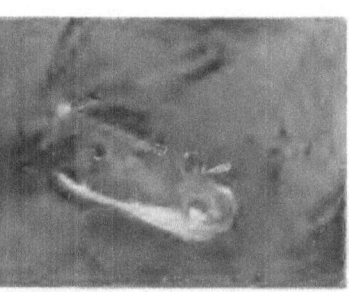

From a painting by W. T. Richards. "THE MILL DAM, NEWPORT."

the grand entrance to a fitting palace where Art is queen.

Pointing with well-earned pride to the long list of world-famed men and women, one time students under the Academy's tutelage, she names Peter F. Rothermel, stirring patriotism in all who stand before his picture of Patrick Henry; Samuel B. Waugh, indicator of attractiveness in American scenery; Christian Schussele, whose surname fitted

Drawn by Jerome L. G. Ferris. "A CHIEFTAIN OF YE OLD SCHOOL."

his life, and whose hand, though palsied, and whose eyes, though dim, directed for eleven years the Academy's classes within his own ambitions, but to possibilities beyond; Edward and Thomas Moran, always delighting with etchings of cheery life; James Hamilton, he of hilarious memory, and scratcher of the sun's secrets; Wm. T. Richards, who coaxes into silent places, and paints Nature's whispers; John Sartain, the grandfather of steel engravings; D. Ridgway

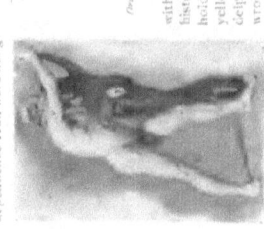

From a painting by Chloe Campbell Custer, Jr. "YE OLD HOUSE."

AMERICAN ART AND ARTISTS.

Drawn by Jerome I. G. Ferris.   A FLANEUR

From an etching by Joseph Pennell.   ST. PAUL'S CATHEDRAL.

AMERICAN ART AND ARTISTS.

Drawn by D. Ridgway Knight.
"HOME IN THE LAKE."

Knight, broad as the Continent in his early portraiture of American subjects, but delicate as the daintiest portrayer of French life and atmosphere, wearer of the ribbon of the Legion of Honor and medals of the French Salon; Stephen J. Ferris, at-

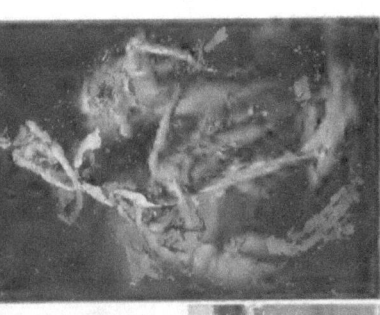

Drawn by William M. Canlin.
"CONDURING."

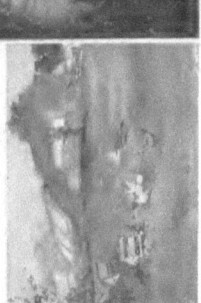

From a painting by Henry Thouron.
"QUICKENING."

indelibility; a score of others equally faithful to their calling as artists and the nest of their bowering—Lovell Birge Harrison, Robert Blum, George W. Plait, John J. Boyle, James F. Kelly, Carl Newman, now member of the Academy's Faculty; Henry R. Poore.

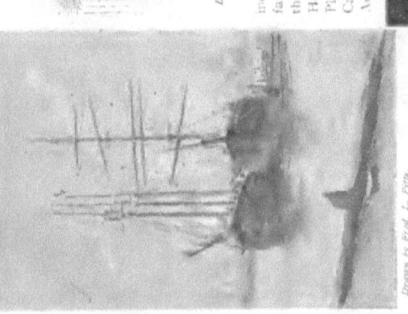

From a painting by Robert Henri.
"FIELD LABORS."

Drawn by Stephen J. Ferris.
"AMATIO CUTTERS."

tractive in whatever he essays; Milne Ramsey, a cherished recorder of pleasant things; Kenyon Cox, full of the *spirituelle*; and Abbey, telling of classics and meadows, and lasses of long ago.

Thomas Eakins, foremost of his school at the Academy, long time instructor, Thomas

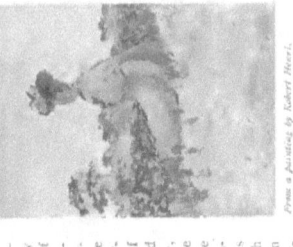

Drawn by Fred L. Pitts.
"COOPER'S FARM."

Drawn by P. Crosson Schell.
"THE BRITISH JACK TARS."

in sympathy with our household pets, Herman Y. Deigendesch, M. K. Trotter, Wm. T. Smedley the illustrator, Benj. F. Gillman—and the list stops not there.

The Academy has not given a Rosa Bonheur to America, but of its women pupils stand forth Ida Waugh and Emily Sartain, as fathered by it. Also

From a painting by Henry R. Poore.
"BEGGING BRUNO."

Anshutz, the conscientious, now teacher of the classes drawing from the antique; Joseph Pennell, whose pencil goes so accurately to the resident what his eye sees abroad, Frank D. Briscoe, at home with brush, pen, or pencil, anywhere where sight is worth

Drawn by Lewis M. Woodman.
"RESTING."

AMERICAN ART AND ARTISTS.

From a painting by Charles Henley.
"A SCENE"

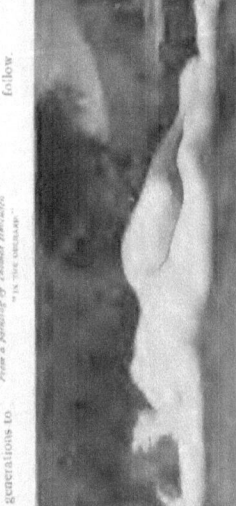
From a painting by Carl Newman.

Drawn by F. E. Gregor.
"IN DEEP WOOD"

Alice Barber Stephens and Cecelia Beau, women loved where art in magazines is dear.

There is revolution in artists as well as in art. America might claim primogeniture of architects in the Cliff Dwellers, bas-relief moulders in the Mound Builders, artists by the Aborigines, She cares not to do that; she is content with her Academy.

Springing, winging, spreading themselves notoriously over the continent are her recent offspring—the grasshoppers as it—those who are chirpy, assertive, devouring, and destined to succeed their fully-fledged predecessors. Among them are F. L. Tubian, doing black and white chromatics most acceptably, from the heights of society to the councils of the chicken yard, for the prominent publications of the day; Geodes, MacCarter,

and Daggy, already climbing to the top of humorous delineators, pointed at fatuity as successors to the inimitable A. B. Frost, with an individuality bred curiously by a common parent mixed with polymorphic genius.

Nosuch church within the country—no other single art holding Keystone State as the Academy has without recognition Academy has ever good work by its own earnings, and of those holding independence of The Academy generation that own and their that will live in follow.

While holding has been hatched tiny from any nest. the name of the first to its title, honored the State tion from it. The been held to its own earnings, and of those holding independence of The Academy generation that own and their that will live in follow.

brooks to-day the will advance her glory—a glory all generations to the blood and honored founders, the contributions

BREAKFAST IN THE COOLIES' FORECASTLE OF A PACIFIC LINER.

Drawn by Milton H. Bancroft.

AN ARTIST IN BUSINESS.

By HENRY MELFORD STEELE

(With original illustrations by James Symington.)

THE old notion that an artist or a man of letters must necessarily be unfitted for a business life has been pretty well exploded during recent years. Perhaps the most interesting demonstration of the falsity of the old theory is furnished by the career of the firm composed of James Symington and F. Hopkinson Smith, who are successfully engaged in the eminently practical business of building lighthouses, breakwaters, sea-walls, and other stone construction. Both these men are painters of established reputation, and one of them is a famous author as well.

James Symington was born in Maryland in 1841, and early manifested a fondness for drawing, in which he was encouraged by a Presbyterian minister who took a fancy to him and who was himself a draughtsman of considerable skill. In 1853 Symington went to Cincinnati, and at the age of fourteen or fifteen found himself engaged in writing out the opinions of the Judges of the Superior Court for the official reports. This occupation gave his thoughts another turn, and he began regularly to study law. But his love for drawing did not leave him; on the contrary, it was strong enough to lead him to enter a night class, where he worked steadily for a year or two, making satisfactory progress.

At the beginning of the war, he joined the 18th Mississippi Regiment of the Confederate army as a private, and served until the war ended in 1865. During the latter part of the war he became an ordnance sergeant, and was quartered for a time near Richmond, where he had charge of some blast furnaces. Iron was extremely scarce in those days, and whenever the Ordnance Department heard of a furnace anywhere in the mountains some one was sent off at once to investigate and report upon the quantity and quality of the output, and upon the facilities for its transportation. Thus difficult, and at times exceedingly dangerous, duty usually fell to Sergeant Symington, and during this period a great deal of his time was spent in the saddle.

On more than one occasion he had experiences which nearly cost him his life. He tells the following story of a winter's adventure: from my quartermaster directing me to look up an iron furnace he had heard of somewhere in the mountains of Patrick property of a man named Samuel Hairson, was one of the richest men in Virginia, and the owner of more than thirty-seven hundred slaves; a veritable colony of servile blacks. Although the furnace was only a small one, the iron produced was exceedingly fine in quality; but it was sixty miles from Danville, the nearest railroad station. I should have taken a horse at Danville, but the quartermaster assured me that I would have no difficulty in finding one at Henry Courthouse, and advised me to take a stage from Danville to that place. I did so. Henry Courthouse was forty miles from Danville. It was winter, and soon after we started snow began to fall and continued steadily all day. When we reached Henry Courthouse the snow was six inches deep, and still falling as if it never meant to stop. I put up at the little country tavern; there were only two stores in it—one in the kitchen and the other in the parlor—but I managed to get through the night in reasonable comfort. The next morning the snow was more than eighteen inches deep. I spent two days looking for a horse, but there was not one to be had, and I finally determined

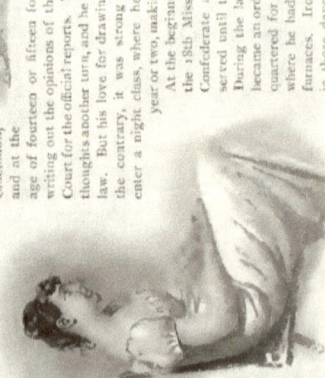

"A HINDOO GIRL."

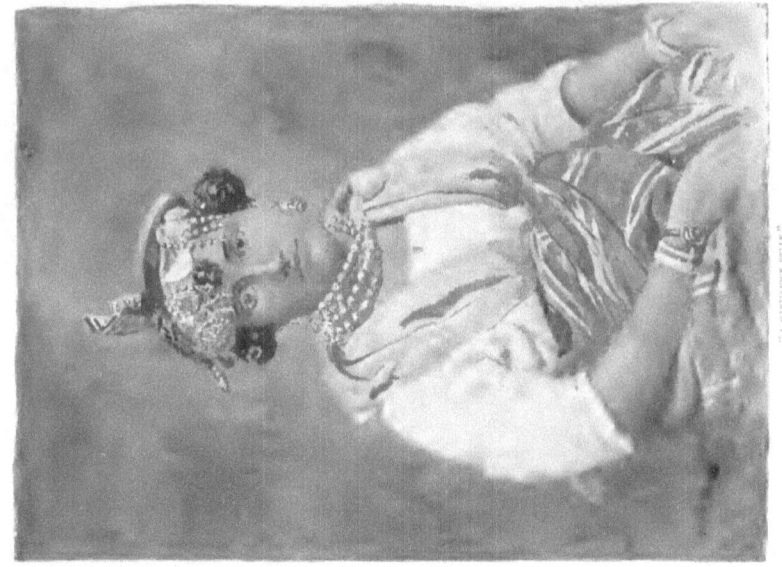

"A NAUTCH GIRL."

AMERICAN ART AND ARTISTS.

to push on afoot. Accordingly, the next morning I set out on my twenty-mile walk. After I had made about six miles I came to a river which I was obliged to ford. The water was fully four feet deep and very cold. I got across somehow, soaked through, of course, and nearly frozen. Here I found that an uncle of Hairson's lived about two miles up the stream, and I started at once for his plantation. I was about the sorriest looking tramp imaginable when I arrived; but I explained who I was, and received the warmest sort of a welcome. I stayed there two days, resting, for I was pretty well used up. They wanted me to stay a couple of weeks, but I knew that I ought to be going.

"My host offered to lend me a horse to go a part of the way, and he sent a darky boy along with me to take the animal back. His parting instructions were to the effect that I must send the boy back as soon as we reached a point beyond which he did not know the road. We started off bravely enough; but at the end of nine miles the boy turned back and I clambered along up the mountain on foot. It was mighty hard travelling. The snow was covered with ice about an eighth of an inch thick, which broke through at every step and made anything like satisfactory progress impossible. Several times I was on the point of giving up altogether; but I floundered on, and at last, to my great joy, and by one of those lucky accidents which sometimes happen, I met Hairson and his son on horseback. Hairson took the boy up behind him and gave me the lad's horse, and together we made our way to his home. I was so completely exhausted that it was all I could do to keep from falling

"A MAP OF BROGDAN."

"FULL DRESS, MARTINIQUE."

off the horse; but we reached the house at last, where I was immediately put to bed.

"It was two weeks before I was able to leave that place."

Mr. Symington's adventures in the wild mountain country of Virginia furnished him with an abundance of material for an unusually interesting book, which it is hoped he may some day be prevailed upon to write.

When the war was over, in 1865, Mr. Symington came to New York and engaged in business with his present partner, Mr. F. Hopkinson Smith, to whom he is distantly related. He studied for some time at the Academy of Design, generally at night, and his water colors soon began to attract attention. He made drawings for Frank Leslie's Illustrated Newspaper, and at one time Mr. Leslie sought to engage him as one of

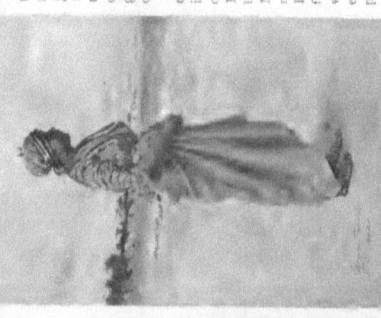

"ALONG THE SHORE, WINDWARD ISLAND."

"A DUTCH COAT, SCHEVENINGEN."

"STARS AND ROSE."

the regular staff of artists permanently employed on the paper. He joined the Water Color Society in 1878, and has been its treasurer for the past nine years. He is reëlected every year, and has come to be regarded as the permanent treasurer of the society.

In 1887 Mr. Symington made an extended trip through Europe, painting industriously all the time. In company with Thulstrup and H. W. Ranger he wandered through England, France, Germany, Sweden, and Norway, and brought back an immense number of studies and pictures. He has travelled all over this country from the coast of Maine to southwestern Texas, investigating different varieties of building-stone, and painting by the way. Mr. Symington is one of the most popular men in the profession, and he deserves it.

Drawn by James Symington. WHAT ARE THE WILD WAVES SAYING?

Drawn by James Symington. SOME NORWEGIAN WOMEN.

AMERICAN ART AND ARTISTS.

A PAINTER OF MARINE SUBJECTS.

By JNO. GILMER SPEED.

(With original illustrations by James G. Tyler.)

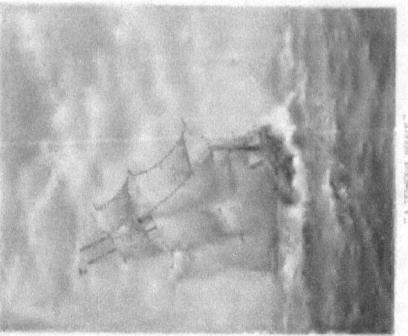

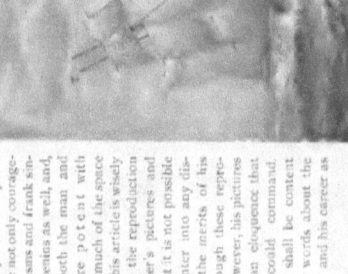

"STORM GULL."

"MARSHES."

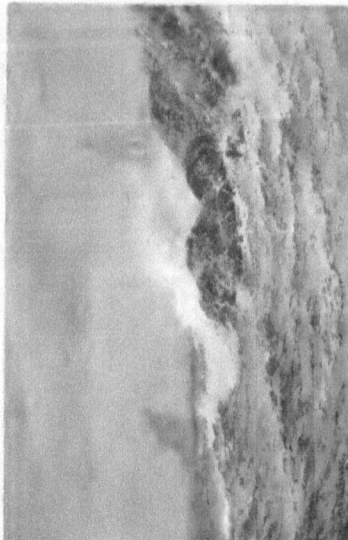

"A TEMPEST SHEEN."

"BOUNDING CAPE ANN."

"IN PORT."

WHEN an artist has enthusiasms, and the courage of them, he is likely to get a good deal of happiness out of his art "whatever woe betide." When these enthusiasms, and the following of them, lead to success, the artist thus possessed and thus guided is to be envied among men. This reflection has been suggested by the work and the personality of James G. Tyler, the well-known marine painter, for both the man and the pictures are alive with enthusiasms which will not be denied, but on the contrary are apt to become contagious.

He paints just the way he thinks he ought to paint, without reference to what critics may say and other artists think, and he speaks out his mind with a manly freedom which seems to count silence as cowardly. One of his friends, commenting on this characteristic in reproving tones, said, "Jim talks too much!" Fortunately for those who come within his circle, Mr. Tyler does not agree with this friend, and therefore has acquaintances are not denied the pleasure and the profit of the thoughts of a mind all untrammelled. Such characteristics can only be accompanied with

great sincerity. In Mr. Tyler's case we have not only courageous enthusiasms and frank sincerity, but genius as well, and, therefore, both the man and his work are potent with charm. So much of the space allotted to this article is wisely given up to the reproduction of Mr. Tyler's pictures and sketches that it is not possible for me to enter into any discussion of the merits of his work. Through these reproductions, however, his pictures speak with an eloquence that no writer could command. Therefore, I shall be content to say a few words about the man himself and his career as an artist.

Mr. Tyler began painting in 1870, when he was fifteen years old. He was then living in his native Oswego. He gained some little local fame before he had been at work a year, and when a

AMERICAN ART AND ARTISTS.

should move with it."

The young man thought that there was a deal of sense in the comment, but at the time he was suspicious that a joke was being played upon him, and that a casual tramp had been pressed into service to play the part of visiting Academician. At his day, some twenty years later, Mr. Tyler is not sure that the shabby gentleman who called on him at Oswego is not the ablest of all American landscape painters. The writer is tolerably sure that he is. At all events he has many admirers.

"THE BREAKWATER."

The next year Mr. Tyler painted about three months in the studio of A. Cary Smith, then well known as a marine painter, though at present he has deserted the pictorial art to be a designer of yachts. This is the only instruction Mr. Tyler has ever had save that which he has given himself. And to himself he has been a hard and exacting master, for never yet has he produced a work that was to himself entirely satisfactory. Recognizing, however, that what he did was as good as he had the time and power to make it, he has given his works to the world with a clear conscience.

Mr. Tyler, like Mr. Albert Ryder, for whom, by the way, he has a very warm

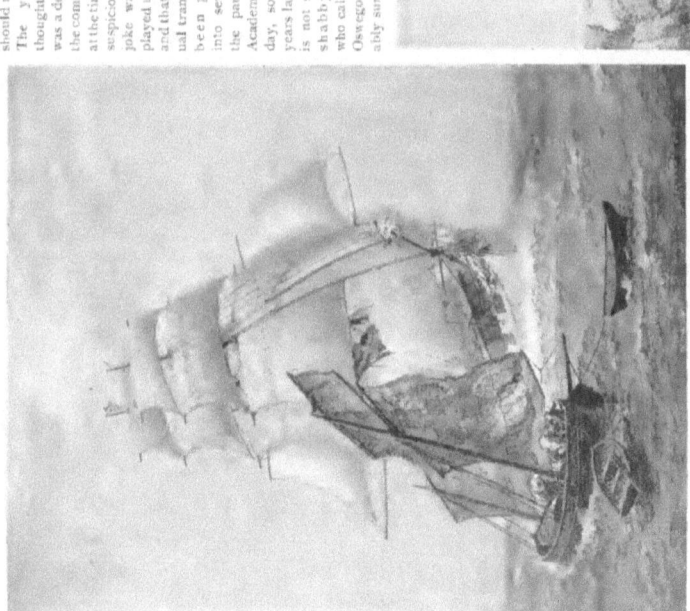

"CREETING A STRANGER."

member of the National Academy visited the town he was taken to see the youthful celebrity. This Academician, though a man of genuinely well earned fame, is not a handsome man in the eyes of strangers, nor does he clothe himself with any degree of smartness. His fame had not reached young Tyler's studio, and the man himself did not look in the least as the boy artist thought an Academician should look. The elder and somewhat shabby man looked at the lad's canvas through his glasses and said kindly: "Your boat moves, my boy, but your clouds admiration, paints from his imagination, and his imagination should be spelled with a big I. He, therefore, escapes the commonplace, and in this achieves no mean distinction. It must not be understood by this that Mr. Tyler is a painter of the uncanny. It is true that in an exhibition at the Academy a few years ago he had a picture of the "Flying Dutchman," and Mr. Ryder, by the way, treated the same subject for the same exhibition. But even in putting on canvas

"A BROADSIDE."

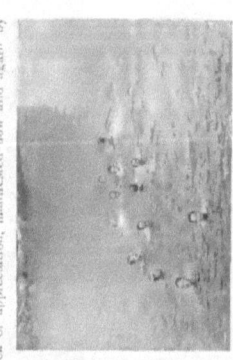

"SKIRMISH."

such a baffling subject as this, Mr. Tyler was equal to the occasion, and came near to satisfying the very severest critics who were gifted with any imagination. It was most interesting at this exhibition to contrast the conceptions of Ryder and Tyler and their methods of treatment. The opinion of connoisseurs was about equally divided, and of critics as well. This was without doubt Ryder's masterpiece, and Tyler has said with characteristic frankness that he greatly preferred it to his own. Tyler's was a study in gray, the phantom ship half revealed in a bank of fog; Ryder's phantom ship was seen in a blaze of glorious color. Both were poetical, both were satisfying. Mr. Tyler's masterpiece, according to his own judgment, is a painting recently finished, and called "The Dawn of the New World." This picture is the result of much hard work and study. It is an effort to represent

the little fleet of Columbus just as land is discovered. Mr. Tyler made this picture before the Columbian caravels had been built, and he needed to find his models in the old records. He has succeeded most admirably, and in this picture there seems to be a happy combination of the real and the ideal. Without this combination, probably no picture is quite worth while to be made. It would be a pity for such a picture as this to be buried in some private collection, and it is to be hoped that the movement to secure it for the Capitol at Washington will be successfully pushed. There is room in that great pile for many pictures, but there are unfortunately not many now there worthy of national ownership.

Mr. Tyler is an impressionist, and sacrifices nothing whatever to the fidelity of detail upon which many realists waste all their time and power. Painting from within himself, instead of copying merely that which he sees, it is only natural that he should frequently produce results incomprehensible to those who have no head above their eyes. But this lack of appreciation, manifested now and again by hanging committees, "bothers" Mr. Tyler not in the least, for he feels that it is his mission in life to point his own pictures in his own way; to please himself and satisfy his own sense of beauty, and what Carlyle called "the eternal verities," without reference to a few busy nobodies who have elbowed themselves into place and authority for the sake of the cheap fame which passes almost as soon as it has come.

From a painting by James G. Tyler.

AMERICAN ART AND ARTISTS.

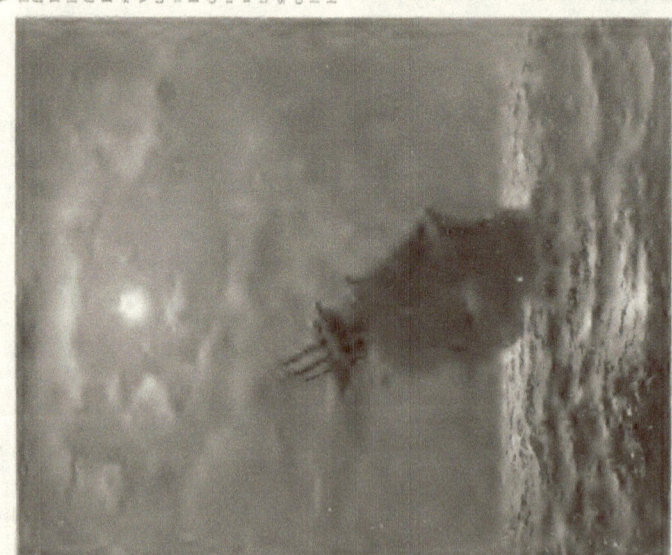

From a painting by James G. Tyler. MOONLIGHT AT SEA.

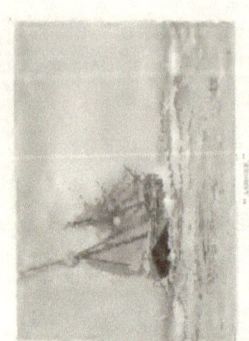

"SUNRISE."

"HOMEWARD YONDERLAND."

When Mr. Tyler sees his own picture rejected, and the half-finished offering of his pupil hung upon the line, he merely laughs and sells his own canvas for five hundred dollars or so. He has his money, and his sustaining enthusiasms remain with him always. These enthusiasms would go far toward making Mr. Tyler happy with his lot, even though he had to do without very much of the money. Not that he despises money—not at all. Even though gifted with an imagination that soars and soars in new er atmospheres, and sails on undiscovered seas, he is too human to despise money, though he confesses freely that he has hated to have to make many of the pot-boilers to which he has signed his name. Fortunately for him and for his art, the pot-boiling era has been passed.

No longer do the skies on his canvas cloud over, and the waves lash in fury at any bidding save that of the inspiration of the moment. His free-winged boats move on a self-appointed mission, and the salt winds have blown away the mists of conventionality. Mr. Tyler loves the changeful sea for its own sake first, and for art's sake afterward; surely much may be forgiven the ardent admirer, if he paint both the realities and the possibilities.

AMERICAN ART AND ARTISTS.

A HALF-HOUR WITH STUDIO BORES.

By CHARLES DE KAY.

(With original illustrations by numerous artists.)

"THERE it goes again!"

The painter strode testily to the door, swept aside the portière, opened a crack and chanted rather than remarked, "Thank you, no, not to-day."

"They are always coming," he continued, craning back his head to look at his canvas. "If it's not a beggar, it's a peddler; and if it's not a model, it's the worst of all—the amateur who wants to pose."

"Danielson told me," I remarked, "that one of the best models he ever had was a young lady, a rank amateur, who earned pin-money unknown to her family. She was shapely as Dian, and as irreproachable."

"Danielson's in luck. Generally they are far from well formed, bore one to death before coming to the point, and hate you forever when you politely say you cannot use them. If they really needed to work, I would not mind. But, any-

By Amy L. Killing. "AN AMATEUR POSTURE."

how, give me a professional, every time."

"They do need the money—oftener than you think," I answered. "But I suppose it's generally vanity of the person. Now, the vanity of women is caution—to men."

"Well, now—see here—I know exceptions."

"Of course—and the men, too. Did you ever notice how

From painting by Bruce Crane. "MIDSUMMER."

Drawn by A. B. Davies. "NUDE IN VERSE."

ing men and boxers, how they stand around stripped after their bath to be admired, puffing out their chest muscles and clinching their fists to brag up the biceps?"

"I'm not much in that line. All I have time for is an hour with the foils round at the fencing club when it's too dark to paint. That gives me just the right glow in muscles, and makes me sleep like a top."

"Carroll Beckwith has a good model," said I, "and Irving Wiles has the monopoly of some very lovely sitter—romantic but not a bit silly."

"Beckwith's a good draughtsman, and no mistake," said he pensively and as if with reluctance. "At one time I thought the French had swallowed him forever—Carolus Duran and all that—but he's struck out for himself,

Drawn by H. B. Harte. "MASK OF ST. THOMAS' CHURCH, NEW YORK."

and be paints now as well as he draws. There it goes again!"

A sound at the door. A timid scrabble at the knocker.

"Five dollars or a dinner it's a lady who wants to pose for the good of art—draped, of course—but will at last condescend to take pay for her services!"

"Done!"

The door opens, and in hobbles a wonderful old trot,

Drawn by Carlton T. Chapman. "A SEA FIGHT."

From a painting by Joseph Lauber.
THE SHORTEST WAY HOME.

who speaks English that sounds like a cross between Cape Cod and Cadgey. She is dressed exactly like one of the old wrinkled countrymarms President Wood paints for the Academy She sits down on the edge of a chair and mystifies us not a little, until I get a chance to whisper in the painter's ear, "Look at its boots."

The painter marches up to the crone, tweaks off a bonnet and wig, and takes by the ear the inhabitant of another studio on the floor above, who thereupon breaks into a yell of laughter and throws himself on a divan.

"I've won," I remark. "So far as exterior goes, it's a lady, and she came to pose. She

"Well, that's just it," said the other. "You never do look at anything, and that's why the public buy your pictures—a fellow feeling, you know."

"It makes no difference," said I, coming to his aid, "whether you artists see anything yourselves or not. All you have to do is to find out what and how much the public sees, and then paint with the eyes of the public. Then you're made."

A wad of paint-rags whistled

by my ear. The masquerading artist sat up very stiff and shook his fist, uttering oaths in Italian, Spanish, French and German.

"Regular art-critic talk. You make me ill."

"Nothing sounds like the truth. I'm only agreeing with you."

"Half truths do more harm than lies."

"You'll acknowledge that artists must live," I interposed, "that few are supported while they are waiting to be discovered as a business way, and that most of you are trying to guess what the public wants. As one journalist of note remarked: 'Yes, cats are still doing something this year, but I think dogs are stronger.' Find out the fashion and plunge in."

and I will dine with you to-night."

"I should think you knew I had interruptions enough," severely, to his friend the painter, "without playing my chest-nuts like this! If I'd taken the trouble to look at you, I'd have seen right through you. Bah!"

"Speaking of animals," said the painter, glad to escape from a painful subject, "did you ever notice how much music Reinhart gets into his Southern illustrations—the sublime patience of his beasts, and the look of waiting for the right time to kick?"

"Reinhart is a Virginian, I believe, and grew up with mules and darkies; or, if not Virginian, he belongs to Southern Pennsylvania, which is

156 AMERICAN ART AND ARTISTS.

From a painting by Hermann Simon.

INNOCENCE ABROAD.

AMERICAN ART AND ARTISTS.

Drawn by G. A. Traver. "TURN TO SEE."

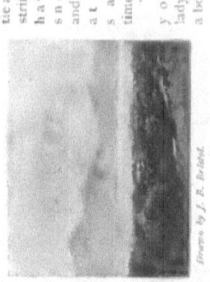

Drawn by R. Birch. "LADY CRUSOE."

Drawn by Arthur I. Keller. "ABOUT TWELVE."

much the same—mules, buzzards, draws, pickaninnies and the rest."

A yawn from the painter is interrupted by a peremptory tattoo on the knocker. There is an obscure sound beyond the portière like the rustling of skirts and subdued coughing. The door is thrown open, and a tall young lady enters, with a most belligerent boa of cock's feathers round her throat; she is followed by a stout elderly lady in furs. They march in with an air of ownership, regard the old woman and me with evident distaste.

Abashed, I retire to a corner of the studio, where I open a portfolio of drawings. Here are a laughing monk, drawn with much pains as to wrinkles, by Fred Webster; a seated youth, by George W. Brock; a "regular boy" with his hands in his pockets, by F. C. Gordon; a Venice water-color by Boggett, and sketches by young Malcolm Fraser, by H. B. Herts, by Edwin R. Child, Morgan Kaees, C. M. Relyea, Archie Gunn,

and others more or less known like them as illustrators or as painters in oil. As I raise my head, the handsome but high-nosed young lady with the boa is surveying the walls of the studio.

"I like that," she exclaims stabbing the air with her parasol before a landscape with pool, lily-pads, partly denuded tree on the right, and a charming effect of distance back to the horizon.

"It is by a friend of mine, Bruce Crane," remarks the painter in an uncertain voice. The dubious one and I exchange glances, and the former feels it necessary to double up and tie a shoestring. I have to sneeze and cough at the same time.

The young lady with a boa regarded us suspiciously through her eyeglasses. Something told her (it was not the fear of using up the painter's time) that it was the moment to leave. I noticed that she lingered in the hall, perhaps apologizing for the queer pair of loafers on his studio.

The silence was thick enough to cut with a palette knife when the artist returned to his easel rather red in the face and preoccupied.

"Neighbor!" squeaked the old woman, in comacoy voice, "a dunt know nathin' boout pictur, but a dew know what a lickt. Now that ther' pictur o' yourn, I swow, it's a cheff-doever!" and he pointed to a drawing by Reginald Birch pinned against the wall.

But the painter was too sulky to rise to this bait. Finally he said.

"You remind me (opposites suggest each other) of a story Geo. Smith tells. He began as a painter of high-bred horses, in Chicago, before he

AMERICAN ART AND ARTISTS.

SALMON FISHING CAMP ON THE RESTIGOUCHE.
Drawn by Henry Sandham.

HAPPY IN GRANDPA.
From a painting by Edward Gradner.

A VERSATILE ARTIST.

By Alexander Black.

(With original illustrations by Carle J. Blenner.)

CARLE J. BLENNER belongs to that interesting group of American artists which we sometimes vaguely describe as "the younger men," or as vaguely again as "the rising men." A Virginian by birth, an alumnus of Yale, he has, within the space of a very few years, exhibited a capacity to be cosmopolitan in style to a degree such as only Americans, perhaps, ever can. He received his art education—or perhaps, in the case of a student so indefatigable, we should say the academic part of his education—at Paris, under Bouguereau, Schenck, and other masters, from whom he returned with a firmly individual style.

"AN OLD-FASHIONED GARDEN, CONNECTICUT."

His work displays a great deal of versatility, ranging from the most delicate forms of landscape to spirited portraiture. At the World's Fair he exhibits "Contentment," and a portrait of Señor Don Roderigo de Saavedra of the Spanish Legation, both admirable examples of his style. That Mr. Blenner will always be effective in portraiture is hinted in the force and character of his figure studies, which contain subtle draughtsmanship and wholesome phases of color. The head of an old woman reproduced in one of the illustrations to the present article is a piece of clever realism in which there is a keen reading of the human nature lying beneath the surface. "Country Life" tells the simple yet always freshly eloquent story of the farm and its unexciting routine. The elements of the picture are skilfully brought together, and the work throughout is sincere and direct. How neatly Mr. Blenner manages sentiment may be indicated by "Afternoon Tea," which belongs to the *terra de société* of painting, and which makes no attempt to

"IN THE CABBAGE FIELD."

retreat with a freshly painted canvas as a shield.

"And the lady in the cock's-feather boa? You were polite enough to her. Social racket, ch?"

"That lady, sir, is my betrothed."

"Great Scott! Congrat— good-by!"

I retired in good order on the door, covering the

Drawn by J. Carroll Beckwith. "A FAVORITE."

Drawn by G. W. Breck. "THE SKEPTIC."

went in so much for cattle. One day the trainer, Splan, introduced him to Rarus loose in his box stall. After seeing him installed (to pun) the trainer went out and happened to be called away from the stable. Rarus got so fond of Gean, or else he was so almightly tickled to be painted at all, that when Gean tried to leave, the horse wouldn't let him."

"And is this yer a parable?" asked the other, feigning not to understand the hint.

"It means I won't prevent your going, as Rarus did," remarked the painter, sourly. He made a dying leap at the other wall, pulled down a duelling-sword with a button on the tip, and, throwing himself into position, began to lunge at me and his friend—who gathered up his skirts and fled.

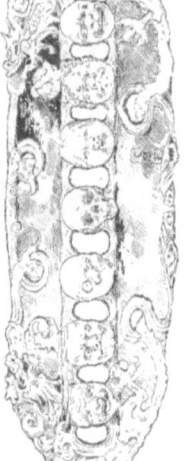

Drawn by Malcolm Fraser. "MRS. THE PURITAN TURNS DOWN."

AMERICAN ART AND ARTISTS.

give to the old romance anything more than its natural charm. This is one of the stories that always are told best when they are told without flourishes—though, after all, it might be difficult to fancy a subject of which this could not be said.

During his residence in Paris, Mr. Blenner appears to have become acquainted with many phases of French life and character. Certainly his studies of Parisian scenes and people are marked by a quite evident appreciation of something more than the shell of things. The "Luxembourg Garden," for example, strikes a truly Parisian note, and the same may be said of the glimpse into the grounds of the Musée de Cluny. Mr. Blenner enters with zest into the treatment of subjects nearer home. He has put real poetry in his "Old-Fashioned Garden," one of those quaint, inartistic but delightful nooks of Connecticut, where there are stone walls

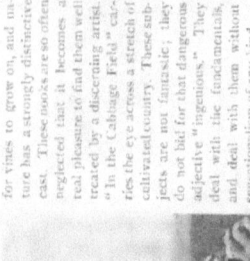

"A STUDY OF SEA."

"LUXEMBOURG GARDEN, PARIS."

for vines to grow on, and nature has a strongly distinctive cast. These nooks are so often neglected that it becomes a real pleasure to find them well treated by a discerning artist. "In the Cabbage Field" carries the eye across a stretch of cultivated country. These subjects are not fantastic; they do not bid for that dangerous adjective "ingenious." They deal with the fundamentals, and deal with them without sensationalism of any kind.

As an illustrator, Mr. Blenner has shown highly favoring gifts. The facility with which he eliminates unnecessary detail gives pertinence and clearness to his work. Illustrators are perhaps particularly under the necessity for studying the element of proportion in the use of detail. Too many of our ambitious illustrators are missing the essentials of the art by overloading their pictures. Mr. Blenner appears to be in no danger of hampering himself by making this radical error. During the past summer he had charge of the Yale art school, and is now settled again in his New York studio in the Sherwood, where the winter days will be too brief to work up the thousand and one sketches treasured in his well-worn note-book. In his wide range of subjects, Mr. Blenner will easily avoid sameness of execution.

"AFTERNOON TEA."

"INSIDE OF THE MUSÉE DE CLUNY, PARIS."

COUNTRY LIFE.

From a painting by Carle J. Blenner.

AN ILLUSTRATOR OF CHILD LIFE.

BY WILLIAM MCKENDREE BANGS.

(*With original Illustrations by Maud Humphrey.*)

"BUBBLES."

So fleeting are the expressions of a child's emotions, that successful and artistic representation of children has always been a difficult task; but when it is successfully accomplished, pictures of children are almost invariably beautiful. And not only are children's pictures, therefore, very pleasing to those who love beauty —whose number, it is to be hoped, is growing and extending—but representations of our future men and women, which are at all adequate, must be interesting and gratifying to all who love children, and their number is certainly legion.

Very beautiful indeed, and very interesting, are the pictures of child life to be found in the original drawings and paintings of Miss Maud Humphrey, or in her work as reproduced in the books she has illustrated for children or representing them. That an artist, or any one else for that matter, should "work along the line of least resistance" to accomplish the largest and best success possible, is a truth so obvious that perhaps to state it is to express a common place; but it is evident that along that happy line has Miss Humphrey worked, for, as her many and various representations of child life are examined, one cannot fail to be impressed with

"PUSSIKIN."

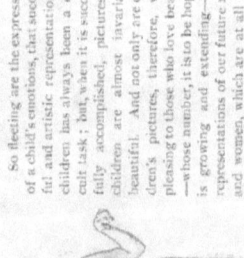

"SWEET CLOVER."

the manifest pleasure she finds in the work, or to feel that her love for her subjects must be very real, and her sympathy with them deep and sincere. Otherwise, I take it, it would not be possible for her to so represent the characters of her little people, and to so suggest their thoughts and quick emotions. Her pictured children are not merely children of handsome faces and pretty clothes. They have something more.

Miss Humphrey was born in Rochester. In her very earliest childhood she drew and made pictures as best she could. Her early hope was to become a painter of animals, and her youthful enthusiasm was for Rosa Bonheur. Before she was twelve she had begun to take lessons in drawing; but her eyes failing her in some measure,

"A TRYING HOUR."

she was compelled for a while to desist. A few years later, however, she had so progressed that she became a pupil at the Art Students' League. While a student here she made illustrations for a children's magazine published in Boston. Her first work in color was done about this time, and soon thereafter, now about six years ago, she was requested to illustrate a holiday book then about to be prepared. Miss Humphrey's pictures were of children, and were drawings in color, from life. This work received favorable notice and attention, and, it may almost be said, determined her aim and the manner in which she should pursue her art. Her efforts, it is true, have not been limited to pictures of children alone. Many other figure subjects, including notably charming pictures of young women, in black and white, and in color, have been the product of her pen or brush; but it is as a painter of child life that Miss Humphrey has achieved unquestionable, and her greatest, success.

"A WEE MODEL."

While it may appear to the uninitiated that the picturing of children is a simple, straightforward task, the contrary is the truth. To begin with, the children's artist has a twofold difficulty to contend with. The brain-whirling restlessness of the young model is a thing to discourage the tyro in this line of art work, and the difficulty of fixing with pen or pigment the ever-changing expression of a child's countenance—the portrayal of the sweet, unsullied soul of such wee characters as engage the talent of Miss Humphrey, is an accomplishment both arduous and thought-provoking.

It is true that the artist here considered often falls short of her ideal; that her pictorial em-

AMERICAN ART AND ARTISTS.

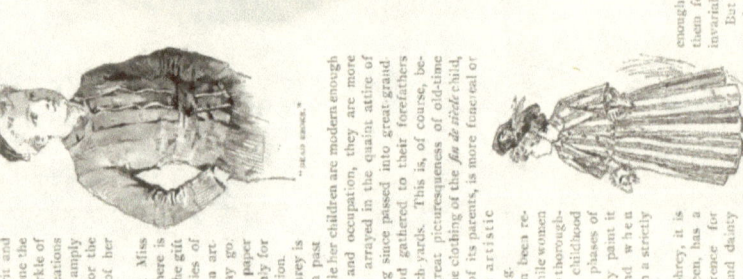

"A RUGBY KNIGHT."

"THE CARES OF MOTHERHOOD."

"HEAD ERECT."

"GOOD-BY."

bodiments of small boys and girls lack spirit and expression; but none the less there is a sparkle of style in her delineations of childhood that amply recompenses one for the missing qualities of her work.

To her work Miss Humphrey brings a gay and joyous fancy. There is an evidence of zest in her drawings. She has the gift of placing rigidly delicate and pleasing qualities of color. She also appreciates the limit to which an artist, dealing solely with one class of subjects, may go. One is convinced in viewing her children on paper and canvas that the artist's heart pulsated warmly for the tiny models from whom she drew her inspiration.

It is clearly evident, too, that Miss Humphrey is partial to the miniature men and women of a past epoch; for while her children are modern enough in face, form, and occupation, they are more often than not arrayed in the quaint attire of youngsters long since passed into great-grand parenthood and gathered to their forefathers in weedy churchyards. This is, of course, because of the great picturesqueness of old-time garbing; for the clothing of the *fin de siècle* child, like the attire of its parents, is more funereal or grotesque than artistic and eye-pleasing.

It has often been remarked that while women are supposed to thoroughly understand childhood above all other phases of life, they rarely paint it exclusively, and when they do, it is in a strictly ideal light.

Miss Humphrey, it is plain to be seen, has a decided preference for child women, and dainty little women at that. The small boy of to-day is not picturesque enough to please her fancy, perhaps, or pranks and naughtiness have no humor in them for her. Oddly enough, however, another child painter, and a man at that, invariably chooses these neglected boys for his most engaging pictures.

But dominating all Miss Humphrey's work is the note of seriousness. Her purpose is the picturing of child nature in its best moods, without affectation or a falsifying of visible facts. In her own peculiar undertaking in the field of art she has attained a much-deserved distinction, and as a student of childhood—its foibles and pleasantries—she is alone among women painters and illustrators.

AMERICAN ART AND ARTISTS.

A PAINTER'S PROGRESS.

By ALFRED TRUMBLE.

(Illustrated from original paintings by Leonard Ochtman.)

SOME ten years since a young artist came to this city from Albany, and established himself in a modest studio under the roof of an old-fashioned house around the corner from Union Square. He was not known among the guild here, but his pictures, which appeared in different exhibitions, attracted some attention, and there were those among our older painters, who are generous in recognizing and acknowledging youthful and new merit, who singled them out as the work of a man with a future. These pictures were landscapes, familiar pastoral scenes, of a charmingly peaceful character, simply painted, without any pretensions to technical display, but fresh and pure in color, and lively with the spirit of the subject. They commenced to figure at the National Academy of Design in 1882, were modestly priced, and found a ready market.

The artist, Leonard Ochtman, was a native of Holland, but had from childhood resided in Albany. It was hereabouts that he began to draw and paint from nature, guiding himself entirely by the suggestions afforded by the pictures which he saw in the art dealers' galleries, in occasional public exhibitions, and in such private collections as he could gain access to. He was, practically, feeling his way, and if his progress was not as rapid as it might have been had he received a regular

"THE ROAD."

"THE GRAPEVINE."

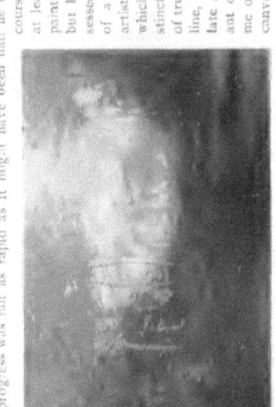

"A SUMMER VISTA."

course of instruction, it at least resulted in his painting like no one but himself. He possessed the advantage of a highly sensitive artistic temperament, which rendered him instinctively appreciative of true beauty in form, line, and color. The late Alexander H. Wyant once remarked to me of one of his small canvases at the Academy: "Here is a young

man, now, who was born to be an artist. He is only learning to paint, and his work is weak and thin. But notice how he grasps the picturesque qualities of his subject, and how tenderly he renders them. He is painting his own heart here, you may be bound. He will soon arrive."

This prediction, uttered by one of the veterans and masters in American landscape, upon the suggestion of an unostentatious study of some bit of an Albany suburb, has been

amply fulfilled. From the time be settled in New York, Mr. Ochtman's progress was rapid. To the slender, reserved young man, with the refined and delicate face, whom many took to be a poet, as, in his way, he indeed is, every gallery among whose treasures he wandered, silently observant and studious, was a school. He had already, by a natural process of development, learned to think and paint for himself. Now, leaving how others thought and painted, he unconsciously gathered strength. His inspirations expanded, his growing confidence strengthened his hand. At each succeeding exhibition his productions revealed more force of execution, and grew steadily upon the favor of those who saw them. One of our dealers in pictures, a man not then much given to encouraging native talent, said to me, at an Academy show :

"Do you know this man?"

I told him that I had met him, and gave him what infor-

AMERICAN ART AND ARTISTS.

A DECORATIVE ARTIST.

By Royal Cortissoz.

(With original Illustrations by Frank Fowler.)

mation I could as to who he was. He listened attentively, with his eyes upon the picture all the while. Finally he said: 'I like his work. He's going ahead. I shall go and hunt him up.'

The artist, however, was beyond his reach. He had accumulated sufficient capital to venture on a trip to Europe, and there he remained a couple of years. The pictures which he sent over from time to time demonstrated that his voyage was not being wasted. They elicited critical commendation and rose steadily in the favor of collectors. Most favorable indication of all, in the practical sense at least, for art must feed on something more substantial than air, the prices his pictures commanded went higher and higher.

I should add, to Mr. Ochtman's honor, that while he returned from Europe with his art broadened and fortified by experience and study, he brought back with him also that individuality which belongs to him as to all men whose education has been self-wise. He paints now, as before, not like a student of the French, the German, the Dutch, or any other schools, but like Leonard Ochtman. I know no higher praise to be extended to him, or I should extend it.

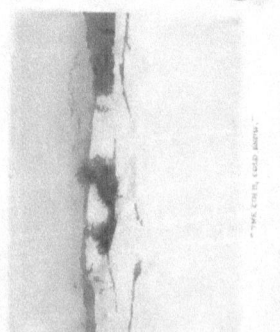

"'GATHERING THE SHEAVES.'"

Sooner or later an artist gets his opportunity. Mr. Frank Fowler returned to America about fifteen years ago, after a sojourn abroad which had been chiefly distinguished by experience under Carolus Duran. He had been chosen by that eminent Frenchman to aid him in the painting of a fresco in the Luxembourg, "The Apotheosis of Marie de Medici." I do not know that the decorative faculty which Duran must have divined in Mr. Fowler had never been employed in this country until lately. I do know that his reputation here has been founded on his work in portraiture. At the World's Fair his contributions to the exhibit of paintings were all portraits. But any one who sought out the section devoted to architecture at the Fair must have noticed some studies of draped and nude figures by Mr. Fowler. A few fragments belonging to the preparation of three panels for the ballroom they represent Mr. Fowler's opportunity.

In his portraits he has demonstrated his acquaintance with truths of structure and his skill in brushing. He has appeared to the same good effect in the figure studies other than portraits, which he has exhibited from time to time. His full measure is given, however, in the frescoes to which I have alluded. In them there is the simplicity of composition which would be expected of one who has position in the measure. A cellist in achieved success as a teacher through the good sense and clearness of his instruction. They have also piquancy and effectiveness. Three figures occupy each of the panels. In the central division are the violin-ist and lyrist reproduced with these remarks, and a oudecheruh, bearing a page of music. The panels to the right and left are assigned to both musicians and dancers. In one the nude trumpeter, illustrated herewith, is accompanied by a maenad in yellow, dancing, and a semi-nude bacchic youth, beating time with a ribboned wand as he joins in the measure. A cellist in bournist the last panel is draped in yellow, and the dancer and tambournist grouped with her are robed, one in blue, the other in white and lavender. Each one of these figures is an image of grace and animation, and they are thrown against a background of fleecy

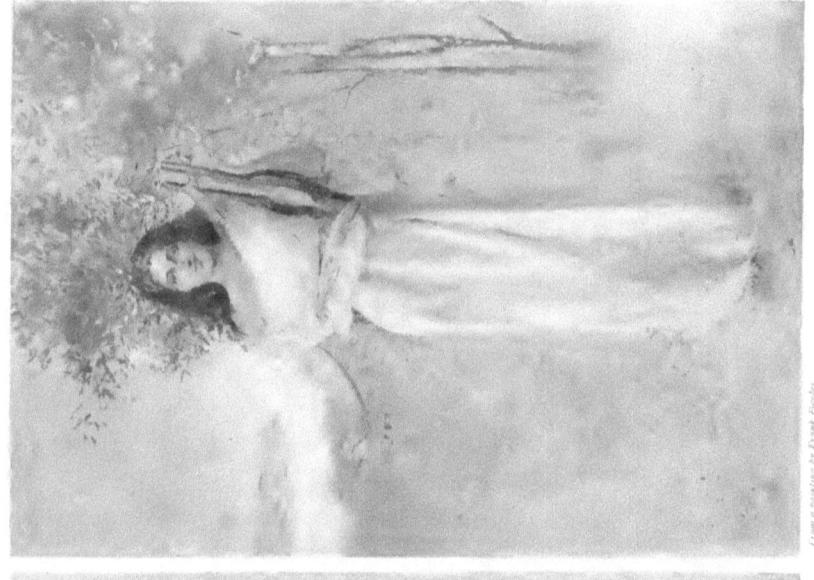

From a painting by Frank Fowler.

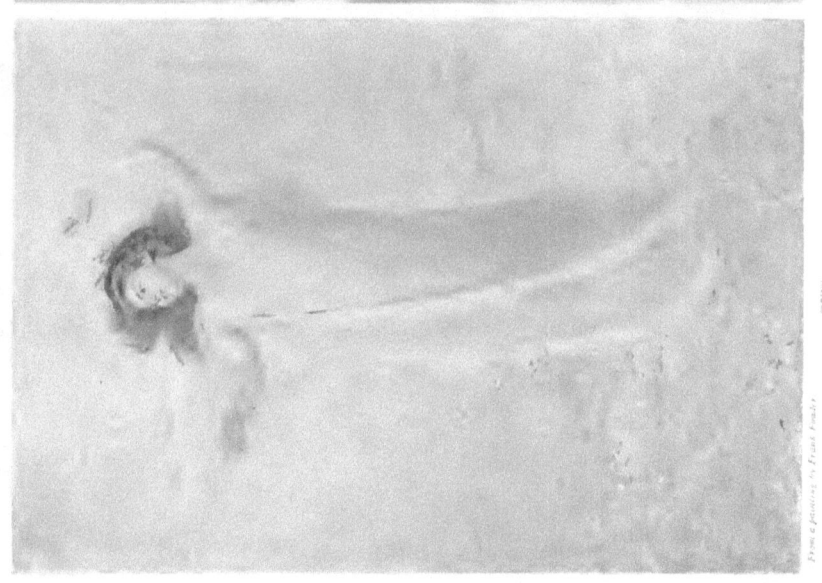

From a painting by Frank Fowler.

AMERICAN ART AND ARTISTS.

clouds and delicate blue sky with a harmonious adjustment to the latter of the flesh tints and of the draperies I have mentioned. The workmanship shows self-possession and energy, and the coloration is delightful. The decorations are extremely clever, in short, and, what is perhaps most pleasing, they are thoroughly decorative. Though Mr. Fowler has not heretofore attained distinction as a mural painter, he has not lacked appreciation in other directions. He is valued as a teacher. He is a member of the Architectural League and the Society of American Artists, and is an Associate of the Academy. At the Universal Exposition of 1889, in Paris, he was awarded a bronze medal. He is still young, having been born in Brooklyn in 1852. On the foundations of an art education, sought first with Edwin White in Florence, and then in the École des Beaux Arts and the studio of Duran, he is building a creditable superstructure through constant cultivation of his gifts.

That in this superstructure there will be incorporated the fruits of further decorative attempts in the vein which Mr. Fowler has recently opened at the Waldorf, is highly probable. In the first place, because these frescos have proven his ability as a mural painter. In the second place, because an ever-widening field is being spread before decorative artists in America years a long dormant impulse and the school of fresco many years ago by William Abbey, is even now in course  of formation. Within the past few years a long dormant impulse has been awakened, painters, prefigured Morris Hunt, at formation. Signs of it were to be observed at the World's Fair, where a group of American artists produced some extremely interesting essays in mural decoration on the domes of the Liberal Arts and Administration buildings. When the new Public Library building in Boston is completed it will be one of the most magnificently embellished edifices in the world, for such artists as Puvis de Chavannes, Whistler, Abbey, and Sargent have been commissioned to people its walls with painted figures. Mr. Fowler's work indicates a welcome movement in American art.

"WITH EYES SERENE."

"MY FAVORITE MODEL."

BY CLARENCE PARSONS LATHROP

(With original illustrations of it by numerous artists.)

Drawn by Mary Rattles.
"BETTY."

WHO, on visiting the studios of different artists, or observing a number of pictures by the same man or woman, has not been struck by the fact that in all of any one person's work there is usually some prevailing type, whether this relate to human nature or some other kind of nature, however versatile the craftsman or craftswoman may be?

In the paintings of Van Marcke we seem to recognize certain "old original" cows whom we can almost call by name, though they appear under slightly varied forms, as clearly as we trace our particular model in all the angelic maidens of Botticelli. So, likewise, it is true of landscapists, that each has his favorite aspects of trees or shapes of cloud;

Drawn by E. W. Kemble.
"WE CAN READ, FIGHT, DANCE, PLAY BALL, OR GET DRUNK."

and among illustrations, for example, the recurrence of a special type or model is very marked in such widely divergent workers as Abbey and Vedder. It was a happy thought, then, on the part of THE QUARTERLY ILLUS-

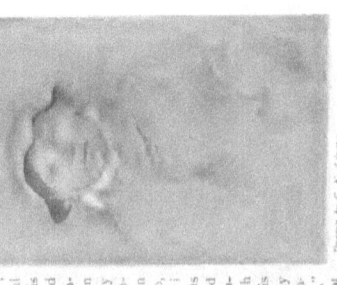

Drawn by Mrs. F. Klepper.
"BATTLE AND SON."

TRATOR, to ask a number of our characteristic and productive artists to send in drawings showing, in each case, "My Favorite Model."

This is, perhaps, a little like asking a poet or a novelist to point out a fixed favorite among his poems or stories. Still, in such a collection as this, we get at a great deal which is suggestive and true.

Thus as Dvořák tells us that the negro has produced the only genuine American music, so E. W. Kemble pins his faith to the negro as an unique, unfailing source of the picturesque and humorous, with capital success, as his many and popular delineations in The Century and St. Nicholas testify. In this field, also, Mary Berri Chapman has planted and packed laurels, although she makes this

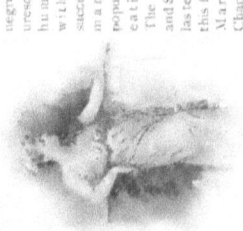

Drawn by Henry Sandham.
"A SCHOOL OF CHERUBS."

confession. "My favorite model is also my latest model, of plural gender as well as number." Yet she admits that a negro "auntie," such as we find here in "Old Kittie," might be called "the favorite model of her friends."

From a painting by Lyell Carr.

DINNER TIME.

AMERICAN ART AND ARTISTS.

"A CAPRICIOUS MODEL."

Drawn by F. S. Rothwell.

Enough of classification. Let us rather look upon these figures and scenes as they appear before us, at hazard, as though we were taking a walk along the street or in the country, a stroll through "society," or, for that matter, making an excursion into dreamland. Is not this world of art, in a fine and lofty way, something like a masquerade? Sundry of the shapes it presents seem perfectly real and well known, others attract us by their strangeness, their air of fantasy. This pretty mare and her pretty foal—are they not familiar to us? Max F. Klepper says they were the result of study on a

Drawn by James Symington.

farm, last summer. We were not there, but we are there now—we are sure of it, and if we could raise live stock as easily as he does, with a few passes of the brush—and such good live stock—we would be content. Next come the man and the horse together, a nude rider, half classic, passably Gallic, with a mythical touch, on a centaured steed. But this does not claim to be Miss Lila F. Bell's favorite, "for, while she generally begins her pictures with a model, she finishes them 'out of her head,' though remaining perfectly sane. From horse and horseman we graduate to the partly human in the next apparition—an abundant yet gracefully posed woman, in simple Greek or goddess garb, whom Mr. Henry Sandham

skilfully introduces to us. It is odd—yet quite in the nature of masquerading—that alongside these representatives of a remoter ideal world we should chance upon the vivid yet phlegmatic "little Dutchman," whom Mr. C. K. Linson makes known, and the serious-eyed young woman with a sort of filleted hood, whom Rona Rado touches for. With her large, firm, yet emotional features she might pass for a Charlotte Corday. Whoever this mysterious personage may be, Iona Rado says she prefers her among many hundreds, and that such has been "the model to many masterpieces."

It will be observed that, as those people pass before us, they do not always unmask. With the very first one in the procession, though, it is otherwise, for Mary Bartles, in an aside, makes us acquainted with her as "Bertie," a native of Alsace Lorraine, as her costume hints. Bertie, now of Paris, is an accredited favorite, "tall, rather angular, with good features and delicate coloring, together with a curious mixture of refinement and loftiness, attractive in many points both artistic and inartistic." She has

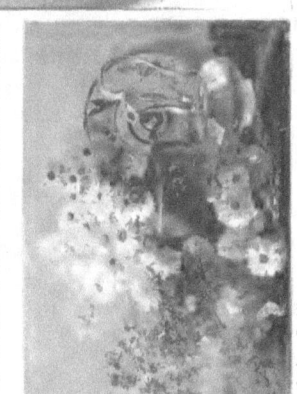

Drawn by J. H. Hatfield.

Drawn by Agnes D. Abbatt.

CHRIST AND THE FISHERMEN.
From a painting by Frank Du Mond.

AMERICAN ART AND ARTISTS.

"a face that is sweet, with an expression both sad and wistful, yet her main effort in life is not to let anybody get ahead of her." Truly it is a curious study, this of the artists models—a study in character not only of the models, but also of the artists themselves, their motives and tastes.

James Symington reveals his sympathy with art in general by his choice of a woman violinist for his subject, or, rather, his representative at this entertainment. Mr.

Drawn by F. A. Carter.
"THOMAS."

Drawn by W. F. Halsall.
"TYPES OF A LOTTERMAN."

wave of some sort, since he is devoted to marine views. So, too, it would appear with Mr. W. St. John Harper, who declares that his favorite is Cynthia,

"That orbèd maiden, with white fire laden,"

the moon. But Mr. Harper juggles with us a little; for he discloses not a man in the moon, but a beautiful, mystical woman in the moon. He finds it difficult, however, to persuade her to pose. "Just as I was about to complete this study I send you," he writes, "she sailed behind a silver cloud. This accounts for the vagueness of the sketch."

Then, again, we are brought face to face with the most intimate of human interests, in J. H. Hatfield's drawing of his daughter Dot, who has figured at the Salon and the World's Fair. "She sometimes wishes her papa was not an artist, but when once interested is willing to lend him a helping hand." From Lee Woodward

Drawn by Miss Georgina Davis. "A MODERN WITCH."

Drawn by George Foxcroft. "THE FIRST CAME."

Daecke sends a little child. On the other hand, Agnes D. Abbatt is inclined to give the human interest a secondary place, claiming a superior and perennial youth for *her* favorite model, who, "as years go on, grows more beautiful. She has become a fashionable lady, with gorgeous costumes. She holds great receptions every year. Do you know her? She is the royal chrysanthemum."

But still more impersonal, more independent of life, even when presented only in outline, mere humanity, is E. M. Bicknell, whose favorite model is possibly a

Drawn by G. R. Dixon. "DOT PLAYING AT REST."

Drawn by Morgan Kheen. "YOUNG WOMAN."

Ziegler's lady in a listening attitude, we naturally await interesting disclosures, which have not yet come to hand. But F. A. Carter is interested in another phase of suspense—that of a man trying to tie his shoe—which, indeed, is one of the problems of life, even when presented only in outline.

Another problem, though by no means vexatious in appearance, is Morgan Kheen's buxom young woman in a bathing dress and scarf-tied hat, standing on a beach; against which we have, by contrast, a young girl in

Drawn by Clara Wagner Parrish. "MELANCHOLY."

173

From a painting by John A. Fraser.

AMERICAN ART AND ARTISTS.

"Marguerite" attire, with a handkerchief in her hand, at a casement which she is about to open. This is a sketch by George Varian, who, rising from the ranks of photo-engraving work, has begun to achieve ideals of his own, and shows romantic sentiment.

A weird woman in black, with her hands clasped, and an open folio fallen at her feet, whom Clara Weaver Parrish brings to our view, has a tinge of decided melancholy; and herein we see the varied scope of artistic vision and sympathy.

Frederic Remington rides into the arena (though he himself remains invisible) on a thin, war-torn steed which looks almost like a hybrid, and he disguises himself further under "A Study of Legs"—"horses' legs," it should be explained. I fancy that Remington also indulges in humor, when he offers this jaded animal

and a few scattered fore-legs as his favorite models. Still he may be quite serious, for, like the famous naturalist who reconstructed an extinct animal from a bone or two, Remington has shown the ability to produce a whole new world of horses in graphic art, from the race of animals that had been going around in a neglected condition before he cast his eye upon them and aimed his pencil at them. William Bodfish treats his two dogs and a pony in a different style. They "keep up the pace," though he complains that

they do not always keep the pose, and he seems to have caught them.

Again the scene changes. Here are two charming young women—one sitting, the other standing with one hand leaning on a window-sill. Who are they? Mr. R. Dixon explains that the fair damsel seated is her daughter and her favorite. The other girl, Georgina Davis's creation, prefers to ask pay for an explanation.

Albert D. Blashfield gives us as his favorite a lady in simple modern cos-

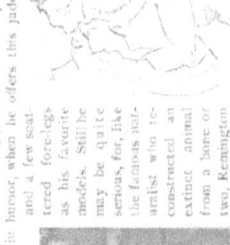

tume, seated in a wicker chair.

C. M. Reyea tells no story, but submits a charming feminine seated figure in cape and hat. Harry Roseland does tell a story of a pretty girl reading a letter under a parasol (and "under the rose"), but the sequel is not given, and Mr. Harry L. Parkhurst vaguely indicates a nude woman dressing her hair.

One is inclined to ask why he should select this as his favorite model. Mr. C. J. Budd, who, as an illustrator of stories of adventure, has used models ranging from the ugliest to the most beautiful of creatures, declares in favor of woman in general, and seems to prefer her as seen in Oriental costume. R. H. Livingstone, however, contents himself with a small boy reading a still

AMERICAN ART AND ARTISTS.

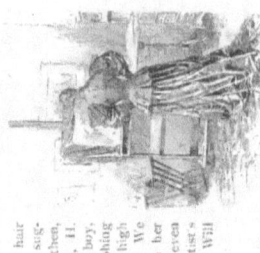

Drawn by Thomas B. Craig. "SHEEP'S HEAD."

Drawn by Frederick W. Freer. "A SUMMER GIRL."

smaller boy how to smoke; but that this does not quite correspond to his ambitions for the future, I judge from the fact that, so far, he has had no regular artistic training, but expects to begin serious study soon. G. R. Drake places before us the modest glimpse of a shyly beautiful yet pensive face, with abundant hair falling and draped over the bust. Albertine Randall Wheelan refreshes us with a quietly joyous little nude boy playing a mandolin, while a kitten, a pug-

Drawn by E. A. Bell. "DOWN."

"WITH HEAD BOWED DOWN."

head bowed, her hair bound succinctly—a suggestion of sadness; then, in the next breath, H. G. Plumb's laughing boy,

Drawn by Will Philip Hooper. "MY FAVORITE MODEL—MY SISTER."

on the broad grin, and George F. Kerr's dashing woman of fashion, in fur-trimmed cape and high plumed hat, reposing on a broad, curved lounch. We also surprise H. Martin Beal's old Pepita, in her Italian costume, asleep near the end of life's toil, even while trying to maintain an attitude for the artist's benefit. And at the same moment we detect Will

Drawn by Peter Moran. "WAITING FOR DINNER."

Philip Hooper's gracefully habited dame of more conventional society, examining a portfolio or a canvas on a working easel. Her back is turned to us. She is a study of draperies. Sometimes draperies are the whole of existence, to cer-

dog, and a newly hatched chicken cluster round his pudgy feet.

Now, what are we to make of all these contrasts and contradictions? What are we to conclude?

Wait a moment! There are some more pictures to be examined. Again the phantasmagoria; again the masquerade. We have here Frederick W. Freer's thoughtfully gay woman, with a broad hat tipped slantingly over her head, and eyebrows slightly strained; E.

Drawn by H. G. Plumb. "TOBIAS."

A. Bell's woman with her

Drawn by Geo. F. Kerr.

From a painting by Jared B. Flagg. THINKING OVER HIS FORTUNE.

tain people; and the artist has perhaps typified this truth here.

But, just as we have become interested in these phases of "the human form divine," we are led firmly to the contemplation of Peter Moran's lean heifer, Thomas R. Craig's strong yet rather mournful sheep, head, Silas D. Dustin's bull belligerently gazing at a leafy background of trees, and Francis Wheaton's charming studies of innocent lambs. The barnyard and the field reassert themselves, in contrast with both the frivolous and the ideal elements of humanity.

Speaking of draperies—there

Drawn by C. E. Burn.
"HER MURSE IN THE DOORWAY."

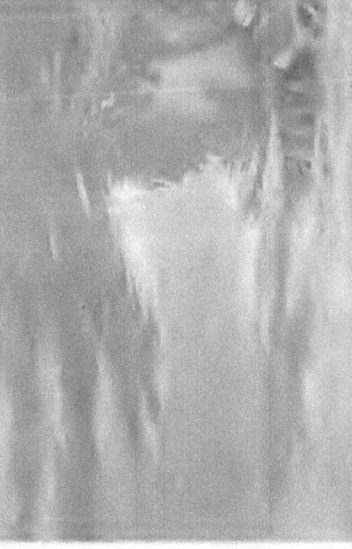

Drawn by Harry S. Watson.
"IN WINTER COMES AGAIN."

are none to speak of, in the case of Charles H. Provost's decorative nude female figure. But in Stanley Middleton's beautiful, serene, and delicately modelled profile head of a woman in her prime, with her neck and shoulder exposed, her back turned toward the spectator, and the fold of a loose garment encircling her, we touch high-water mark of purity and sweetness. The seriousness of W. Middleton's artistic purpose is well indicated in these words of his: "Of the many models I have used, there are but two or three, perhaps, that I could call 'favorites'—owing to the fact of

Drawn by Stanley Middleton.
"A NOOK DREAM."

model about me, who comes merely for the dollar and a half, is not in the least calculated to stimulate my inspiration, and I give a sigh of relief when I can bow them gracefully out of the studio forever."

It is pleasant, also, to be reminded that there are keen, sympathetic eyes always on the watch for the humbly or

always deriving better results from them, their refinement, and, above all, the interest they show in the work they undertake. To have a so-called

AMERICAN ART AND ARTISTS.

domestic, and skilful hands to depict the same, as in G. F. Burr's old time American farmhouse by the highway, with its immense tutelary tree (an elm, I suppose) and its quaint well-sweep. That bit of bucolic landscape is fitly companioned with the excellent old lady, bonneted, bespectacled, and wrinkled, whom Harry S. Watson so faithfully portrays. Mr. Burr says openly that his favorite model is landscape, and that the old farmhouse which he puts in evidence is the sort of theme which most appeals to him. Mr. Watson says nothing, except with his crow-quill, but his drawing speaks volumes for his love of the wholesome, the domestic, and of integrity in character. He is good. Mr. Archie Gunn goes to quite another extreme, and one may be forgiven for smiling and staring to think of the surprise and horror with which Mr. Watson's decorous old maid or matron

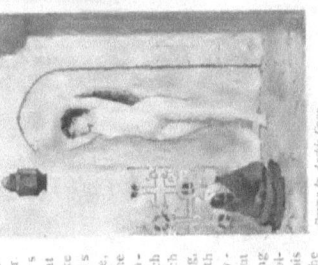

a very different and a grim phase of truth which Mr. D. D. Smith illustrates in the still—very still life sketch below, if it be proper to speak of bony structure as having life; for here the artist sardonically shows us an empty skull lying upon a perhaps equally empty dailypaper, with an empty pipe, an idle pen, and equally idle banknotes close at hand. Who shall say this is not "Treth," as much as the lovely woman above? But that the grimness hinted here is not Mr. Smith's habitual mood may be inferred from his writing to us: "All models are favorites of mine who can, by distinction of pose, motion, or expression, throw themselves into the character represented." After these two very decided unmaskings—one of the bare body, the other of a bare skull—one turns with interest and appreciation to Maria Brooks's charming and cleverly characterized little girl "in the Dumps," her face forever hooded and concealed. Who is this tiny incognita? Why, she may be any one of our friends or ourselves—are we not always much like her at times? F. S. Lesley's odd group of a

able (whichever she may be) would regard her next door neighbor as gathered in by Mr. Gunn, without a stitch of clothing. This is but another episode in the bizarre masquerade of art, at which we are glancing. Mr. Gunn's reason for presenting this delicately rendered study is that his chief and favorite study is that of the female figure. But we do not quite understand why it should be the function of "Irais" to reveal herself precisely in this form to a small Nubian slave squatting in the foreground. It is

AMERICAN ART AND ARTISTS.

YORK HARBOR, MAINE.

From a painting by Harry Fenn.

tumble-down chair supporting a travelling bag, an umbrella, and a feminine hat seems, however, to warn us that the time of departure is near, that the show is almost over. And here, once more, we note the universal interest, the lively perception of graphic art, which can invest a plain bit of furniture and two or three ordinary articles of use or wear with so much movement and suggestion of story.

"A DUTCH PEASANT GIRL."

Drawn by George Wharton Edwards

"A SPRING SONG."

Drawn by Francis W'exton.

"A SUMMER SHOWER."

Drawn by Francis W'exton.

Mr Hugh M Eaton is both quaint and discerning in his effective drawing of a medieval noble or gentleman holding in his two hands, by hilt and blade, a sword.

Illusion leads to fairyland, whither Curier Barnes now transports us, in his delightful conceit of a lovely girl reading from some legendary volume, with her feet resting on a live tiger, who obligingly offers himself as a rug, while a child, desired

"AN OLD FRIEND."

Drawn by Frederic Remington.

on the floor beside him, is goatly enfolded and supported by its tail.

And now the masquerade is over. It ends, aptly enough, with a humorous small boy, and a dog, devised by Frank P Bellew ("Chip"), who bring up the rear in the manner usual to processions, together with Remington's forlorn and hungry quadruped, which we have spoken of before. Bellew's small boy seems astonished and inquiring, as his canine friend is, also, yet somehow they both appear to have a secret knowledge concerning this whole riddle of illustrative art

"LOOK YER, WHAT YE DOIN."

Drawn by Frank P. Bellew.

THE ARTISTIC DISCOVERER OF LONG ISLAND

By LILLIE HAMILTON FRENCH.

(With original illustrations by Charles H. Miller.)

THE most important art movement of recent years among us owed its immediate inspiration to an action by Mr. Miller, who was then, with Mr. Wadsworth Thompson, on the hanging committee of the Academy of Design. This was in 1877, we think, though possibly a year earlier. The vitality and breadth of the younger painters having strongly impressed these two gentlemen, they at once broke through the long-established customs of the Academy. The pictures of the new generation were hung upon the line; those of the Academicians were hung in the spaces left, without regard to the sanctities of ancient precedent or privilege.

This action on the part of Mr. Miller and his colleague won from the younger painters an immediate response, while it created among the elder men both indignation and dismay. The Academicians met and agreed upon a rule by which each member should hereafter be entitled to so much space upon the line. The younger artists also met, but out of their agreement developed that which with its noble building has since been known as the "Society of American Artists."

For this early recognition of their work the younger painters have always held

"SUNRISE LEAVES."

"THE MILL ON THE BAY."

"STEWART'S POND, NEAR JAMAICA, LONG ISLAND."

Mr. Miller in loyal regard. One feels that whenever his name is mentioned among them. That for which the public who have lost recollection of these things esteem him, however, is his sympathy for the picturesque and beautiful in the Long Island landscape, a picturesqueness and beauty of which he has been so distinguished an interpreter. Bayard Taylor used to refer to this lover of the out-of-doors as the artistic discoverer of that interesting country. But Mr. Miller has grown to be something more, so strongly is he imbued with the spirit of its quiet loveliness, so eager a student is he of its old landmarks and traditions, and with such appreciation has he translated them on canvas for us. His effects in color, the richness and depth of which bear testimony to the better Munich influence, are lost in their reproduction into black and white, the splendor of his sunsets fades, but one has always left the charm of the composition, and that which nothing destroys, the sense of a very delicate and rare appreciation of the picturesque felt in all of Mr. Miller's works.

NOTE.—In person Charles H. Miller is ruddy, robust, and royal tempered. His laugh is as vigorous as his painting. He is a man of versatility—a versatility that extends outside his own immediate profession. He is an enthusiastic worker to political and social fields. His studio in New York is more of an artistic workshop than a mere painting parlor; no cumbrous bric-a-brac belitters his walls or floors. Mr. Miller has made a life-long study of the picturesque part of old Long Island, and many are the artistic records he has torn from the leaves of nature's book, spread open upon this rich little continent—torn, not rudely, but with careful, sympathetic touch.

AMERICAN ART AND ARTISTS.

THE OLD MILL.
From a painting by Charles H. Miller.

184

AN ENGLISH-AMERICAN ARTIST

By CLARENCE COOK

With original Illustrations by George Henry Boughton.

WHEN an artist owes his reputation to the genial environment of an English mother-country, and is at the same time indebted to his foster-mother, America, for the early impressions which crystallized into a natural bent and influenced his subsequent career, he is apt to be somewhat divided in his allegiance. English in his methods he may be, but the American inspiration persistently creeps into his pictures, giving them an international interest.

Few living painters have enjoyed so wide-spread a popularity in our country as George Henry Boughton; a popularity with which, it may be said, a feeling of something like personal friendship is mingled. Until the question was finally settled at the Philadelphia Exhibition in 1876, when Boughton's work was shown in the British section, there had always been a belief that he was an American, transplanted for a time only; it was hoped, to England; and even now it is likely that nine out of ten of our people outside the profession, who enjoy his pictures, think of him as a countryman and have a patriotic pleasure in the belief.

Nor are they without a reason for their belief. He was born, indeed, in England, at Norwich in 1834, but his parents brought him to this country when he was three years old and he lived here until he was twenty-five. In 1859 he went to Paris, where he studied for two years, and in 1861 took up his residence in London, and has remained there ever since. He is a great favorite among the artists and literary men in London, as well as in general society; he has married an English wife, and in 1879 he was elected an Associate of the Royal Academy. It is understood that he wishes to be considered an Englishman, and, to emphasize the fact, he chooses to pronounce his name English-fashion, calling himself Bough-on, instead of Bough-ton, as is usual in this country.

With the exception of a few

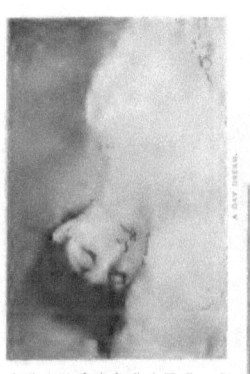

A DAY DREAM.

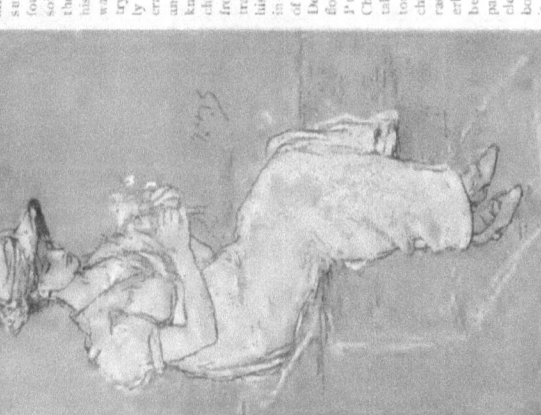

"COMING NEXT"

less important pictures, almost all Boughton's subjects have been found on American soil; and this, added to the fact that during all his formative years he was living in this country, has added naturally enough to the general belief that he is an American. He is known in this country chiefly by engravings from his pictures illustrating scenes in the history of the Puritans in America. The March of Miles Standish, The Departure of the Mayflower, New England Puritans Going to Church. His subjects taken from the "History of New York," as chronicled by the veracious Diedrich Knickerbocker, have not been so successful, partly because that clever and amusing book is less read than it ought to be, and partly because as a mere

AMERICAN ART AND ARTISTS.

story-teller the artist is not altogether in his element. Sometimes, too, he errs, as may another painter has done, in taking a story or anecdote that no skill would suffice to tell with the brush, except for those who already know the story. Thus in one of his most important pictures drawn from this source: "The burghers of New Amsterdam protesting against Governor Stuyvesant's decree forbidding tobacco-

A SOLDIER'S REST.

"AN ENGLISH IVY."

smoking, by sitting down in a body before him and smoking with might and main"—it would be impossible for any one who had not read

ROSE.

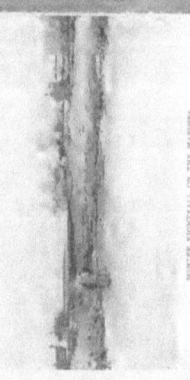

THE DAYS THAT ARE NO MORE.

illustrations that accompany this notice belong— Black-eyed Susan, "Coming, Sir!," A Spring-time Posy, Rose, and Care-free. In these sketches the artist's ideal of the female figure and of female beauty is indicated; the seeming too-great height; the square jaw, often unduly pronounced; the pose, sturdy rather than graceful, the hands and feet strongly modelled, and somewhat larger than suits the more attenuated taste of our time. The excessive height of his figures, with which Mr. Boughton has often been reproached, in some cases is due, we believe, to the clinging draperies and tightly adjusted details of the dress. The period most affected by the artist for illustration is the latter half of the eighteenth century; in this he is most at home, and we opine he would spend

CARE-FREE.

WINTER NIGHTFALL ON THE MARSHES.

his time there if he were allowed, with Pamela and Sophia Western, Clarissa, Olivia and other gentle heroines of that day's romance, rather than paint historical anecdotes for the market. He must not, however, be charged with subordinating his talent to the will of others to any reprehensible degree. His interest in the England of Goldsmith's day is very genuine and hearty, and his pictures furnish a pleasing accompaniment to the stories of a day not so distant as to be strange, and not so near as to have lost its power to charm the fancy and touch the heart.

Irving's history to understand what is the relation between the crowd of smokers and the angry man who stands gesticulating before them.

We are inclined, however, to seek for the real Boughton, not in these semi-historical subjects, but in the pastoral and idyllic themes he has found in the rural life of England, Holland and Brittany, to which some of the

PICTURES THAT HAVE INFLUENCED ARTISTS.

By Charles M. Skinner.

THE growth of the big oak from the little acorn is a trite symbol of development, but it is apt to the case of the mental life of almost every human being. Some trifle, seen, heard, or believed, has given a new turn to thoughts, ambitions, and convictions, and from that germ of experience the individual marks the deciding point in his career. There are men who start out as sneaks who end by becoming philanthropists, and there are men who begin life as good boys who

Drawn by Agnes D. Abbott.
"A FOXY FACE."

Drawn by Forbein d'Après.
"THE NORTHEASTER."

bring up in Congress, or the penitentiary. In this article we find how and why it is that certain painters are what they are, and these disclosures have a deeper interest than they realize —the interest of a psychologic revelation. Had not Irving R. Wiles seen a Fortuny, he might have been playing in an orchestra or raising watermelons, and but for the fortunate attraction of a Chinaman done in colored chalks, in a tea store window, Mr Howarth might at this day have been putting up oolong in half-pound parcels behind the counter of that very shop ; and where, then, would Puck be? A successful man says that he owes all his prosperity to a kick. His father gave it, instead of a blessing, when he led him to the door and told

From a Painting by George H. Boughton.
"BLACK-EYED SUSAN."

188 AMERICAN ART AND ARTISTS.

From a painting by Agnes D. Abbatt.

IN PASTURE GREEN.

him to "hustle" for his living. He had to earn that living or die. Artists, poets, musicians, actors, all interpreters of the beautiful, are not to be kicked into greatness of efficiency. Art is a tender and lovely mistress, and to work for her is a delight.

But the same causes operate to make a good painter that produce a good farmer or an esteemed President. Those causes are largely assimilative. Such of us as are occasionally tempted to the unhealthy exercise of introspection touch a point of lucidity in that view when we exclaim in astonishment, "For goodness' sake, have I an age? Is there anything to me? I knew that I got my complexion from my mother, and my temper from my father, and my squint from one grandfather, and my miserly habits from the other; but now I find that I owe my political views to the Daily Terror, my choice in eating to my cook, my religion to disgust at a tract that I found in a horse-car, my poverty to an accidental talk with an acquaintance in school, my taste in music to an accidental talk with a second rate fiddler, my pugnacity to a thwack on the sconce that I had twenty-odd years ago, my way of shaving—but there! I am simply a feeble prey of influences. There isn't enough originality in me to choose the pattern of my own trousers." At that moment the consolation suggests itself that our neighbors are as petty and imitative as we are, and that humanity is, after all, but a large machine composed of many parts, but doing the same work year in and year out, and leaving the best things that tempted

No, friends, that is not the way to look at it. The assimilative faculty is a divine one. If we accepted no teachings, followed no hints, the safe and proper conservatism that holds us together could not be, and instead of society we should have anarchy. It is the glory of every one who is living usefully and honorably, that he has, though unconsciously, absorbed something good of other men and is endeavoring, again unconsciously, to create something better for his successors to copy. All advance is but a series of improvements on old models. There would be no artists to-day, had there been none yesterday. This series of confessions is of especial moment, because the impressions made on the emotional nature of artists are deeper than those projected against the more callous consciousness of ordinary mortals. They are more highly sensitized than the latter. Suppose it had been a plumber instead of Mr. Bolmer, who, on his day of inspiration among the lonely dunes and marshes, had felt that affiatus through which nature fights and glitters as in apotheosis; what

then? He would merely have reckoned it in to the next man's bill. Would that bleak lake shore that lingers in Mr. Meeker's memory have so pursued the imaginings of an alderman? Nay, say. Would the Corot, that Mr. Lander owns and loves so, charm the stentor who roars fish through our street? Alas and alack, and again, nay In certain cases these impressions have been vivid and fleeting, but in others the effect has been of life-long and fortunate endurance. Who does not see the relation between Thomas Moran's early admiration for Turner and his "Dream of Venice," and his western landscapes? Who that has felt

AMERICAN ART AND ARTISTS.

A STORY-TELLER ON CANVAS

By CROMWELL CHILDE.

With original Illustrations by W. Taylor & Birney.

IF there is one fault in the world of art to-day, it is the tendency toward "faddisms" of impasto and the worshipping of mere "prettinesses" of subject and style. The grand and simple methods of coloring and treatment in the old masters too often find their echo nowadays in catchy trivialities of the moment, clever bits of painting indeed, born of undoubted facility with the brush, but of little definite value. Art in its broadest and truest sense needs a plain *motif*, and each canvas as it leaves the easel is fulfilling its purpose if it shows not merely a surface of dainty tints and tones, but a thought.

There is literature in art, as there is in literature. The exquisite canvas of "The Last Token," at the Metropolitan Museum reveals, in its portrayal of the girl stooping for the rose among the savage beasts, a whole history of human passion—

"WHILE THE SUN IS SETTING."

the poetry of Mr. De Haven's pictures of evening glow needs to be told that he has responded most quickly to the charm of sunset pinks and yellows playing over the westward faces of sand-dunes? It will usually be found in pictures, as in other things, that the exceptional and surprising are not the things that live with us longest. We assimilate most quickly what we feel to be the normal and the true. Iona Rado and Mr. Poore illustrate one of the inevitable and educating experiences. In no set of pictures, then, has taste and character been more exactly discovered than in these illustrations. Tranquillity is the theme in the sea views by Agnes D. Abbott, as it is in Frances Wheaton's shepherdess. A. W. Van Deusen is a soldier *in esse*, as you see from his choice of Morot's fiery battle-piece. H. Martin Beal is more the soldier *in posse*, his booted and girded swashbuckler expressing strength in repose. The thoughtful charm of Corot is repeated by Benjamin Lander; and in the great skies and leafless trees of F. L. Field and F. J. Meeker we have the sad sentiment of November. Grace and feeling pertain to the figure by Miss Rado, and violent feeling without grace is the expression of Will Phillip Hooper. It is obviously the homely beauty of life that allures Mrs. M. E. Bignam, while the majesty of the classic is potent with W. St. John Harper. Ella F. Pell summarizes, in her drawing, the arts that have influenced the world for good, taking for her types the Venus of Milo, the Moses of Angelo, and the paintings of Raphael, Corot and Turner.

"ASPECT OF INSPIRATION"

Drawn by Elsa F. Pell.

From a painting by R. Verplanck Birney.   LOVE LETTERS.

AMERICAN ART AND ARTISTS.

love, religion and the faith of the Christian martyr. In brief, it tells a story.

A story, told in its salient facts and not left to be guessed at by the viewer with his *peace-see*, implies a thought, and an intellectuality that is literary and of the world of men and women, behind and directing the brush. The story-teller in art, far from sacrificing his devotion to color and form, needs both of these as aids to his success. They are the stage accessories to the drama he is about to "ring up."

The art exhibitions and "private views" of the past few years have given to W. Verplanck Birney, beyond the cavil of a doubt, a recognized

SIR HENRY'S RETREAT.

THE TWILIGHT PRAYER.

AN ENGLISH ALE-CELLAR.

and a representative place among story-tellers on canvas. Should his tale be one of modern times, his maids are in the dauntiest of furbelows and would charm without adventitious surroundings. Like the silk frocks of the ladies of early in this century, they can "stand alone." But Mr. Birney makes them, each and all, show a glimpse of their lives and of themselves.

Should he portray a bit of peasant life, the mainsprings of human action, whatever may be its trend at that moment, are unfolded. In one of his recent canvases, "Deserted," a village girl, her whole frame shaken with grief, kneels at a bench beside a tiny paned window. An elderly woman rests a pitying hand on the girl's

AMERICAN ART AND ARTISTS.

shoulder. Without is seen a vine-covered English church, and a wedding party is entering. In the figure of the groom one recognizes the girl's lover of the past.

The story is different in "Decorating the Old Flag," where a table is spread with gay flowers, and a band of bright-eyed children and girls are fastening them on the Stars and Stripes. "A Place Wherein to Think" shows a bewitching

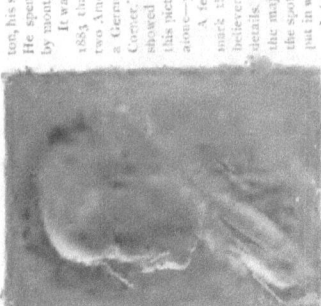

PLEASANT THOUGHTS.

girl in the brown-toned parlor of a quaint old English inn. Once more, in a Tyrolese sitting-room, a queer capped old woman sits and knits, while a dove, the symbol of the Holy Ghost, is above her head.

THE GERMAN CORNER.

top, his student-days in Boston, Philadelphia and Munich. He spent four years in this latter city, varying the time by months in England, Italy and the Tyrol.

It was at the International Exhibition in Munich in 1883 that he scored his first success, being one of the two Americans who sold pictures there. His canvas was a German peasant scene—an interior called "A Quiet Corner." In this, even so early in his career, he clearly showed the *motif* of his art life. A story was told in this picture—a simple one, a tale of girlish day-dreams, alone—yet it determined his course.

A few of the articles in his "creed of the brush" mark the trend of his thought. First of all, he is a believer in truth—the truth that exists even in the tiniest details. To accomplish this the majority of his studies are the spot, and each bit of "nature" is put in with the most reverential care.

It is this that gives his pictures their value and their strength. In "Wherein to Think" he has conveyed bodily to canvas the inn of romance that little town of Worcester, an abbey of a modern day has hallowed and taken for his *mise-en-scène*. In his Shakespearian black and white, in "Deserted Shakespeare's the bed that is seen is Inn," executed with all own, copied faithfully, exfidelity. Nor is con- dy beyond the reach of his britsh. "I like to paint comical ideas," he told me once, "laughing expressions, jollity, and wit." Perhaps the best canvas of this kind he has turned out is "A Fool and His Lunch," in which a merry jester smacks his lips and winks his eyes over a frugal meal of onions and sausage.

TARD MOON LIVES.

DUTCH KITCHEN.

OSTLER KITCHEN.

As a colorist he is strong and virile, as a composer graceful and observant of detail, but his name will go down as a master of ideas.

Few Academy exhibitions of late have lacked a message from his easel. He is one of the young men on whom Academicians have their eye when they consider recruits for the jealously guarded rank of Associate.

From grave to gay Mr. Birney's stories go. He runs the whole gamut, but most truly, most delicately, does he touch the notes of sentiment and sadness. His range is unrestricted over Europe and America. Germany, Italy, the Tyrol, France, England, especially are the sweet rural life of Britain, all these are as familiar to him as is his own land. His birthplace was Cincinnati, and so he, too, has "come out of the West." But it has been the East that has inspired him, for his school-days were spent in Washing-

AT LAST.
From a painting by W. Verplanck Birney.

WOMEN ARTISTS IN CANADA

By ALEXANDER BLACK

With original illustrations by members of the Woman's Art Association of Canada.

THE tendency toward organization which has become so general and so conspicuous during the last few years is quite as characteristic of the arts as of the trades, and it must be admitted that the results of the tendency appear to be beneficial in more than one direction. An artist may choose to look slightingly upon the sentiment of association with its fellows, but he cannot afford to despise the practical advantages.

This fact is one that women, perhaps more particularly than men, have seemed to be prompt in taking into account. The associations of women which have sprung into life within the years of this twilight decade, not to go so short a distance backward as the preceding decade, have abundantly justified their own existence. What is true of the United States is probably true of other countries in which the same conditions prevail. Certainly the most important instance offered by our neighbor Canada emphatically supports this view.

The Woman's Art Association of Canada, the first and only national art association of women in that part of our continent, was organized at Toronto in April, 1890, holding its first exhibition in the same month. There had long been an obvious need for an organization of this sort in Canada, and the success of the initial movement left no doubt of the wisdom of the plan, even in the minds of those who wish to be extremely sure before they go ahead. The women artists of the Dominion had needed a rallying point. The Royal Canadian Academy and the Ontario Society of Artists are not constituted so as to permit the encouragement of which the women artists as a class felt themselves to be in need. With a view to taking practical steps, Mrs. M. E. Dignam, who had studied at the Art Students League in New York and afterward at Paris, called together a company of women at Toronto and the Woman's Art Club was organized. Within a short time more than one hundred prominent women had become

patronesses and honorary members. Aid and counsel were given by a number of women artists in the United States, including Mrs. Julia Dillon, Mrs. E. M. Scott, Mrs. E. L. Coffin, Mrs. C. B. Coman, Mrs. Rhoda Holmes Nichols, Miss Rose Clark, Mrs. Emma Lampert; and the gratifying success of several exhibitions suggested the extension and incorporation of the club. Thus the club became the Woman's Art Association of Canada, and carries with grace and dignity the honor of being an incorporated and a national body.

The Association is supported entirely by members' fees, and the proceeds of

AMERICAN ART AND ARTISTS.

lectures and exhibitions, the business being transacted at the monthly meeting. An interesting feature of the Association's plan, and one that certainly is to be considered eminently practical, is the providing of studios for the members, with a view to supplying, as far as may be possible, the needs of those who have studied abroad and who wish to keep up their academic training. The classes have been excellently supported, and they have naturally tended to popularize the Association.

The output from this centre of art activity is marked by considerable variety. Portrait painters, landscapists, illustrators, copyists, decorators, all find community of interest in the now flourishing enterprise. The exhibitions show a growing tendency to work by direct methods. Studies from nature out-of-doors become more frequent, and improve in quality. A glance at the accompanying sketches will reveal the earnestness of the work these ambitious Canadian women are doing. The disposition to be faithful is sufficiently apparent to require no comment. The

Drawn by M. E. Henshel.
TWILIGHT GREY.

Drawn by Clara D. Oslee.
ON THE MEADOW.

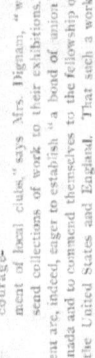

Drawn by Clara D. Oslee.
THE MOWING LOT.

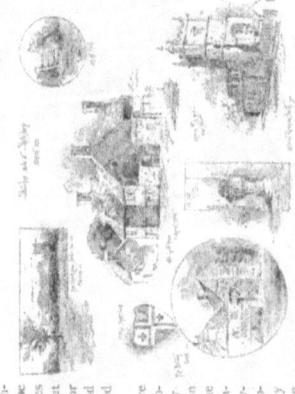

Drawn by Mildred Grayson Smith.
SKETCHES AT OTTAWA.

Drawn by Daisy K. Cherie.
"NO OBJECTION TO CREAM."

From a painting by Clemence van den Broeck.
READING THE FUTURE.

figure work is simple and effective. Miss van den Broeck's student of destiny in a coffee-cup is a charming figure. The field studies are quite as felicitous in displaying a candid and unaffected habit in looking at nature.

The Association is young, but full of vitality. Already it has enjoyed the sincerest flattery of imitation. An association in Indiana is said to have been organized upon the same lines and another in Ohio is now forming. "For the encouragement of local clubs," says Mrs. Bignam, "we send collections of work to their exhibitions," eager to establish "a bond of union" among women artists in Canada and to commend themselves to the fellowship of women artists throughout the United States and England. That such a work, even for those who have happened upon "a long felt want," is accompanied by many discouraging difficulties need scarcely be said. But Canada does not seem to be without women who are ready for pioneering in art, and unlikely to be distracted by first successes.

This is all the more notable because the political air of Canada favors that of Great Britain in matters of the fine arts. There is a tendency to look to the Governor General for support and benefits. Many Canadians have been knighted; why not an artist? But these ladies

From a painting by Mrs. M. E. Dupuy. FEEDING THE HEIFER

AMERICAN ART AND ARTISTS.

look only to their own energies and bright, capable minds.

A peculiarity of the work of Canadian artists in general is the absence of any appreciable influence upon it of the leading artists of Great Britain. Neither the old Pre-Raphaelites nor the later school of London, which may be called the classical British school, neither the interesting outpost of Sir Edward Burne-Jones, Bart, newly ennobled, nor the Flemish archaeological

From a painting by Mary McConnell
SPRING FLOWERS.

Drawn by Mary M. Phillips
STREET IN A CANADIAN VILLAGE.

school, ably represented in London by Alma Tadema, seem to find much response among our cousins to the northward. French art has had more influence, but, singularly enough, the French population of Canada furnishes hardly any artists. Canadian art seems to be moving exactly on the same lines as the art of the United States. Examination of the sketches after work by Canadian women in this paper will show that the same is true of the feminine side of the house. English tendency to anecdotic art is not apparent. Whether this is a good thing or ill need not be discussed; it is enough to mark the fact.

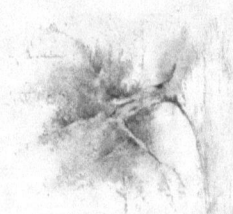

Drawn by Nina Wedlock
QUINCES, NOT APPLES.

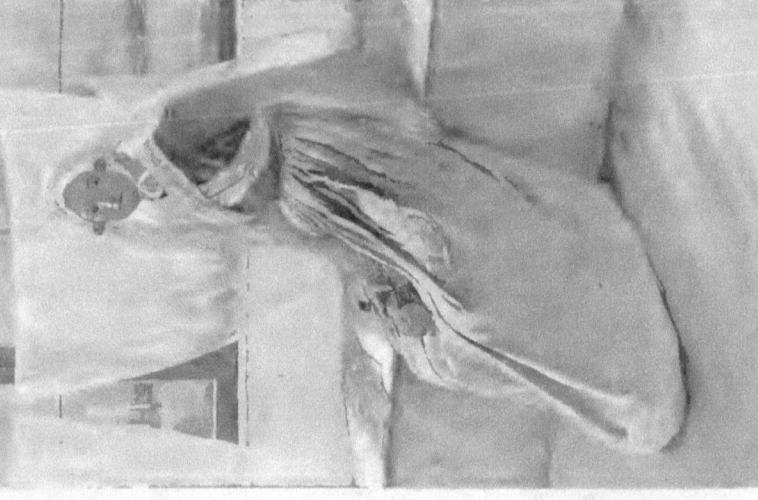

Drawn by Anna Campbell
ROSE THE NATIVE.

From a painting by George Wharton Edwards
"ALL IN THE CLEAR GLORY OF THE WORLD"

There was a time when Boston artists were infected by a suspicion that they were not welcome guests at New York Exhibitions; but the acceptance of thousands of pictures, the winning of many prizes in New York, have broken down this imagined grievance. Why should not Canadians try their chances in New York?

PEASANT AND PICTURE.

By GEORGE WHARTON EDWARDS.

With original illustrations by the writer.

In the clear dusk that was upon the dike I saw her first outlined against the dark mass of the village church. The roofs of the small one-storied peasant houses that lined the crooked way along the dike were blurred against the tender sky, and here and there a thorn-bush showed its ivory-like blossoms, shaking in the wind. The tiny pools of water beneath the willows at the edge of the polder were yellow as topaz. Swallows whirred against the light and skimmed the eaves, and there was the sound of voices and laughing from a group of peasants at the edge of the sea. I was sketching with the last light, and a maid stood beside me, her cap ends stiffly starched and brown curly back at her temples, where gleamed two shining plates of gilded silver marking the head-dress of Breskens. Across her bosom lay a kerchief, its ends tucked cunningly between the buttons at her waist, and her skirts were ample and of a blue woolen stuff. Her arms were bare to above the elbow and were burned brown by the sun. There she stood against the yellow of the sky, smiling down in wonder at my rapid brush strokes. The wind blew salt from the sea, and from the inbound boats, blunt bowed, lee boarded, and brown sailed, came clinking of chain and rattle of block, in harmony with the softened voices of the fishermen. "Stand thee well before me, little Misje," I said in her tongue, "and I will give thee a silver gulden for thy pains." At which her eyes twinkled, the gilt ornaments above them gleamed in the light, and she became part of my picture.

"Who is thy father, little maid?"

"My father was Stofrnik Appel," she said, "and one day he went forth in his boat from the dike end, upon the early tide. It was the herring season, and the storm came up, the great storm of '87,—the Heer will remember, perhaps. The wind blew, the water swept the dikes, and his boat came never back from the sea. So all that night and day did the bells ring at Breskens, at Vyte Vliet, at Hoornen, and even Hulswlyk. Thus were forty boats lost, and thus I am an orphan it is now six years since. My name is Lovje Appel, and of brothers I have two, Jan and Arrie. 'Twas Jan that brought thee here before yestereen in his boat from Hoornen."

The light failed fast, and from the harbor reach came forth twinkling flashes from the beacon light, that broke into dancing ruddy sparks at the wet edges of the dike stones.

I packed my box with moist uncleaned palette and brushes, and my easel in its convenient straps, while the maid tightly gripped a silver gulden as we parted, she to come to me at early day for a fresh pose indoors.

Days passed; as I painted I had no thought of time. Sitting in the wide window-seat, against fresh lawn curtains, all in the clear light, she posed while I sought the solution of the problem of tone I had set against my hand's cunning, and it availed me much that she truly kept her pose.

Often came to us the curious villagers to watch the progress of the picture, never failing to properly and respectfully leave their clumsy wooden klompjes (shoes) at the doorstone, and doff the lat as they entered, and I knew of their presence only by their heavy breathing or a chance whispered criticism of the picture, so quiet and considerate were they as they watched its growth. Thus and so the picture grew and was finished, and the reason of my stay among them was at an end.

So one morning I came away from Breskens, when the wind blew fresh, the gulls flew nigh, the tawny yellow waters of the sea were tumbling and tossing, and the white-caps showed far out, while the few boats that the harbor sheltered were rocking in a fine, all headed to the westward, tugging at their moorings. My luggage was snugly stowed in Appel's bluntbowed tjalk. I had said farewell to little Lotje and the villagers, of whom some had a hand-grasp and God-speed for me; the red roofs of Breskens and the pier head where the peasants had foregathered in my honor became blurred in the distance, and Appel held the tiller in his strong hand as the tjalk, well heeled over and her brown sails rounded out, bounded away for the distant shore.

AMERICAN ART AND ARTISTS.

Drawn by Katherine Pyres. ORIENTAL SKETCHES.

Drawn by H. E. Dixson. A SEQUESTERED NOOK.

study of *grande peinture* with Gérôme, and her negro studies in the Southern States are as characteristically rendered as her memories of Venice. We do not know that she accepts pupils; but if so, her many-sidedness, admirable training, sympathy and magnetism would make her a most desirable teacher.

Another woman who has had the advantage of the best European training and has profited by it is Mrs Marie Guise Newcomb. Her studies of dogs and horses show in their handling the virile strength of her master, Schenck, plus a womanly sympathy in her understanding of the individual character

WOMAN IN ART.

By ELIZABETH W. CHAMPNEY.

With original Illustrations by Numerous Artists.

ONE of our prominent instructors in art, during a class criticism, wishing to deprecate the excessive finish and delicacy of the work of one of his students, a young man, said, with equal truth and gallantry—

"A few years ago we would have called such painting that *effeminate*. We no longer use the word, now that the women do so well."

When the very masters, the pupils' work, are convinced, and the girl and business it is to find students carry off the prizes at art schools and exhibitions both at home and abroad, they have won the right to be considered seriously.

That such an artist as Gérôme, a sceptic in regard to the mission of women in art, should have been won by the genius displayed in the oriental sketches of Miss Katherine Hoeger to accept her as his pupil, is ranking her at the outset very high, and Miss Hoger has more than fulfilled the prophecy of her master. She is an all-round painter. Her exquisitely decorated fans were the vogue in Paris when she began the

Drawn by Florence Marsdahle. (MY MOTHER, YOU KNOW)

of her models, a quick—almost humorous—and a fine enthusiasm for the horse, which she considers one of the noblest of creations. She is our best known animal painter among women, and well deserves her honors. Elizabeth Strong, whose skill in painting dogs has won

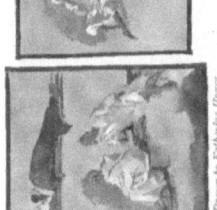

Drawn by Ellen Lesley. A LOCCA BRED

Drawn by Marie Guise Newcomb. A HAPPY COMPANY

Drawn by Clara W. Ludlow. NO ONE OWN FIRESIDE

From a painting by Katherine Langdon Greene.

BROOK WILLOWS.

AMERICAN ART AND ARTISTS.

recognition in Europe, and who was a pupil of Van Marcke, is also in New York this winter. No other American women have studied animals more seriously, though Florence Mackubin shows much facility in her portraits of dogs, and Grace Hudson introduces them cleverly in her illustrations of Indian life, as does Ethel Isadore Brown in her dainty sketches of society.

After Paris, more of our art students go for instruction to the Netherlands than to any other country of Europe, drawn, doubtless, by the excellence of

the academies, in which women have an equal footing with the men, by the art movement among the younger painters, by the exquisite Dutch landscapes depicted in the amber reflections of the quiet old masters. We have two women of exceptional ability—Clara T. Wetherbey and Clara W. Lathrop—who have responded to this fascinating Dutch influence. Miss Metchester's water-colors have the charming tone of the Dutch masters, quiet and serious, with a delightful feeling of earnestness and conscientiousness in their simple subjects, mostly dim interiors of peasant houses painted with a sentiment which has nothing to do with sentimentality, and gives "a sense of nearness" to the poor people represented, which the artist must

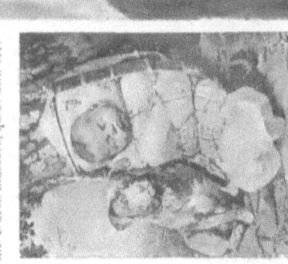

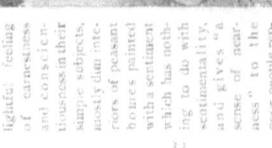

AMERICAN ART AND ARTISTS.

have felt in painting them. Miss Lathrop, describing the sketching grounds which she has so charmingly rendered, writes:

"We were in a little out-of-the-way fishing village, known only to artists, where the peasants were willing to pose in their own homes. The color was charming, with the dull red walls, shining copper pots and pans, and rows of old delft plates over the fireplace. There was always a low, wide window, and often a quaint old clock, and his of pottery in dull yellows everywhere and greens."

Mrs. France is another artist who loves to touch the heart and who has the power to do so.

Miss Sophia Walker treats portraiture from the stand-point of the genre painter, and such a portrait of a loved face must be inexpressibly precious to its possessor. How the blessed tears must spring to the eyes in weary days of absence to see mother in the old familiar corner, breaking the seal of a letter from her boy, or taking tea from grandmamma china which she brought into the family as a bride, or father in his easy-chair at his writing-table looking up from his newspaper, with his pet books about him. Such canvases will never be sent to the garret or the auction-room, for they are full of living associations to friends and are interesting as pictures to strangers.

Another portrait-painter with another style, distinctively manly (in its best sense) is Grace Randolph. She has but recently returned from the Parisian ateliers, and her figure paintings and portrait busts have the latest traditions. Possibly her study of modelling has contributed to her skill in depicting the planes which give her painted heads their sense of roddity as all-round objects and not flat surfaces.

The drawing of the human figure, conceded to be the most difficult branch of art, is also the favorite one with the ambitious student, and one in which she frequently succeeds. Mary Buttles is a portrait painter. Edith and Ellen Lesley, Helen E. Keep, Gertrude Greene, Florence K. Upton, Helen Jeffrey, and Abby E. Underwood draw figures very cleverly for illustration. Martha S. Baker, of the Chicago Art Institute, is interested in illustration as a teacher.

From a painting by M. R. Dixon. DOCTORS, TEN PENCE.

From a painting by M. R. Dixon. OLD AGES.

AMERICAN ART AND ARTISTS.

Drawn by *Kenyon, M. Hager.*   AMUSEMENTS OF THE GRECIAN MAIDENS

AMERICAN ART AND ARTISTS.

pastels and water-colors have been received with enthusiasm by the New York Water Color Club when those of many an old professional were rejected. She is a woman of conscience as well as feeling, and of a fine scorn for all shams. When asked what style she proposed to adopt, she replied: "If I cannot have a style of my own, I trust I may be spared an adopted one."

Drawn by Rosa Koch.

It is a little tie remarkable that landscape—usually first attempted by the tyro in art as its easiest branch (an inch or two more or less on the branch of a tree does not signify, but on a man's nose it does)—landscape, so overrun by men, should be affected by few women painters. Mrs. M. E. Dignam, Mary B. Chapman, Ida C. Haskell, and Eugenie Heller, indeed find figures and landscape of equal interest; but Mrs. Charlotte Whitmore is one of a few in her devotion to landscape pure and simple. She dislikes to have figures introduced in landscape, and says that for her they take away the real restfulness of nature. "Figures are a constant reminder of suspended animation, and are even more tire-

From a painting by Charlotte Whitmore. ON THE MC CRACK.

A DISTRACTIVE DOLL.

Mrs. Dixon's skill in the composition of important figure paintings has obtained for her a wide and enviable reputation. Her pictures of young girls and of child-life are also deservedly popular—a field in which she meets a rival worthy of her steel in Miss Maria Brooks, an English lady, who has captured New York by her charming rendering of children. It must have been before one of Miss Brooks's canvases that the poet wrote—

With merry dancing eyes
And flying curls,
And robes of shining white,
Oh! very beautiful are little girls,
And lovely to the sight.

From a painting by Clara Weaver Parrish.

Drawn by Mary Jeffries.

Drawn by Mary Sedwick. A STUDY.

Drawn by Lucia Leslie. AN OLD SCOTCH COTTAGE.

From a painting by Francis Coates. THE OLD BELL.

Some of the most talented of the women of the day are among the youngest, and some who have never profited by the European schools have yet found their own expression in a most acceptable manner. Mary R. Williams is one of these, an artist with rare poetic instinct and feeling. Her

AMERICAN ART AND ARTISTS.

some than real people, and almost everyone is glad to get away alone."

Emma K. Lampert, herself a landscapist of merit, advises women not to make landscape a specialty, unless they have great physical strength and perfect health. She says: "The difficulties encountered by a woman working alone in the fields is rarely realized by one who has not had the experience.

Drawn by Mdy C. Hazlett.

WINTER THOUGHTS END.

snow, making festoons of swan's-down on the bare branches, of glittering ice, and dark pools of freezing water, safe alike from tramps and rheumatism. She has another for the spring-time, a little house eight by ten feet, which can be taken apart and put up in any place, in which the easels and other paraphernalia of sketching may be locked overnight.

Mrs. Whitmore's prejudice against figures in landscape will be voted down by all who know the paintings of Lydia Field Emmet. The *plein air* of the school she represents, with its dazzling effects of scintillating light, the best of

Drawn by Mary E. Hart.

CORONATION.

The weight of the necessary outfit, the long walks in the hot sun, and the danger of working alone in pass the wild sort of places that are especially paintable, are reasons why so few women elect this branch of art."

Katherine Langdon Corson has overcome these difficulties by her portable studios. She has two; one on runners for snow, fitted up so that it can be hauled, and with a glass front. From this she can paint the charming effects of soft

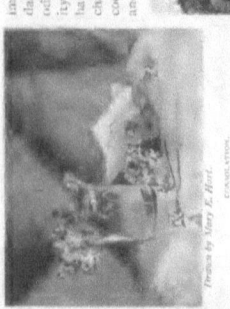

From a painting by Emma Lampert.

OZARK SUMMER RAIN.

impressionism, a realism which does not disdain beauty, a knowledge of *fin-de-siécle* methods, with a touch of her own sweet personality, will bring back in her canvases, to all who have been so favored as to know them, the charming girls and sunny downs of Shinnecock. Annie R. Shepley, who is very skilful and successful in portraiture, also testifies to

her liking
for figures in
landscape. "The
effects of sunshine,
air and color, to me
make out - of - door
work the most desir-

Drawn by Jennie Lea Southwick.

FIGURE IN TRAMS.

able existence in the world." Among other ladies notably successful in this field are Mrs. Julia Henshaw Dewey, Emily Slade, Josephine Wood Colby, Lucia Fairchild Fuller, and Ellen F. Stone. Mrs. Montgomery Sears, of Boston, and Mrs. Egerton Adams, of Chicago (E. I. S. A.), are accomplished water colorists, and have won laurels for their dash and finesse in the treatment of the head and figure.

From landscape with figures there is but a step

Drawn by Ellis F. Peel.

EVOLUTION OF THE SOUL.

to land-
scape with architecture, and for such
subjects Venice is the Queen city.
Jennie Lea Southwick is one of a doz-
en or more of our American painters,
among whom Rhoda Holmes Nicholls
is a shining example, who have felt and
interpreted acceptably the charm of
this bewitching city. Miss Southwick's
nature is intensely artistic. Everything
Venetian is dear to her, from a row of
old fish-baskets to the Salute, shower-

From a painting by Claude Raguet Hirst.

AN OLD COPY.

From a painting by Lucy D. Holme.

A FIELD LABORER.

ROSES.

From a painting by Mrs. F. M. Scott.

AMERICAN ART AND ARTISTS.

ing back all the glory of an Italian sunset from its dome and marbles and reflected again in the iridescent water.

Vedper is the connecting link between landscapes and marines. Few of our artists, men or women, attempt the changeable, difficult sea; but Helene

From a painting by Mrs. C. E. Coxon.
AN ISLAND.

Drawn by Abby Underwood.
A WOMAN.

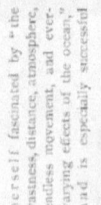

Drawn by Henrietta Bannon.
A CUPID. CENTRE.

Cox's charming figure studies, and Ella Condie Lamb's noble designs for church decoration.

Every one of the exhibitors at the Woman's Art Club deserves mention, as well as other artists whose work is represented in this article, but of whom we have not space to write. Many another highly

From a painting by Rhoda Holmes. THREE NUNS.

From a painting by Lydia Field Emmett.
SNOWDROPS.

herself fascinated by "the vastness, distance, atmosphere, endless movement, and ever-varying effects of the ocean," and is especially successful in harbor and shore subjects. Our review is as little more than a catalogue. We have no space to tell of the high ideals and achievements of such artists as Mary Cassatt, of Mrs. A. McG. Herter's playful fancy and beautiful pictures of Japanese life, of Dora Wheeler Keith's admirable portrait and decorative work, of Louise

gifted woman whose name will occur to the reader of this article, may seem an almost unpardonable omission. They have proved their right to wear the paint-bedaubed apron, and to thrust paint-brushes-like Japanese hair-pins in their pretty Psyche knots, for in nearly every woman who paints, as was said of Madeleine Lemaire, there are two women — "the drawing-room woman, who smiles at compliments, and the atelier woman, who will not listen to them." They have won their place in art without sighing a single womanly duty or losing a single womanly charm.

In still life women have done some re-

Drawn by Maud Stumm.
IN GREEN SPIKE.

AMERICAN ART AND ARTISTS.

Drawn by Katharine Hoyt.
CORAL-OF THE SAXONS.

markable work. Claude Raguet Hirst, who, by the way, is generally supposed to be a man, has made a reputation for "bachelor subjects," collections of bachelor comforts, particularly pipes and rare old violins (copying the worn and stained places exactly). Two such pictures were in the spring water-color exhibition, suggestive of college life, the toil and solace of the book-worm and the grind.

Frances Catherine Challener is a student of still life and flowers, with a preference for Venetian glass and all delicate and exquisite objects, and possesses a fine touch in representing them.

Frances S. Carlin paints roses in a broad and simple manner, but has lately made very acceptable studies of the homes of French peasants and of the peasants themselves.

Mary E. Hart has made the violets her very

Drawn by Mary K. Williams.
A FORTUNE TELLER.

own, because she loves them and has found

A daintiness about these early flowers
That touches one like poetry.

Agnes D. Abbott enjoys the distinction of being a member of the Water Color Society. Her flower paintings are too well and favorably known to need comment here,

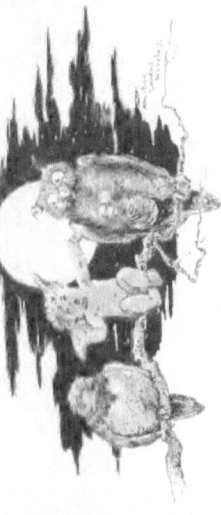

Drawn by Josephine Cook.
JACKS QUEEN.

but she has lately taken up a new line in landscape and architecture.

Marguerite Lippincott is frankly and simply a flower painter, for she feels that "to no more delightful practice can be found than in the rich warm hues of flowers."

Maud Stumm, though successful in this line, enjoys most of all studying the figure in Grecian drapery. Frieda Redmond uses flowers decoratively, and loves the freedom given her by large wall spaces. Josephine Cook treats a rose tenderly, as do Mrs. E. M. Scott and Mrs. Dillon, as though it were a *gage d'amour*.

The sweetest flower that grows
I give you as we part.
To you it is a rose,
To me it is my heart.

Drawn by Fanny Trowbridge.
VENICE "EMBARKING."

This indeed can be said of nearly all of woman's work in art. To the critic the canvas is a display of brilliant virtuosity; to the artist, more particularly if she be a woman, it is often her heart.

Drawn by Emily S. Moon.
OLD FISH HOUSE.

Drawn by Almerian Rowland Wheeler.
"OH, DON'T GO AWAY!"

Drawn by Frieda Voelter Redmond.
WHEN THE FROST IS ON THE PUMPKIN.

AMERICAN ART AND ARTISTS.

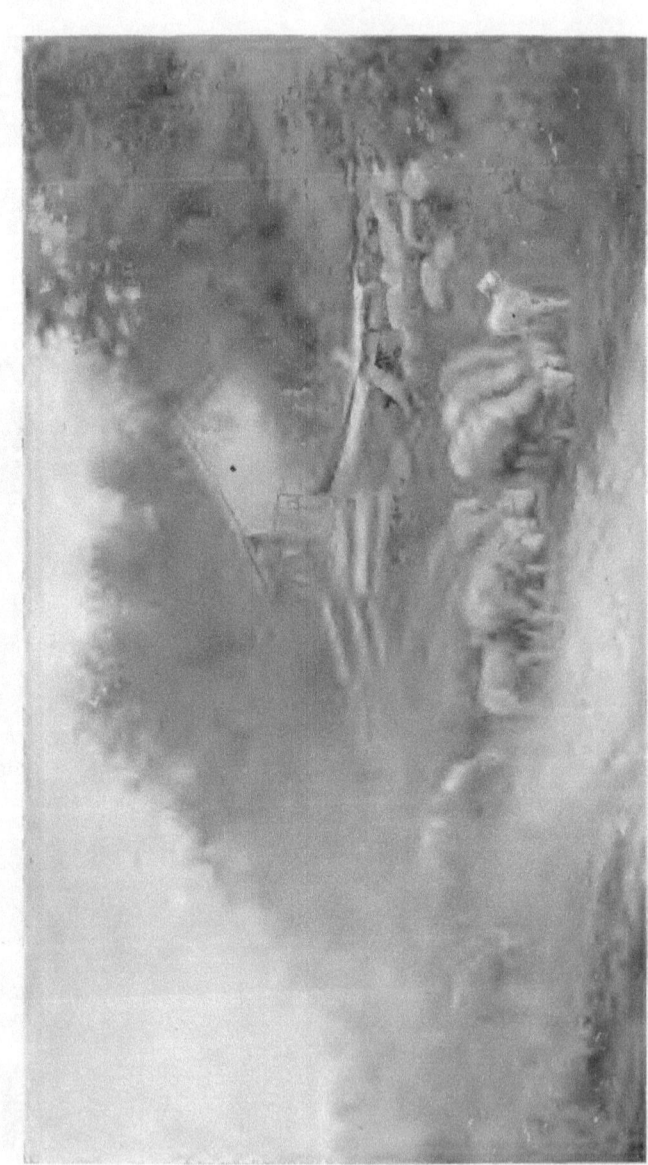

From a painting by *Maria Goza Nixcomb.*

GRAZING BY THE ROADSIDE.

FROM FINANCE TO ART

By CHARLOTTE ADAMS

With original illustrations by Stanley Middleton

THE fine flower of idealism flourishes on the most arid soil, or rather on soil that seems and to the class that does not possess or sympathize with the insight of genius. It is given as yet to but a small circle of writers and painters to appreciate the fact that the highest of all forms of idealism, namely, that which springs from realism, lies at the root of American literary and artistic expression to-day. The quickening of the American creative faculty came at the time of the great war of freedom; and in the case of a few strong individualities, like that of Winslow Homer, for instance, the subjective and objective sides of American life met in splendid harmony. Then followed a period of factitious or eclectic cosmopolitan development, which by degrees resolved itself into the study of the national life, without reference to the impulse from without except as regards technical methods.

The existing art system contains numerous individualities reacting upon American life and reacted upon by it, all going to form an inchoate,

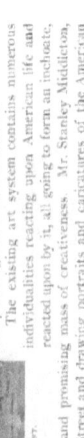

A FRENCH PEASANT.

chaotic, but hopeful and promising mass of creativeness. Mr. Stanley Middleton, clerking it in Wall Street and drawing portraits and caricatures of the American

ROWING PARTY, LAKE CHAMPLAIN.

A CATTLE PAINTER FROM FRANCE

By HENRY ECKFORD

With original illustrations by Aymar Pezant.

CHARACTER in beasts and birds — the bovine in cattle, the swinish in pigs, the self-complacency betrayed by geese in their waddle — is one of the traits of Japanese art. It is largely due to the glad, unfettered study of external nature by artists of Japan that men of the West have taught themselves to see character in animals. At the same time, the great movement of philosophy on the track of evolution has made the public more tolerant and observant of our humble fellow-mortals in fur, feather, and scales. Artists have helped in this work by showing that beast, bird, and fish are beautiful and worthy of deep study for their colors and forms.

Among the French artists at the World's Fair new to Americans was the maker of "The Road to Vaudancourt," a cattle piece with the herd coming forward by the dusty road. Realism is at its best in the varied groups of kine by M. Aymar Pezant. Cows prone and standing, cows in movement and sluggishly chewing the cud, fetlock-deep in water. The lively gait of steer and heifer, the slow, sagacious look of udder-bearing kine, the menace in the uplifted muzzle and wide-spread ears of bull or ox — all these traits he knows how to give in summary scratches of the crayon and to paint in oils. M. Pezant is a worthy successor of Troyon and Van Marcke.

AMERICAN ART AND ARTISTS.

types of character that unconsciously posed for him, was himself unconsciously developing, in his modest individual way, the nationalistic side of American art. There are many such men in America, all working along the same lines of nationalism, with varying depth of purpose and under different conditions, but

FIDO.

all animated by the same conviction, that the period of organic production in American art has arrived.

Mr. Middleton has not been spoiled by his foreign studies. His preliminary training in American art-schools led him to Paris, where he developed himself on all sides under Harpignies, one of the most significant of French landscape individ-

EXCELSIOR MILL, MILFORD, PA.

INDIAN CAMP.

ualities; Dagnan-Bouveret, a famous realist and modernist; Benjamin Constant, who feels beauty in woman even more keenly than most painters, and apotheosizes it, and under Jacquem de la Chevreuse. Excellent influences for a broad-minded painter— none better. The result of this choice of instructors has been the formation of a well-rounded, evenly balanced talent, as much at home in the rendering of Nature as of Humanity. There is no trace of imitativeness in Mr. Middleton's work. One feels that the painter has placed himself face to face with his subject, has grasped it solidly and with due regard to detail, and with absolute truth. In his landscapes he shows special feeling for light and atmosphere, and is, moreover, entirely without the mannerisms of which the pupils of distinguished masters are frequently unable to rid themselves. Very fresh in color and true in atmosphere and tone is the Rowing Party, Lake Champlain, with its three figures in bright costumes. The foreground is carefully studied, and the sky with its fleecy clouds, shows brilliant painting. In the Indian Camp, Excelsior Mill, Milford, Pa., Old Toll-bridge, Middleburg, N. Y., the style is fresh, true, sparkling, and, above all, exact, the result of French training as well as personal temperament. Returning from the Woods has excellent work in the foliage, and is a very good example of this painter's landscape style at its best. "As She came Over the Stile"— a pretty girl standing on a stile under interlaced tree boughs— is crisp and strong in treatment and well painted.

From Benjamin Constant Mr. Middleton has caught the spirit of the eternal feminine in its most gracious aspect. How charming are these heads of young beauties; these delicate, well-poised heads of the highbred American type—blonde, auburn, chestnut, thoughtful, gracious, and charming Beau-

OLD TOLL-BRIDGE, MIDDLEBURG, N.Y.

AMERICAN ART AND ARTISTS.

SOME FRANCONIA MOUNTAINS.
From a painting by Stanley Middleton.

tifully poised and balanced in composition and general style is the quarter-length called A Poem, an auburn-haired girl reading from a book. The purple dress is kept well subordinated to the head, which is delicately and strongly modelled against a dark background. This is a work full of distinction. A Flemish Belle is a graceful head encased in a quaint Flemish bonnet, trimmed with a broad red band of figured ribbon and a white cape curtain. A reddish shawl round the neck sets off the delicate oval face and fine straight profile. An Oriental is a head somewhat in the Constant vein, with a black and gold veil bound about the hair. Mr. Middleton should devote himself to painting beauties of a classic and romantic type, for in this line he shows the distinctive temperament, combined with technical skill and fine comprehension of his theme. En Soirée presents a fair example of the painter's ability in the direction of portraiture. The dusk, graceful head is seen in profile against a luminous dark-blue background. A white lace bertha is tastefully disposed over the yellow gown.

More important is the large portrait reproduced in these pages, which for grace in composition and nice balance of line may be warmly recommended. The pale blue dress, the crashed strawberry and ermine cloak, form a scheme of color that commends itself to the beholder at first sight. The head is dignified, well-bred, and graceful. Allowing for differences of age, time, and method, there is something of Copley in the manner in which this portrait is handled. We recommend to Mr. Middleton the study of the suave and beautiful female portraits of the eighteenth century in England and America. There are few accomplished painters of high-bred women in America, and the demand for them is on the increase. Mr. Middleton has the suavity of the last century combined with the élan of the close of the nineteenth. In A French Peasant an example is given of Mr. Middleton's ability with charcoal—an artist's achievements in that direction is often more useful to the student than his more finished work. If asked whereto Mr. Middleton is liable to fall below the level of his own best work, one may answer that his danger lies in a certain facility, which is partly natural, partly the result of training. All that teachers can do is

A FLEMISH BELLE.

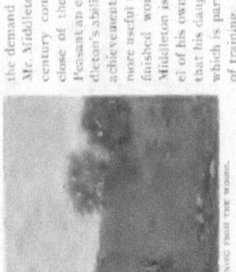

LA SIESTA.

to encourage their pupils to ascertain processes of composition, drawing, and painting. They can give them a good example sometimes if they possess the necessary brains and hearts, but this example is a silent one. Paris is the place to learn how to use the tools of art, but when they are learned comes the question: "What have you to say?" Most of our young artists in Paris have nothing to say except what the Frenchmen round about them are saying. They get into a habit of thinking processes everything, and sneering at "literary" art. Now Mr. Middleton is not exactly in this category, for we see how he has taken hold on American scenes and American types. But his danger lies in that abyss all the same. He is now so facile, so quick and smart with the brush, he may readily forget to keep a firm hand on the helm, and steer that difficult course between art for the craftsman and art for the public, between art for art's sake and art with a message to the world. Summing up, we may say that Mr. Middleton has already shown the qualities which go to form an accomplished artistic personality, and it is probable that the maturity of his talent will present still more credible results.

AMERICAN ART AND ARTISTS.

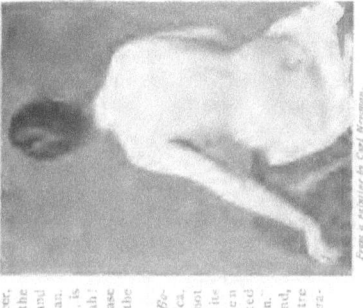

SKETCH CLUB SMOKE-TALK. *From a photograph.*

From a painting by Carl Newman. SPOOK.

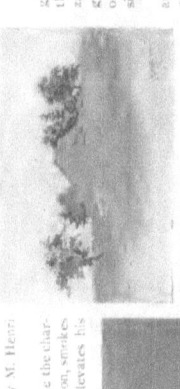

"IN THE GLOAMING." *Drawn by C. Andrew Hutton.*

PHILADELPHIA IN SOUTH RIVER, NEW YORK. *From a painting by F. Octavius Sokol.*

nose at the very mention of vulgar beer, and, because he deprives himself of the services of a valet, declares himself, and is recognized by many as, a Bohemian.

This, naturally, is an extreme. Bah! "To what base uses, etc., as the poet cried.

La vie de Bohème in America, however, is not dead, though its name has been misappropriated by "weldon."

It exists, and, magnet-like, draws to a common centre the student and graduate in art, literature, music and the sciences.

From a bronze relief by George Morgan. PRYOR.

A BOHEMIAN ART CLUB.

By HENRY RUSSELL WRAY.

With original illustrations by many members.

The word Bohemian, in its modern application, has been robbed of much of that romance which was wont to cast a halo about it in the times written of by M. Henri Murger in his *Scenes de la Vie de Bohème*.

The word in our day has been dwarfed to illustrate the character who sips champagne *frappe* with a souvenir spoon, smokes only imported cigars, wears foreign-cut clothes, elevates his

Drawn by Peter Moran. HARD MUSHER.

To one of these groups credit is given of forming and maintaining to this day one of the oldest art organizations in the United States, and of graduating from its garret rooms some of the brightest lights in the profession.

To said old Philadelphia, then, attention should be directed, while a review is made of its now famous Sketch Club, where Bohemianism is

Drawn by George E. Essig. BEACH PATROL.

not forced, like a hot-house plant, but thrives in a natural state, and where fellowship exists without becoming tiresome.

The Philadelphia Sketch Club was organized November 20, 1860, by six young enthusiasts who met in the studio of George F. Bensell. Meetings were to be held every Saturday night, and, as one of the rules stated, "when the treasury

A QUARTETTE.
From a painting by Hermann Simon.

AMERICAN ART AND ARTISTS.

A COUNTRY LANE.
Drawn by A. M. Lindsey.

A WAYSIDE INN.
Drawn by Daniel Wilson Jordan.

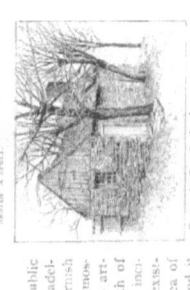

SKETCH, A LEVEL.
Drawn by Frank L. Pitkins.

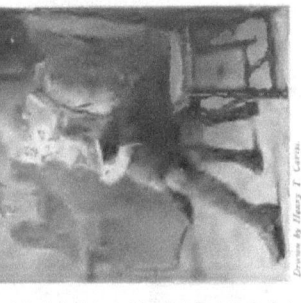

Drawn by Geo. B. Wood.

BELVEDERE.
Drawn by Charles H. Stephens.

Drawn by Henry T. Cariss.
FIRST LESSON IN DRAWING.

dale, the lawyer-artist president of the club, wrote as follows of its early life: "The club was planned at a time not conducive to the growth of the germ of an artistic association. The civil war broke out before it was six months old (and almost every member enlisted), and during the next five years matters æsthetic had but little place in the public mind, nor did Philadelphia at that time furnish the conditions or atmosphere congenial to artists and the growth of art. It is to the Academy of Fine Arts, incidentally, that the Sketch Club owes its existence, for it was at her classes that the idea of founding a club was first thought out, and it was the students who furnished the first material of the membership, and have aided in replenishing it ever since."

The rise of the club into the realm of prosperity and influence dates from December, is in need of funds it is to be replenished by a subscription levied on each member, not exceeding twelve cents." The struggle for life was hard, despite such devices.

The first exhibition of the club was held April, 1865, and to make a better display it moved from the studio to a room on Chestnut Street. This very nearly cost the organization its life, for one year later it stood on the brink of disbanding, and only saved itself by moving back to garret quarters. William Moylan Lans-

AMERICAN ART AND ARTISTS.

1869. In 1874 a journal called the Portfolio was published, and lived a trifle over one year. About this time a life class was inaugurated, and has existed to this day. Thomas Eakins was instructor, and anatomical lectures were delivered by Dr. Harrison Allen. A trust fund was also started, and placed in the hands of two trustees, the disbursing of this fund, the manner of which is known only to the trustees, has saved many an artist member from going to the wall.

Herkomer, the English painter and etcher, after visiting the Sketch Club, wrote of it: "I have never seen its equal for hospitality, good-fellowship, picturesqueness, and typical Bohemianism, although I've been in almost every art and social club in America and abroad." Before touching its life of to-day, mention should be made of some of the artists, now known the world over, who are either active or non-resident members, and whose enthusiastic support forded the club over trying times. F. T. Richards, Camille Piton, Alexander

From an etching by Henry Russell Wray
AT ANCHOR.

Drawn by Gustave A. Gilabert.
OLD STREET, LYONS, FRANCE.

Drawn by William A. Poore.
THE TANGLED PAIR.

Drawn by Milton H. Bancroft. CLOISTER OF CHESTER CATHEDRAL.

From an etching by Joseph Pennell. IN THE HARBOR AT VENICE.

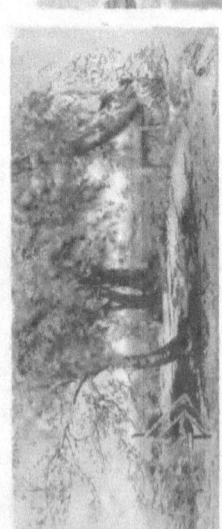

Drawn by Fred H. Schell. SURF AT HIGH TIDE.

From an etching by Edith Loring Getchell. A DAY AT SUNSHINE.

IN THE BRUSH.

From a painting by HENRY R. POORE.

222

AMERICAN ART AND ARTISTS.

A FARM-HOUSE BY THE SEA.

Drawn by F. F. English.

AMERICAN ART AND ARTISTS.

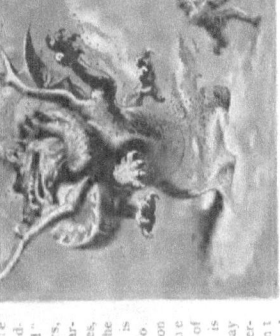

From etching by William Sartain.

Drawn by Walter M. Dunk.
A SCORE MORNING.

Drawn by Marion A. Wirt.
A STUDY

From a sketch by Howard Roberts.
IN PROGRESS FROM.

Drawn by J. L. Clapper.
IN MAIDEN MEDITATION.

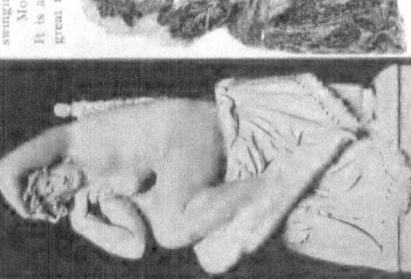

Drawn by E. B. Bensell.
THE DRAGON AND THE BEGGAR.

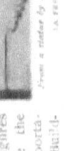

Drawn by F. T. Richards.
SAPPHO.

ing at the World's Fair. About this great fireplace members smoke their long clay pipes and sip beer from earthen mugs, or mix a toddy from the huge kettle swinging on the crane.

Monday night is the life class, and Saturday night the regular club gathering. It is about eleven o'clock that members and guests ascend the many flights. A great table is filled with art portraits and periodicals, with a part cleared for the groups working off impromptu sketches. Another table has the modest "spread" of crackers, cheese, sardines, olives, etc. In the other room is the piano. Every person crossing the threshold of the club is bound to pay for his entertainment when called upon by story,

Harrison, Clifford P. Grayson, A. M. Lindsay, Henry T. Cariss, Leon Delachaux, Fred. Schell, Fred. Pitts, Birge Harrison, D. Ridgway Knight, Fred. James, Chas. F. Dana, Milne Ramsey, F. Cresson Schell, Joseph Pennell, prince of henand-ink men, Frank Moss, A. B. Frost, Peter Moran, Proper L. Senat, S. J. Ferris, Will Lippincott, Bernard Uhle, and a score more.

Two rooms on the fourth floor of a building at Eleventh and Walnut Streets, Philadelphia, form the attic abode of the club to-day. Moneyed men have offered to erect a building for these Bohemians, but it is safe to predict that a garret will always mark the club's prosperity. Hanging on the walls are sketches, etchings, models' coats and armor, tapestries, draperies, and trophies, in artistic disorder. A huge fireplace in one room was designed by members, and the central figure was modelled in clay by John J. Boyle, the sculptor who made the figures outside the Transportation Build-

AMERICAN ART AND ARTISTS.

SURPRISED AT THE WAYSIDE INN.

Drawn by W. T. Thuston.

AMERICAN ART AND ARTISTS.

song, recitation, or criticism, and lights of the drama and opera are gathered together weekly in the rooms.

There is a club within this club known as the Grub Club (one of the Life variety). It numbers to-day thirteen. These men, for reasons of fellowship with a suggestion of economy, meet daily in the rooms at noon, prepare coffee, consume their lunch, and enjoy the after pipe. The "shot" per man per lunch is too small for mention.

HARVEST TIME
Drawn by J. Henderson Eddy

VINTAGE A FAMILY AFFAIR
Drawn by W. J. Thompson

STILL LIFE
Drawn by Benjamin R. Elliott

CARICATURE OF SKETCH CLUB MEMBER
Drawn by Henry R. Poore

A subject is given out monthly in the club for a competitive sketch, work is brought in at the stipulated time, and thoroughly criticised before ballot for award is taken.

The active membership of the Sketch Club numbers over four hundred, including such names as Thomas P Anshutz, Charles H Stephens, and Henry R. Poore, instructors at the Academy of Fine Arts, Frank D. Briscoe, the marine painter; John J Boyle, Thomas Robertson, and George Frank Stevens, sculptors, Henry

F Cares, David Wilson Jordan, Joseph P Reed , F F Jungish, the water-colorist, C Few Seiss, the illustrator of scientific journals at home and abroad, Alex F Harmer, who illustrated Crook's campaigns and Captain King's novels, George Wright, T S Sullivan, William Thompson, Carl Newman, professor at Academy of Fine Arts , F Cresson Schell, G B Wood, Herrman Simon, C H Spooner, J Liberty Tadd, Wilson Eyre, Jr, among the cleverest architects of the country, Lewis E. Faber, Hal Hurst, A M Lindsay, A Houston, J Neely, Fred. Pitts, Cola Campbell Cooper, D A. Partridge, Angus Wade, Joseph Day, Julius Neeker, F P

A SKETCH CLUB HORSE
Drawn by Frederick Engle

NATURAL WILLIAM
Drawn by Lewis Baumbach

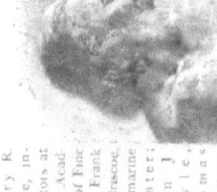

THE OLD BARN
Drawn by J. Neely, Jr.

IN DEEP THOUGHT
Drawn by Horace Wells Sellers

SMOKING UP
Drawn by Joseph R. Day

A STUDY OF A FOOT.

Drawn by Horace Wells Sellers.

Chandler, Walter M. Dunk, Frank H. Taylor, John V. Sears, and George Morgan and James Blake, both Mint designers. The range of ideas which pictures the artist as a being who ekes out a scanty existence on cry bread in a garret; or which portrays him as princely being, living in luxurious apartments, decked out with velvet coats and Tam-o'-Shanters to correspond, is focused to the truth when meeting the real being at such a club.

He does not prove to be a half-starved creature nor a reveller in luxury, but one with a jovial nature, a strong handshake, a big heart, and a versatile spirit.

If we seek for reasons why Philadelphia should have kept so long a club of this informal type, there are many at hand. Notwithstanding its constant growth, Philadelphia changes less than the other great American cities; all its institutions have a permanency not found in other great centres of population

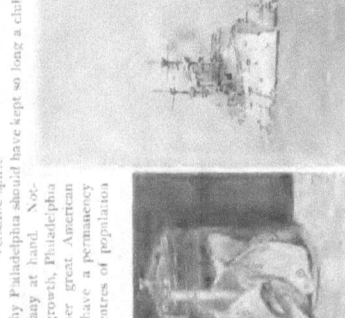

Drawn by B. D. Pietro.
A WOODEN SCHAE.

Drawn by W. Meglan Lansdale.
AT GRAND RONDO.

Drawn by C. Fro Sea.
WARM FISH.

From a painting by Thomas Hackett.
A BIT OF THE LAST CENTURY.

From a painting by W. Verplanck Birney.

AMERICAN ART AND ARTISTS.

A COZY CORNER. *Drawn by Fred. R. Gruger*

SUNNY DAYS. *From a painting by Hermann Simon.*

GIPSIES ALLEY. *Drawn by W. Vogbach Kidney*

A TWOLIGHT SITTING-ROOM

in America. Dull and monotonous social horizons, which make Philadelphia like London without Mayfair, seem by no means unpropitious to the formation of artists.

The rough-and-ready character of the Sketch Club is seen to be a natural reaction from certain things in the social fabric of the Quaker City which are not less unchanged. On the one hand we have a large population of steady-going, dull citizens, formed on the stamp set upon Pennsylvania by the Germans, those "Dutch" for whom Charles Godfrey Leland devised a jovial hero-type in Hans Breitmann. On the other, we have a small, exclusive, and very worldly society, whose members, when they emigrate to New York, out-do the most snobbish natives in snobbery. Is it any wonder that the artist and journalist, the musician and architect, must have some place where he can escape the choking atmosphere of these two bodies of citizens? It was at the Sketch Club that Thomas Janvier learned to write his "Ivory Black" stories. Bohemia existed in New York thirty years ago, with headquarters at Pfaff's, but with the destruction of the old intolerant, narrow social spirit among the rich, and a broader culture that rose from the breaking up of all the old social lines, by a swamping of old social factors and fetches of Bohemianism disappeared. In Philadelphia it lingers. *Vive la Bohème!*

AMERICAN ART AND ARTISTS.

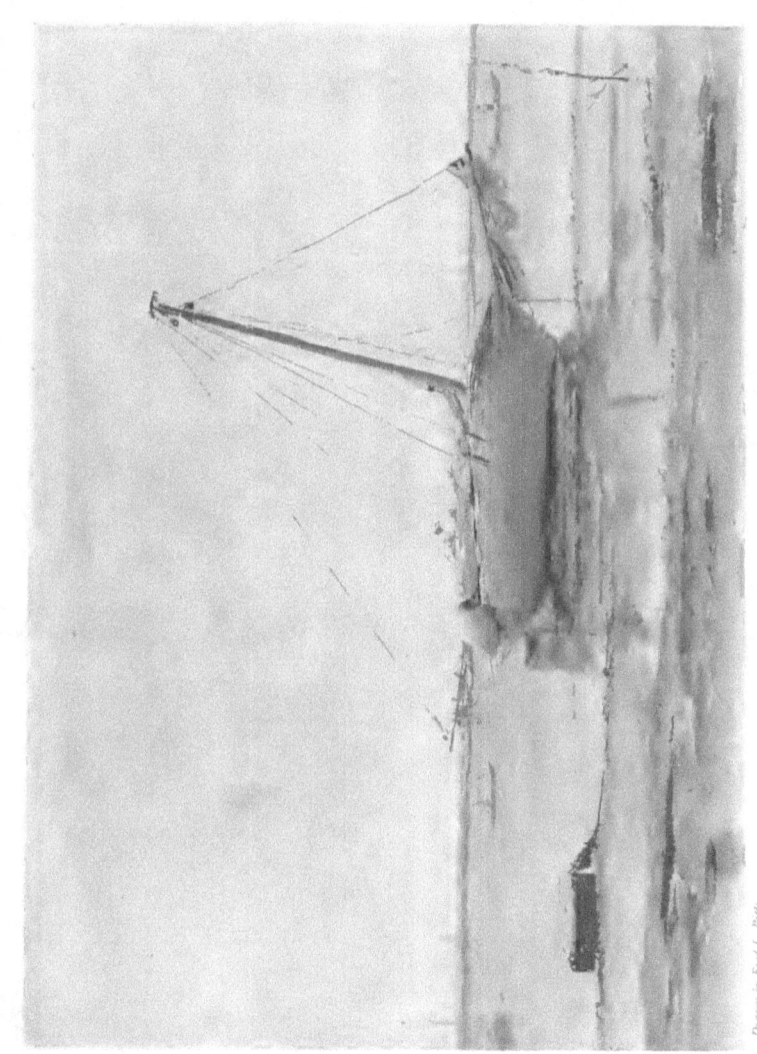

LOW TIDE AT SOMES'S POINT.
Drawn by Fred L. Pitts.

230   AMERICAN ART AND ARTISTS.

RUINS OF THE CASTLE, HEIDELBERG.
Drawn by W. Meylan Lansdale.

AN ORIGINAL MARINE ARTIST

By Edgar Mayhew Bacon.

(With original Illustrations by Frank De Haven.)

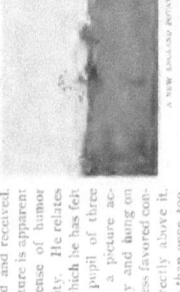

"AN OLD CABIN IN SUSSEX COUNTY, NEW JERSEY."

Unlike the old-time voyagers, whose journeyings were commenced with salvos of artillery and concluded amid popular acclaim, Mr. Frank De Haven goes on his voyages of discovery so quietly that not one of the black bottles on Governor's Island salutes him, and it is doubtful if even the mayor and city fathers know when he returns. But where his prototypes were well content to fetch back reports of what they found, he fetches from the Maine coast whole acres of sand-dunes and miles of breaking surf and brings them bodily to New York. The sea breezes to which he sets his canvas are perpetuated by some magic which the earlier navigators did not know.

Mr. De Haven's face is familiar to the readers of the ILLUSTRATOR. The early struggles, of which he had his share, have only served to strengthen his character, and the upward growth of his forehead alone tells of approaching middle age. The quaint Marine studio, cooled by the sea breezes, has also been pictured in these pages, and we have learned from his own pen how his best picture, of sunset and sand-dunes, was painted and received. His serious artistic nature is apparent in his work, yet a sense of humor brightens his personality. He relates with relish a joke of which he has felt the point, as when a pupil of three months' standing had a picture accepted at the Academy and hung on the line, while his own less-favored contribution was skied directly above it. This has occurred more than once, too.

He is a musician as well as a painter, the violin being his favorite instrument, and his collection boasts one priceless Germana. The alembic in which the raw

"A NEW ENGLAND POTATO FIELD."

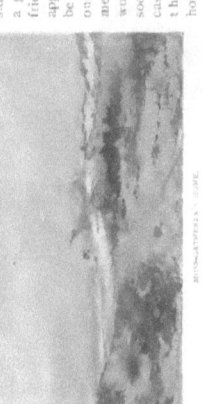

"A DYE HOUSE."

SURF NEAR MARBLED CLIFF.

MOONLIGHTED LOCHS.

material of art is converted to its finished product is his Twenty-fourth Street studio, dedicated to the god of work. In this studio, or in the home where his charming wife presides, Mr. de Haven is a genial host and his friends are many and appreciative. He may be fairly said to be only at the commencement of his career. It would require a bold soothsayer indeed to cast for him any other than an auspicious horoscope.

AMERICAN ART AND ARTISTS.

From a painting by Frank de Haven.
SPRINGTIME.

AMERICAN ART AND ARTISTS.

THE ARABS OF NEW YORK

By NYM CRINKLE.

With original Illustrations by J. G. Brown.

I THINK J. G. Brown though English born is more distinctly a New York painter than any other of our well-known artists.

I should not like to have you think I am circumscribing or localizing his genius in saying that, because in painting what is characteristic and true of New York he has shown the veracity and ability to paint anything that comes within the measurement of that ability.

I remember once hearing a vivacious young lady at an exhibition say, while standing in front of one of his canvases, that she loved Mr. Brown because he painted the ballads and not the laws of art.

That, on the whole, is a good criticism, because it is instinctive and not pragmatical. Most of Mr. Brown's pictures sing themselves, as one might say do "Sally in our Alley" and "Bonnie Doon." Their messages are concrete, direct and simple. I cannot at this moment recall one of his canvases that tried to make a sentiment welter in paint with mere technique. One and all they transferred some gleam of humanity from the street to the studio, and then kept it burning like one of those lowly, but inexhaustible, tapers that Devotion used to leave upon its shrine.

I said to a New York painter: Well, will you kindly tell me of another who has so successfully caught what one might call the eftlight of New York—that flickering phantasmal humanity of our streets and alleys? You know his boys when you see them, don't you? not because they are all alike, but because they have all flitted before your eye in real life. You don't have to be introduced. There is no need of an explanation that this is a New York boy. You could not by any possibility mistake him for a Chicago, or a London, or even a Philadelphia boy.

It doesn't make any difference where you are—say you are at an exhibition in Munich, and you come upon this boy—presto! you will hear the cry of the *Evening Telegram* and feel the throb of the Seventh Regiment band, and sniff the hot waffles on the corner.

I suppose the New York street boy has more

liberty and more incorrigible independence than any other boy in existence. He is very often a nuisance, but he is always a self-supporting and immeasurable possibility. The late Chas. L. Brace once taught me to tolerate, if not to respect him, for he took down a register in the Newsboys' Home, and pointed out to me a long line of respected and influential men who had fought their way up from the New York pavement.

There are great possibilities of sturdy life in the school of the street. It pounds sentimentality out of a fellow to begin with. I never knew one of these fellows to

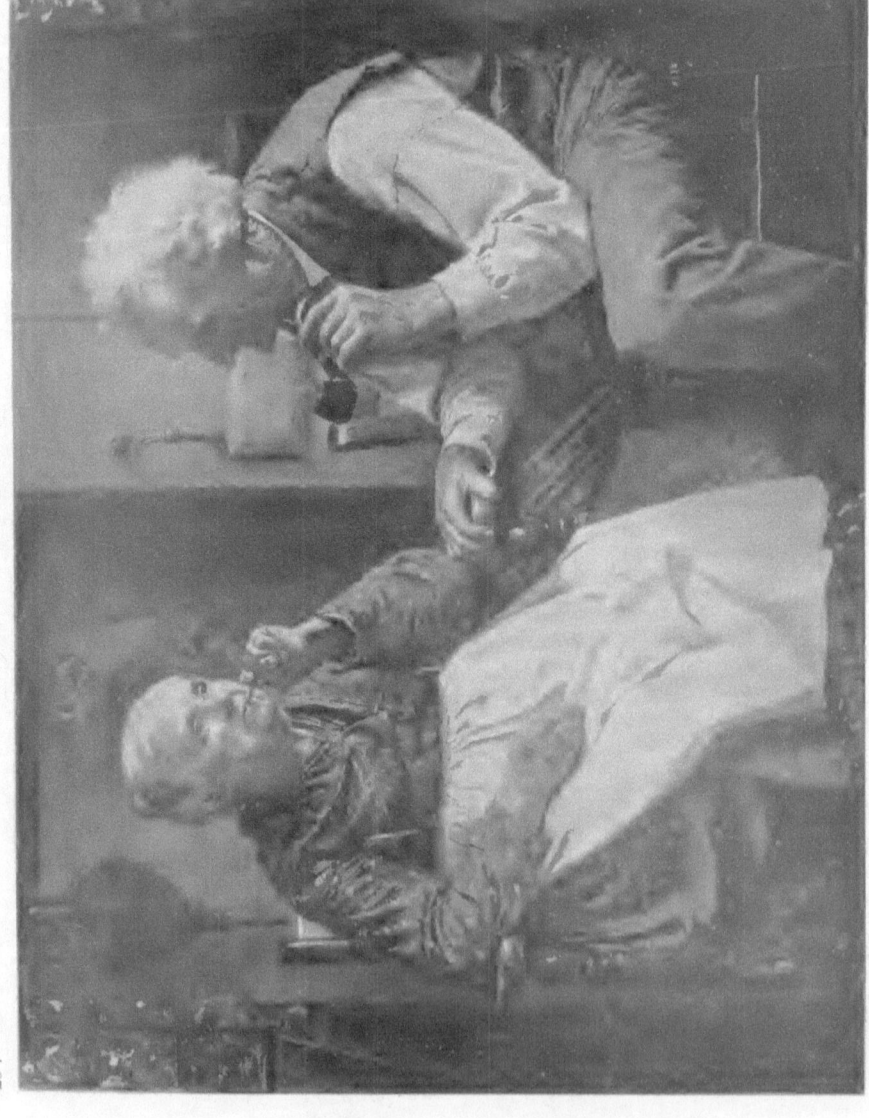

A SOCIAL PIPE.

From a painting by J. G. Brown.

AMERICAN ART AND ARTISTS.

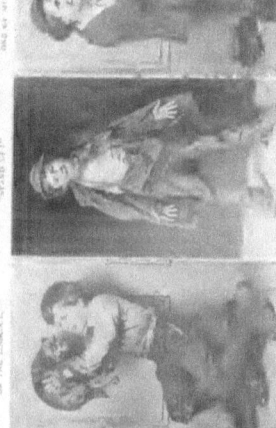
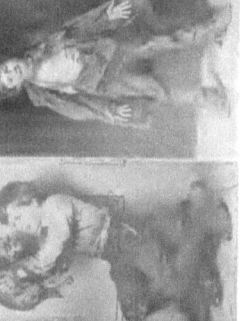

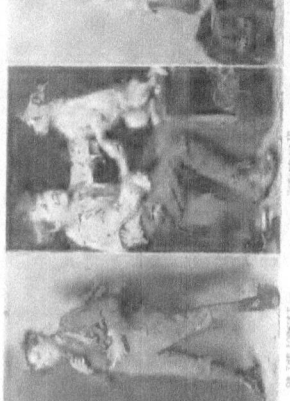
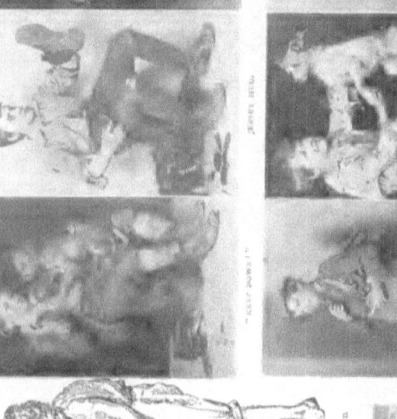

be mawkish. It brings an urchin ruthlessly up to the awful but benign law of the survival of the fittest.

Brown's picture of "On Dress Parade" is more than an octave of vital tones. One might call it a jolly madrigal, in the major key of course. I don't think it worth while to subject it to a spectrum analysis, because the character is more important than the coloring, and I am chiefly delighted at the delicious way in which the artist has made each boy in that platoon look his own unmistakable individuality. After all, as Emerson says, "It is only man that interests us, and

AMERICAN ART AND ARTISTS.

here are as many men as will make up a proverbial sailor, who have been put into line with quite as many characters, temperaments and shades of conscience, as clearly marked and distinctly separated as are the black and white keys of some softer and politer instrument.

There is a delightful essay for somebody who has sympathy and sense, and no knowledge of hue and color and "arrangements," if he will sit down and pick out the bully, the brains, the self-consciousness and the waggishness that are differentiated in that platoon.

Of course I know that most of Mr. Brown's compositions are story pictures, an objection that holds good against certain groups in the Sistine Chapel, and that being story pictures they appeal less to the technical critic than to the sensibilities of the human being. But I for one persistently like the story picture, just as I like story poems or story marble. I don't suppose Mr. Brown undertakes to paint allego-

ries any more than Burns undertook to write epics, and there is a two-volume romance in Burns's "wee, crimson-tipped daisy." But what Mr. Brown undertakes to do he does unmistakably, and nearly always delightfully. He can summon the boot-black from the curb-stone and make him tell his own story. I don't think anybody has unloosed this fellow's lips as Mr. Brown has. Take any one of those studies or finished pictures and see how frank and direct it is. Sometimes it is like one of Beringer's songs—oftener it is like one of Whittier's minor poems. (Do you remember Whittier's "School Days"?) The charm of the fellow accoutred with muffler

AMERICAN ART AND ARTISTS.

REFORMER AND ICONOCLAST

By WILLIAM J. BAER.

With original illustrations by William M. Chase and others.

IN THE STUDIO.
Drawn by William M. Chase.

"Euripides expressed to the Athenians, who criticised his works, 'I do not compose,' says he, 'my works in order to be corrected by you, but to instruct you.' It is true, to have a right to speak thus a man must be a Euripides. However, thus much may be allowed, that when an artist is sure that he is upon firm ground, supported by the authority and practice of his predecessors of the greatest reputation he may then assume the boldness and intrepidity of genius, at any rate, he must not be tempted

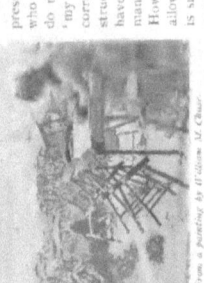

THE END OF THE SEASON.
From a painting by William M. Chase.

and armed with shovel; for the "Clean your side walk, ma'am?" lies in the subtle story of the situation no less than in the verisimilitude of the type, and the handsome urchin who is being "made up" by his pal is about as limp and submissive a victim of superior skill as you can imagine.

In most of these bootblack studies Mr. Brown sees only the jocund side

AN EARLY CALLER.

ON DRESS PARADE.

of youth, which laughs at misfortune. He has portrayed the boy's love for a dog in almost every attitude. He figures as the master, the trainer, the prophetor—never as the persecutor or enemy. Nor do we detect in these urchins the dark side of their lives. For the most part Mr. Brown sees them in the sunshine. They are exuberant, sportive, reckless, mischievous, never vicious, deformed, or awry with an inheritance

AMERICAN ART AND ARTISTS.

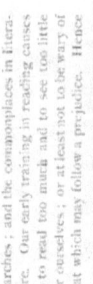

INTERIOR.

From a painting by William M. Chase.

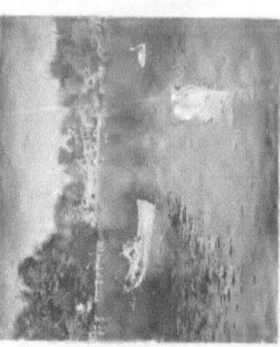

ROBERT BLUM.

From a painting by William M. Chase.

part contained in it, or cannot justly discern which qualities are to be considered accessory, or even superfluous, in the work undertaken, will surely be robbed of much pleasure as well as instruction in viewing such art as has strong tendencies toward individual interpretation.

The ordinary conception of the public agrees on three points, viz., literary art; topical songs, waltz music and marches; and the commonplaces in literature. Our early training in reading causes us to read too much and to see too little for ourselves, or at least not to be wary of that which may follow a prejudice. Hence our views on art are rather apt to be too literary and out of balance to appreciate anything not descriptive. No one will deny that subjective matter cannot lend special interest. There is, however, no great art, nor will there be, which will require an explanatory text to aid its interpretation. The Venus of Melos is just as fine to us, without knowing what she may have represented. Michael Angelo's Moses is equally great, apart from its subject. Velasquez was Velasquez whether he painted Philip

A LADY IN BLACK.

From a painting by William M. Chase.

out of the right path by any tide of popularity that always accompanies the lower styles of painting."—SIR JOSHUA REYNOLDS.

The subject of this sketch is so well known that nothing we might say of his life and struggles would be new. Nor shall the accompanying illustrations be enlarged upon. Let us rather consider how we may better appreciate the living presence of one who is at once a master in his art and in his capacity as an instructor. That individual or public whose love for music or painting is limited by the literary

AMERICAN ART AND ARTISTS.

From a painting by William M. Chase.
SUNLIGHT AND SHADOW.

From a painting by William M. Chase.
THE LADY IN WHITE.

From a painting by Georgiana Brisland.
A SUMMER PATH.

while he may have added he has never intruded. Because of his strong convictions as to his domain, he has been praised, and on the other hand railed over coals of literary fire. To do this is to rob Peter to pay Paul, so that we are all unhappier for the doing, losing much that is both beautiful and profitable to contemplate.

As suggested in the introductory quotation, Mr. Chase has looked neither right nor left, and has "arrived," even for some who once denied him his proper place. To-day he is successful in many ways. His sitters and patrons are people of judgment in art matters, who do not carry with them the air of the "generous patron." His landscapes have found a ready place in many collections of art. His studios are visited by promising talents, both men and women, anxious to

From a painting by Elizabeth Curtis.
A QUIET NOOK.

Drawn by Howard Chandler Christy.
A LANDSCAPE.

learn something from their gifted master. And does not the summer school on the Shinnecock Hills assure us of his prowess? Furthermore, to hold and have held the high distinction of President of the Society of American Artists, is an honour second to none.

The art of Mr. Chase may be said to base its existence on form and color. It affects us more like music than any other kindred art. Those of us who are familiar with such musicians as Schumann or Händel can feel better what is meant when it is said that many appreciate but

From a painting by William M. Chase.
A GIRL IN OWEL.

From a painting by Howard Chandler Christy.
A SHINNECOCK GARDEN.

or a Spanish beggar. But does not the Sistine Madonna lose much of its hold when we rob it of its divine sentiment? Mr. Whistler's portrait of his mother moves us by a something —we sometimes think we know—but we don't worry about the why. In short, the domain of art is strongest where it depends on its own peculiar strength, and I hold that he who can manage his art in its own peculiar field, and allow kindred art to simply add and not supplant, is surely on neutral grounds. Mr. Chase has gone his own way, and

240　　　AMERICAN ART AND ARTISTS.

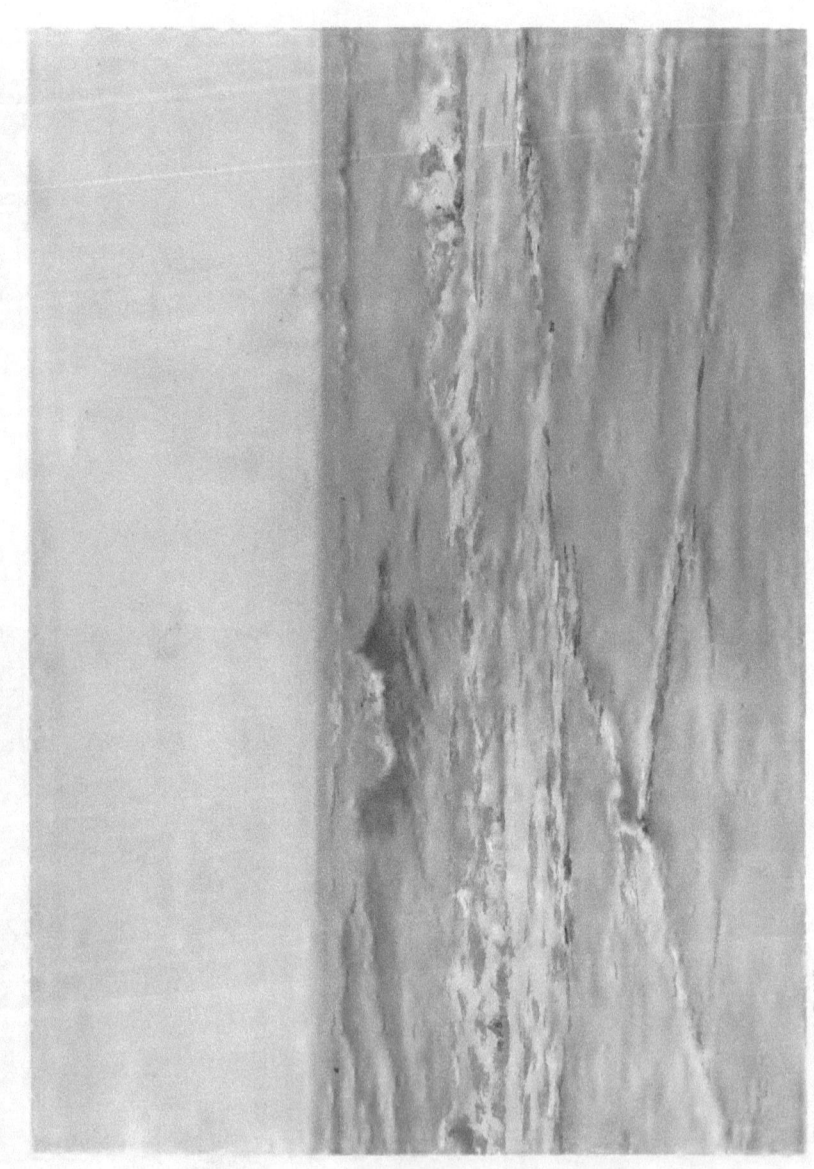

From a painting by A. T. Miller.　　　A SUMMER DAY SURF

few quite understand. There are those masters who are matter-of-fact and scientific, and produce as successfully as the dreamers do. Handel wrote his "Messiah" as he wrote operas before it, in an apparently matter-of-fact way—why? because he could turn anything into music and had no need to await an inspiration.

Like them Mr. Chase possesses a freshness of spirit that is uncompromising in its convictions; always happiest in large and simple comprehension of the color schemes which he resolves into a unity of effect. Nothing seems to enter such work which could be dispensed with. As it is fresh,

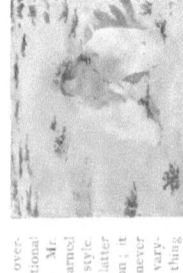

From a painting by Jane Fawcett.
OH SUMMER DAYS.

power of absorbing other qualities cannot overcome its force enough to make it additional rather than supplanting or superseding. Mr. Chase has not forgotten anything he has learned in passing from his earlier to his present style. Too many of our talented men have, in latter years, made appalling changes of conviction; it has accentuated the worth of those who never forget that art and its phases are ever varying, and that no art is bettered by anything

short of its broad and elemental truth. Impressionism and *plein-air*, so called, are truths—great truths—but surely not the only ones.

To Mr. Chase many things have an artistic value, for he is an ardent student of Nature in its every phase. Lavater said: "The enemy of Art is the enemy of Nature. Art is nothing but the highest sagacity and exertions of Human Nature; and what Nature will be honor who honors not the Human?"

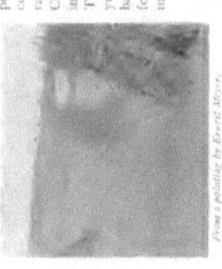

From a painting by Matilda A. Browne.
A NEWBURYPORT MEADOW.

From a painting by Reynolds Beal.
ON SHINNECOCK BAY.

From a painting by Charles E. Langton.
WASH DAY.

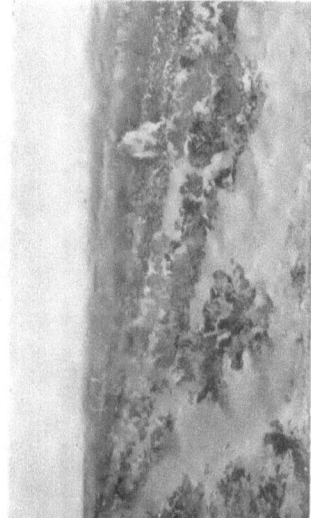

From a painting by A. T. Mills.
THE FARMYARD PATH.

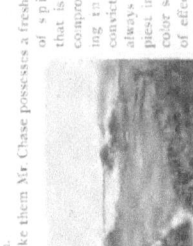

From a painting by Lydon Field Emmett.
WINDS WILD SOLO SONG.

From a painting by C. L. Weidekamm.
FLOWERS AND TREES.

it is to the painter free from foreign support, suggestive of any school but Nature's. While it is fate to throw away that which modern impressionism has given us, it is death to the painter whose

A STUDENT OF DRAWING

By HENRI PÈNE DU BOIS

With original illustrations by Alfred Paris.

A GREAT man of letters—William Dean Howells, to be precise—said to me, "The artist, the only person in the world who is in the right, is made by our social system the only person who is in the wrong." He said it in his profoundly sympathetic, persuasive manner, and I, the veriest Philistine, had never thought that the artist was in the wrong!

The artist lives in the midst of our civilization in a desert hermetically closed to everybody, but pompous, charming, varied, strange, splendid and ever surprising, which he calls his studio. There, in a vast and silent solitude, where nothing recalls housekeeping, politics, visitors, sayers of nothings and vile preoccupations—everything—antique and sumptuous furniture, tapestries representing gods and heroes, Oriental stuffs the color of sulphur, of pale azure, of dolorous and

STEREOTOMIZING THE OLYMPIAN.

A PILLAR OF THE SEA.

THE LAST LOAD.

tender pink that gold and silver traverse like shivering rays, fine coats of mail, swords which were at Culloden, bows and arrows of monster-killers, musical instruments refined or barbarous, playthings of the eighteenth century, everything has the calm and triumphant seduction that the quality of complete uselessness gives to things.

It is there that one may and one must forget the abominable mechanism of utilitarian civilization, drink the nectar of dreams, careless as shepherds of Laconia listening to the murmurs of fountains in the shade of hedges of laurel-trees. There is in the life of every artist, however, a symbolical aspect. Theodore de Banville relates that in a corridor which was dimly lighted by three gas-jets he saw Ingres seated near an open box which had a sort of Hercules was engaged in filling with huge logs. In the box, which was empty and sonorous, the wood fell by violence the sovereignty which others had usurped, but artists have a graver pretension. They propose to themselves the superhuman problem of *learning how to draw*.

To draw is to realize an impossible miracle. It is, with a line, purely chimerical, with traits that have neither form nor color, to represent forms, colors, movements, life, nature, and beings a prey to their appetites and to their passions. It is a marvel so difficult in itself that most artists never attempt it; or, having attempted it, abandon their project and resign themselves to amiable commonplaces.

It is evident that Alfred Paris has not yet renounced the ambition which was that of Ingres. He knows that the slightest sketch must rhythmically vibrate, and have, like a poem, its special beauty. He is quite incapable of perpetrating the heads encircled with wire, so neatly shaded that they seem to be made of velvet, which Academicians give as models. He prefers the Eclogues of Virgil rather than the Æneid. Evidently, he went from the drawing class in to the fields. He tramped over many leagues and when he saw a beautiful scene, without weariness, on any piece of paper that he found, he drew what he saw with the ardor, the ignorance and the marvellous instinct of genius.

There were: a cavalier on a horse at full gallop coming straightway toward him; a peasant bent on a plough drawn by two horses in a landscape lined by trees blent in an indistinct mass of foliage; a two-wheeled cart overflowing with its weight of hay, drawn by two horses in tandem; a man patiently building a fence at twilight round a sheepfold to be protected against the wolves in the night, and two dogs on guard—one a stolid sentinel, the other an interested spectator of the man's labor.

There were: a big Norman boy in wooden shoes rolling a  wheelbarrow filled with fruit, away from trees the branches of which were still bent by their loads that a woman, bent toward the ground, picked up when they fell; a young surveyor in his uniform, the ample folds of which fell gracefully; the magnificent gesture of the Curé of Barseilles, kneeling between the angry loutalion of gendarmes

and desperate workingmen on strike, pointing to heaven with his wrinkled hand, firm as a steeple of granite.

There were many more: some of them may be studied in the drawings herewith. The artist immediately immobilized on paper movements, impressions, expressions of faces, in sketches rapid as the flying in-

AMERICAN ART AND ARTISTS.

THE ARTILLERYMAN.

were not exactly similar to those he had heard in the first place, he tore his design and began a new one. Soon he worked with self-assurance, reading sonnets like an ox. He carried an umbrella, an easel, a folding-chair, all the apparel of a painter, and a lunch-basket. He perpetually thought

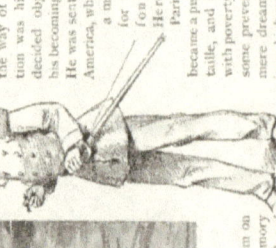

SOWING THE GRAIN.

He walked in the forests, joyful, his pipe between his teeth, and loaded like an ox. He carried an umbrella, an easel, a folding-chair, all the apparel of a painter, and a lunch-basket. He perpetually thought of the harshness, the ferocity and the tenderness of Nature. He perpetually said to himself that man is never pure enough, faithful enough, sincere enough to deserve the name of artist, which is grander than anything.

Alfred Paris was born in 1848 at Tarbes, the birthplace of d'Artagnan, whom Dumas immortalized. The first block thrown in the way of his vocation was his father's decided objection to his becoming an artist. He was sent to South America, where he was a merchant for twenty-four years. Heretumed to Paris in 1885, became a pupil of Detaille, and is blessed with poverty, a wholesome dreaming, lacking which one may never become an artist

THE TROMBONE.

stants. Then he trained himself to carry images in his brain, and to put them on paper at home. He questioned features of the passers-by and noted in his memory the tales that he had read in them. Then, when with his pencil he had reproduced the images of these passers-by, he questioned them in their turn, and if their tales

AMERICAN ART AND ARTISTS.

A LOVER OF THE SEA

By Jno. Gilmer Speed.

With original illustrations by F. M. Bicknell.

In going through a gallery of paintings a student of art does not need a catalogue, nor even examine the signatures, to know the painters of very many of the canvases. The style, the coloring, the method of treatment and the subject are usually so marked in one who is possessed of a haunting ideal, that the authorship of the work is as characteristic and easily identified as familiar handwriting.

The first impression one gets in seeing any number of paintings by Mr. F. M. Bicknell is that he has this haunting ideal. By way of practice, like every sincere student of art, he has tried many and varied subjects, and he keeps on trying them. He makes a study in portraiture, and again the vine covered cot of a French peasant; he paints a landscape, and then an interior; but even a casual observer will note very quickly that from each and all of these Mr. Bicknell quickly parks back to the sea—to the sea of which he is a genuine lover. He paints many kinds of craft upon many kinds of water; and though there is a loving touch in all, we feel instinctively that even yet Mr. Bicknell is not doing that which he best loves

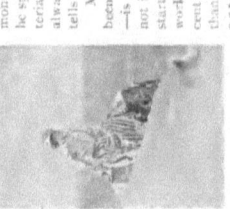

STUDY IN FRANCE.

to do—he is not embodying his ideal on the canvas, though he is near to it. He always achieves a certain measure of success, but his pictures of the breakers rolling in, and the wash going out over the sand, are so capitally done that the others seem almost amateurish in comparison with them. During the summer months that

IN THE SEA.

he spends on the Maine coast he accumulates ample material for the winter work in his studio, about which there always seems to be something nautical, something that tells of the sea with almost audible force and directness.

Mr. Bicknell, who is a native of New York—having been born in Westchester County about thirty years ago—is not an artist by accident or chance, though he was not intended for his present profession by those who started him out in the world. For eleven years he worked in a banking office, and heard much more of cent per cent and the quotations from the exchanges than of that art patter which is the language of the studios—a language the full meaning of which no outsider, however much he frequent those pleasant places, ever entirely masters. While in the banking office, he spent all his leisure in painting, and also attended the classes of the Art Students' League in the evening. Even as an amateur he sent pictures to the exhibitions of the Academy and of the Society of American Artists. These he had the

BEAR BUTTING.

LANDED.

ON THE BEACH.

satisfaction of seeing hung on the line, and thus encouraged, he determined to say good-by to the banking office and depend upon his art for both fame and fortune. This was seven years ago. Mr. Bicknell is not yet famous, nor has he yet made a fortune; but as he has lived graciously upon the sales from his studio, and as he bids fair to make a great name for himself, he does not in the least regret the step he took when he gave up uncongenial work for an employment to which all of his inclinations called him. Friends shook their heads when the step was taken.

245

NOT FAR OFF SHORE.
From a painting by E. M. Bicknell.

AMERICAN ART AND ARTISTS.

GERALD C. PRATT.

G. A. TRAVER.

ALICE BARBER STEPHENS.

F. W. EDWARDS.

V. G. ATWOOD.

KNOX CRAIG.

GEORGE WHARTON EDWARDS.

HARRY ROSELAND.

ALBERT D. BLASHFIELD.

Before settling down to work in a studio in New York, and after throwing off the binding commercial garments that he had worn so long, Mr. Bicknell went to Europe for a period of study and preparation. He sketched and painted in both France and England, and some of the pictures that have been reproduced to accompany this article were made during this stay abroad. The picture of Barbizon shows us whither his footsteps led him in his wanderings in France, and many sketches in his studio show that he must have lingered long in this neighborhood, even though the music of the sea was ever in his ears and its fascinations called him to its shore.

It is a gratification to write of Mr. Bicknell's work for more reasons than one, but the chief pleasure is because we have, in an unreassuring way, become somewhat in the habit of thinking that the workmanlike professional could not grow out of the gifted amateur. This really never was the case, and Mr. Bicknell's pictures illustrate the falseness of this foolish assumption—an assumption, however, which amateurs themselves have had more to do in creating than the skeptical professional or the unbelieving critic.

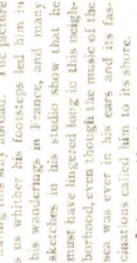
NEWBURYPORT SHIP YARD.

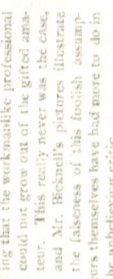
AMONG THE WEEDERS.

INDIAN BY THE SEA.

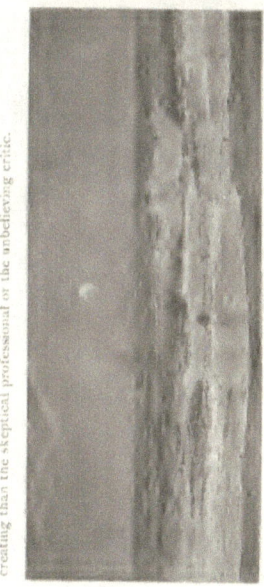

AMERICAN ART AND ARTISTS.

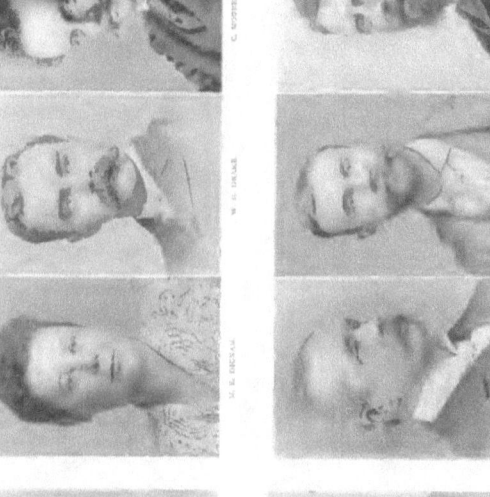

AMERICAN ART AND ARTISTS.

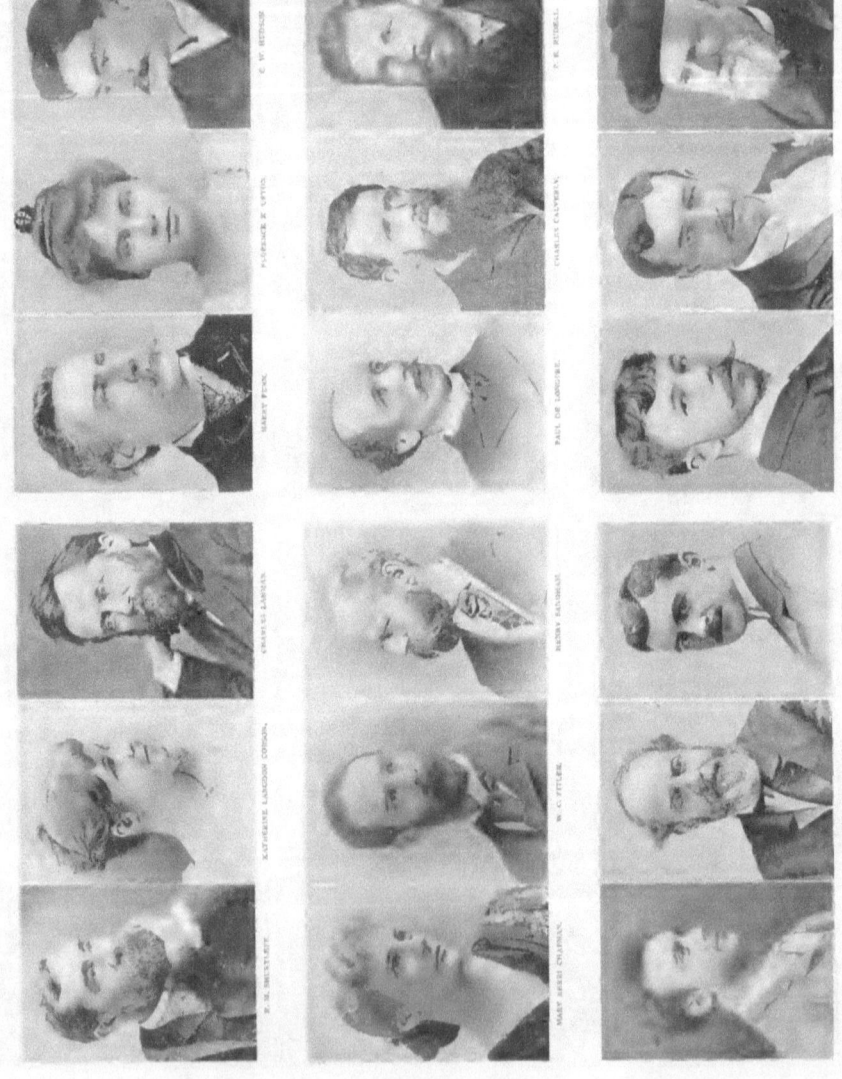

252

PHOTOGRAPHIC APPENDIX.

CONTRASTS OF LIFE AND ART.

By WILL H. LOW.

(With Parallel Illustrations.)

THE world in general agrees beyond doubt with Robert Burns when he opines that Nature " her prentice hand she tried on man, and then she made the lassies," and no class appears to share this opinion more heartily than the painters if we may judge by their choice of subjects, in which woman predominates to such a marked degree. Again, if one happens to be a painter, the fact that nine out of ten models who knock at the studio door to offer their services are apt to be women, must, by the law of supply and demand, be an indication of the average painter's taste. The direct relation between a given picture and its model is naturally dependent on the temperament of the painter; if he is an uncompromising realist the similarity

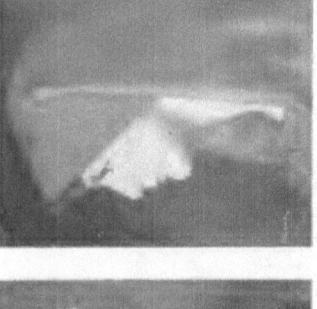

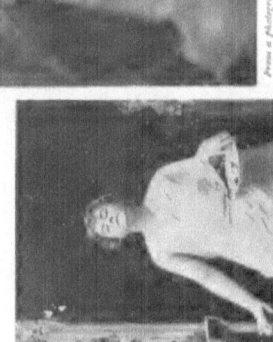

From a painting by C. v. Bandenhausen.
"Nydia, the blind girl of Pompeii."
Copyrighted, 1890, by Harry C. Jones. All rights reserved.

From a photograph of Miss Caroline Miskel.

between the model and the picture may be very great, but if on the contrary he is possessed of a certain idea and works as it were from within outwards, his indebtedness to the model may be quite as great as with the realistic painter, but the result is less obviously portrait-like. In these pages, however, we have a problem which is neither that of the realist nor, for want of a better word, that of the idealist. Here we have certain well-known pictures in comparison with which we have direct photographs from nature as nearly identical in position, costume, and expression as possible, and the few words which follow in an attempt at the critical considerations suggested by the contrasting pictures are hardly necessary, so vividly do the pictures speak for themselves. At the outset, indeed, a difficulty offers itself, for while one can speak without fear or favor of the painted picture, how can one treat the fair women who have lent themselves to these contrasts in the same impersonal manner? Fortunately, it is chiefly in a complimentary way that the charms of the

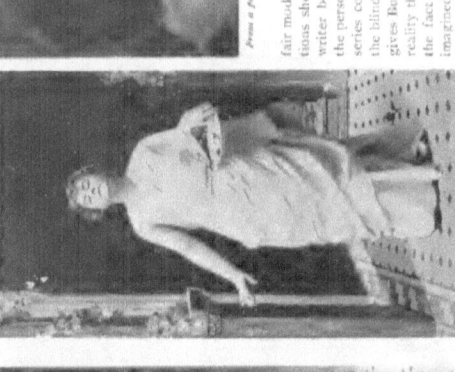

From a photograph of Miss Teresa Vaughan. "FABIOLA." From a painting by J. J. Henner.

fair models permit one to speak, but if in the course of this paper critical considerations should overweigh the scale of judgment on the less gratulatory side, the writer begs pardon in advance and pleads in his favor the fact that for the nonce the personality of the model is merged in the character portrayed. The first of the series contrasts the well-known picture by C. V. Bandenhausen, entitled "Nydia," the blind girl of Pompeii, with a photograph of Miss Caroline Miskel, who certainly gives Bulwer's heroine quite as much grace and sentiment and considerably more reality than the original picture. The slight difference in the pose of the head, and the fact that Miss Miskel is somewhat less "divinely tall" than the painter has imagined "Nydia," only serves to show that painters as a rule are more generous in the proportion of length in comparison to the size of the head than nature.

The next of the series reproduces "Fabiola," by J. J. Henner, in contrast to which Miss Teresa Vaughan has lent her gracious personality. The difficulty of so simple a subject is that no two heads are likely to be of exactly the same type,

AMERICAN ART AND ARTISTS.

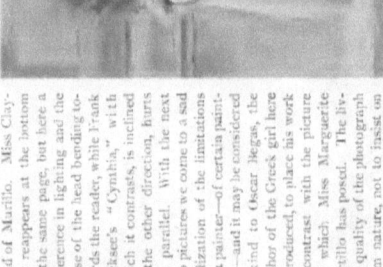

From a photograph of Miss Teresa Vaughan. *From a painting by Murillo.* "MAGDALEN." *From a photograph of Miss Estelle Clayton.*

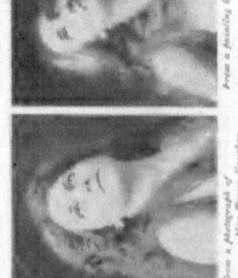

From a painting by Frank Dicksee. "CYNTHIA." *From a photograph of Miss Estelle Clayton.*

From a painting by Oscar Begas. "THE GREEK GIRL." *From a photograph of Miss Marguerite Cortillo.*

head of Murillo. Miss Clayton reappears at the bottom of the same page, but here a difference in lighting and the pose of the head bending towards the reader, while Frank Dicksee's "Cynthia," with which it contrasts, is inclined in the other direction, bursts the parallel. With the next two pictures we come to a sad realization of the limitations of a painter—of certain painters—and it may be considered unkind to Oscar Begas, the author of the Greek girl here reproduced, to place his work in contrast with the picture for which Miss Marguerite Cortillo has posed. The living quality of the photograph from nature, not to insist on

and the difficulty is added to in this case as the painter habitually renders an arbitrary and somewhat artificial effect of light. In the painted head the shadow under the chin is quite as dark as the dark drapery and represents a degree of shadow to which Miss Vaughan's fair complexion—very properly, one must admit—refused to descend. The question of similarity of type again arises in the reproduction of Murillo's "Magdalen," and is further complicated by the fact that Miss Estelle Clayton appears in friendly rivalry with Miss Vaughan in rendering the fair penitent. Both of the ladies appear rather to the disadvantage of the original picture in point of character, the greater firmness of modelling and the slight angularity of certain lines in contrast with the rotundity of others, making either of the heads preferable from a realistic point of view to the over-pretty and softened-to-nonentity

more evident superiorities to the original in point of beauty, make Begas's painting seem commonplace to the last degree.

Siche's Pompeian girl on the next page finds two prototypes, in the upper one of which Miss Miskel reappears, while Miss Vaughan furnishes the other subject. In both these, charming as they are, will be noted a certain variation in line and proportion, which if the object sought was an exact reproduction of the original would be difficult to avoid, but the painter would have been fortunate had he found such models to his hand. A few pages back Miss Miskel was told by inference that she was not "divinely tall," but the head for which she has posed in imitation of Joseph Sieck's "Lydia" affords the opportunity of finishing the quotation by adding "most divinely fair" in reference to it. In the reproduction of the "Judith" of Ch. Landelle, Miss Teresa Vaughan appears in a tragic rôle which we fear certain souvenirs of her success in "1492" have disturbed. Holofernes would hardly need fear such an ap-

From a painting by N. Sichel.
"THE MAGDALEN."

parition, and in truth in such subjects as this one finds the defect of the system which has afforded these charming pictures. Where the subject of the picture is mainly occupied with "existing beautifully," results as good as these can be arrived at; but in pictures of a different, or possibly a higher grade, where action or strong emotion is to be expressed, the quality must, in almost any case, reside in the painter; and be expressed by him on the canvas. It would only be by the most

From a photograph of Miss Caroline Miskel.

From a photograph of Miss Teresa Vaughan.

fortuitous circumstances that the elements of exact reproduction of line and movement would coincide with that of expression, and not once in a thousand times would the inconscient camera render what the emotion of the trained painter would detect in the same model. To bring to a closer this review, to which a strict sense of truth has given an almost fulsomely complimentary tone, mere mention must be made of a reproduction of Baudenhausen's "Listening to the Fairies," for which Miss Miskel has posed. It is with pictures like this, even with the result as in this case is most successful, and the re-variations which are obvious here, that this system is certain to produce an agreeable picture.

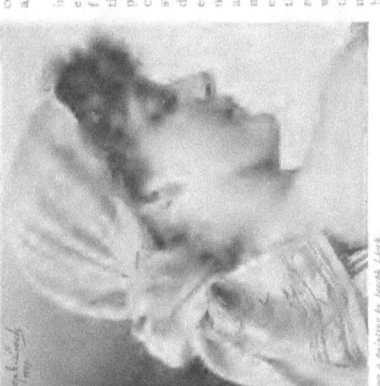

From a photograph of Miss Caroline Miskel.

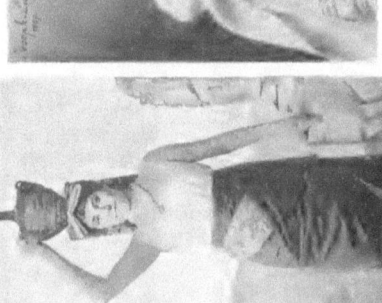

From a painting by Joseph Sieck.
"LYDIA."

In a certain sense, indeed, from the novelty of the idea and from limitations of time, the pictures reproduced here may be considered as first steps in an interesting direction. With great expenditure of time much more might be attempted and be made as successful, or even more so, than these. The *tableau vivant*, crystallized as it were, and by the aid of the camera made permanent, offers a wide horizon of possibilities. The limitations noted above, in speaking of the "Judith," could be in a degree overcome by careful consideration of subject and sentiment. It would, doubtless, require much preparation in disposition of backgrounds and the manner of lighting, and on the part of the model a complete submission of personality, to enter into the exact sentiment of the figure represented. Pictures representing groups or several detached figures would still increase the difficulties, but with time, patience, a studio capable of affording a variety of lights, and, above all, that quality of genius which we name taste, the task would be an alluring one, and would undoubtedly give most interesting results. In these days, when the amateur photographer is abroad in the land, no better means of acquiring one of the qualities which cannot be purchased, with even the most expensive camera, could be found than in thus endeavor-

From a painting by Charles Laudelle. "JUDITH."

From a Photograph of Miss Teresa Vaughan.

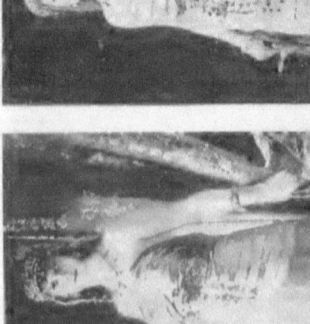

From a Photograph of Miss Carmen Michel. "AWAKING TO THE FIESTA."

From a painting by C. von Bundersdamen.

ing to reproduce good pictures. In this way principles of composition, of light and shade, of that which we must retain in nature, and that which we must reject or relegate to a subordinate place, would be learned, and unconsciously the amateur, in attempting original work, would after such a training apply the principles thus acquired. When once we approach the subject of originality, however, we step beyond the limits of this article, though the transition is a natural one. The amateur takes upon himself, with each new plate, to make a picture which has never existed before, and, if by careful attention the discernible qualities which go to make up a work of art are acquired, each of these plates might represent the result of such study. Leaving out of the question absolutely original subjects, such as would require on the part of the amateur the creative, imaginative faculty which is not lavished on the first-comer—few artists even possessing it—there remains the whole range of subjects to be gleaned from literature and illustrations by the camera of such themes would more than repay him who would attempt them. No hard-and-fast rule can be given for such picture-making, but one would go far in first looking over the range of subjects, choosing that which really interests one, the simpler the better at first, and then making an effort at realizing how such a character in the story would naturally live, move, and have his being. All details given by the author should be noted and followed where such detail helps to make the character visible, or suppressed if such details are more individual than typical, for it must be remembered that the author only has to do with the mental vision, and cannot always be followed when it comes to the realization of the picture in his mind's eye. Then, a characteristic type of model having been found (no easy task), there would come in the considerations of placing the figure on the plate, the effect of light and of line, the thousand and one considerations which must all be taken into account if you would make a work of art. Repeated attempts would be necessary, and many plates; but the growth of appreciation, resulting from study, would lead one on until, in the hands of the intelligent amateur, the camera would become more than the inconscient toy which is too often at present. Hence I may conclude in saying, think for yourself; and then—and only then—let the camera "do the rest."

SHADOWS OF THE ARTIST'S IDEAL

By MARGUERITE TRACY

With illustrations selected from our last photographic prize competition.

> He would fain
> (But could not) see me always, as befell
> His dreams to see me, plucking asphodel
> In saffron robes on some celestial plain."—E. R. SILL.

THROUGH its ever-changing environment the poet looks straight into the deeps and shallows of human life and reproduces them unhampered; but the artist, forced to interpret through the visible form, longs for another day when dignified and simple folds shall drape without distorting the figure.

The artists, the poets, the historians of Greece have preserved for us the type of a perfection in form and costume from which we have strayed—the artists among us looking back regretfully. And it is their looking back that has kept the Greek influence alive through all the excesses of elaborateness and severity that have overshadowed it. It has been a restraining hand, invisible and seeming to accomplish little; but who can tell to what a pass we might have come without it?

Among the accompanying illustrations "Are They the Real That Blossoms and Passes," photographed by Gertrude Kasebier, to which was awarded the prize for selection of model, pose and general composition in our prize competition, fulfils the requirements of this type in many essentials. It possesses an intrinsic charm of poetic composition. As the girl in "Are They the Real" looks down on the blossoms in her hand, one cannot think of Echo, the wood nymph who loved

Photographed by Gertrude Kasebier.

"Are they the real that blossom and pass,
The flowers that fade and die without grace,
Or only the shadows of them divine?"

Narcissus and pined for him, growing day by day more ethereal, until she became only a soft voice calling him through the woods and by the river brink. Narcissus never answered. With heart breaking for his dead sister, he haunted the streams and fountains, dreaming that his own reflection was the lost face that had resembled his. In sweet compassion the gods changed him at last into the flower which bears his name and that still loves to bend its head above the water edges.

The costume, with its simple, ungirdled chiton or tunic, belongs to a well-known form of Greek dress which consisted of two very long pieces of cloth pinned or clasped at the shoulders, letting the superfluous length fall like a mantle over the breast and down the back. The chiton was sometimes shortened by being drawn up over a girdle, and sometimes, as in "Are They the Real," left to hang in its own full, loose folds. Often two girdles were worn, the widest one very low and the narrowest very high, giving a new set of folds between. Miss E. F. Farnsworth's picture "When Evening Cometh On," which received the prize for historical accuracy, shows the double girdle, although, as she explains, it does not consist of two separate belts. "The dress," she says, "was pale violet trimmed with silver—the metal belt in front being continued with braid which crossed in the back and went over the shoulders. There is little I can add besides the picture. It is a correct dress of a Greek lady when Greek art was at its height."

Photographed by Miss E. F. Farnsworth.

"When evening cometh at anchor doth the small bo the great unknown,
In silence reaching to the endless land."

And indeed there is little that one need add about a picture which speaks with such lofty, serene eloquence. While very different in thought, the beautiful harmony of costume and composition is even more felt than in "Are They the Real." One sees the hushed tones of the western sky, the deepening purple of the hills, the

AMERICAN ART AND ARTISTS.

dim shadows that steal across the lingering glory of the water, and one feels the insistent mystery of twilight pressing close.

The chiton was the most important garment and was worn next to the body. For greater warmth the himation, or cloak, a little shorter than the chiton, was worn above, and sometimes the himation was worn without the chiton. Sometimes the free, mantle-like drapery of the long chiton was separate and often much modified in form into cloak or fitting jacket. The peplum, a long shawl or scarf, was wound outside all the other garments according to the taste and convenience of the wearer. The chiton, the himation and the peplum are the elements of the Grecian costume, their many changes and modifications showing the rise and fall of Grecian art. Great richness of ornamentation marked the early, more barbaric, years,

Photographed by Charles E. Fairman.

"What elates him,
Or saddeneth. Beats in eager softness,
Or beats firm, stout and twilight-thinking around?"

Photographed by Carrie S. Hibbs.

"There my thought sees thee,
All ears would feel it warm at heart."

and was recurred to in more refined form in the extravagant centuries just preceding the Christian era. At the time of its highest development, however, the costume was extremely simple and unadorned, its beauty depending on the softness of the material and the exquisite grace of its folds.

As in "Are They the Real" this simplicity is observed in "Thine Eyes too Wise," photographed by Miss Dora Winter Jaiven. She says of it "I wished to portray the idealistic and spiritual in one subject, and perhaps a touch of the Byzantine school."

The Byzantine traces, if any, are very slight, as Byzantine dress was much influenced by oriental taste — weak-hearted, shuttle-cock Byzantium, always

Photographed by Dora Winter Jaiven.

"Thine eyes, too wise, are heavy with life's take."

being swayed by new conquerors and isolated by enmity from all that could teach it; yet it was through Byzantium that the art of the East was first taught to the West, and the prosing Byzantine historians alone have kept record of this connecting link in the great general chain of art.

Returning to the Greek, however, Miss Jaiven has succeeded so well in portraying the idealistic and spiritual that one could fancy her Greek woman to be Helen, looking down on the battle-scourged plains of Troy.

"When Hope is Enthroned Above," photographed by Charles E. Fairman, is another model of Greek simplicity, showing only the twice-girdled chiton without the shoulder drapery. There is exquisite grace in the figure, but the type is not as perfectly Greek as that of " Are

"When Hope is enthroned above."

AMERICAN ART AND ARTISTS.

Photographed by Wm. E. E. Stafeldt.
"Who is Sleeping?
Who is Watching?"

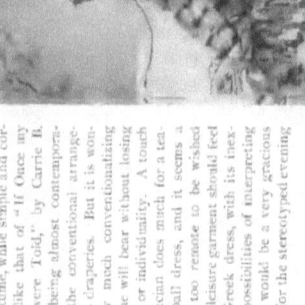

Photographed by Wm. H. Kidd.

"We know not whither the dove with the olive leaves,
And how we know must to the haven.
When the clouds of the twilight thaw
And the moon gleams but in her grows."

Photographed by Jennie C. Peet.

Photographed by W. E. E. Stafeldt.   "After Repose."

They the Real," and the general feeling of the figure is more modern, in spite of the plain robe and sandalless feet. Sandals, by the way, were often the most expensive items of the toilet; the thongs, and the ribbons which bound them by intricate windings to the feet, giving opportunity for exquisite extravagance of ornament.

"Only as Dreams," photographed by Miss Jennie C. Peet, is full of the Grecian spirit which strives to make all calm and beautiful that is connected with death. The dead have drunk in the waters of Lethe, forgetfulness of all sorrow and strife, and perhaps, when the peace of Elysian fields has entered their souls, they will return for another life upon the earth. The Athenian maid carries a funeral urn to be placed with the dead, and the bough she holds must

for the costume, while simple and correct, errs like that of "If Once my Thought were Told," by Carrie R. Hicks, in being almost contemporaneous in the conventional arrangement of its draperies. But it is wonderful how much conventionalizing the costume will bear without losing its beauty or individuality. A touch of the Grecian does much for a tea gown or ball dress, and it seems a thing not too remote to be wished that every leisure garment should feel it. The Greek dress, with its inexhaustible possibilities of interpreting its wearer, would be a very gracious substitute for the stereotyped evening costume.

If students are correct in gathering from Pausanias, against the authority of other historians, that virgins were admitted to witness the

be the golden one which alone entitles a living being to cross in Charon's boat.

It is much to be regretted in this picture that the chiton escapes in folds of such even length from under the mourning-bordered himation or cloak, giving the effect of a single garment with the unpardonable anachronism of a ruffle on the hem.

William H. Kidd's enraptured figure does not have the wreath of Erato, and is undoubtedly Euterpe, the giver of pleasure. She does not hold the characteristic double flute, but then Euterpe was not confined to that, making music on many instruments.

The expression of the face and the pose are what give charm to this figure.

AMERICAN ART AND ARTISTS.

"*Tell us, maiden blushing roses,
Are these blushing hearts as well?*"

Photographed by Charles M. Carter.

Photographed by Charles M. Carter.

"*Wake less oxen each other day,
And sweep the rippling lyre.*"

Photographed by Charles E. Fairman.

SALUTE OF THE ROSE.

Photographed by A. W. Wilson.

"*Athena, hear thou my prayer, obey!*"

Olympic games, then W. B. E. Shafelt's first group is one of maidens watching the contest; the second, the confidential discussion of it afterward.

The bands worn about the head, as shown in "After the Games," often rivalled the sandals for extravagance. There are no examples among the illustrations of the mitra or bushel-shaped crown, which women copied from Ceres, nor of the tiara worn by Juno and Venus; but the net supporting the hair at the back appears in "When Evening Cometh On," and Charles M. Carter's "Maiden Binding Roses" wears, in addition to the fillet, the wreath of flowers which the Greeks loved so well.

None of Mr. Carter's pictures have any fault of modernism in robe, but it could be wished that the general tendency of the hair-dressing, not only in these, but in most of the photographs, had been more toward the softly waving locks about the forehead of the blousic in "After the Games." The dress which Mr. Carter's figures wear returns to the long chiton with ends folded over, forming drapery at the shoulders. This drapery is shorter than that of "Are They the Real," with a plain, unbroken border and a loose girdle. In the last of his pictures given here, the chiton is shown dropping from the shoulder, as it was free to do if the wearer desired, for there was great liberty as to the amount of fastening about a chiton. Sometimes the draping was brought over the arm and fastened by buttons or clasps, so as almost to form a sleeve, while often among athletic women there was only one shoulder-clasp, leaving the other side entirely free. Spartan women at one time left one or both sides of the skirt open for greater freedom of motion, and the huntresses drew the chiton through their girdles, shortening them to their knees.

In "The Salute of the Rose" Mr. Fairman gives us another of his spirited, graceful figures. At once it takes us wandering fara-field, amid the beautiful emblematic customs of the Greeks, who fitted everything with a symbol and found no beauty of form without its corresponding beauty of thought, no thought without its expression in

AMERICAN ART AND ARTISTS.

Photographed by Charles M. Carter. "The front of repeatedly gestures everywhere."

—perhaps unformulated—"what is fittest, what is most beautiful for this use?" They knew well that beauty means fitness if it be true beauty, and they would not cumber their rougher tools, crockery and garments with the awkward burden of ugliness, nor fancy that ugliness was strength. When even the common people of a nation know this priceless lesson of art, the influences that surround genius are such as to foster its fullest development. Yet the fascinating " Salute of the Rose " has the same latter-day expression in the face that is seen in " When Hope is Enthroned Above," and to a less degree in "What Vision?" The setting of Mr. Fairman's pictures is so correct,

Photographed by Gertrude Käsebier. "Divinely taken as earwards thought"

however, and their sentiment so clearly expressed, that he is even forgiven for their one lack, since ancient Grecian faces are not met at every turn in our nineteenth century.

The photograph sent from England by A. W. Wilson, like two of those by Mr. Carter, has palm-leaves as an appropriate background for the face. The girl's wrapt eyes are fixed on something beyond our sight, and though her costume is not as perfect in detail as many of the others, she seems to be seeing some shield-bearing hero of old Greece whom the rest of us may never see, even though we haunt the world like Echo, looking as well as calling for him.

These fair visions of another day have occupied the space of this article almost to the exclusion of a word as to their conjuring. They are shadows in a double sense: they give only a suggestion of the form which had a variation for every mood and thought, and like marbles they leave color to the imagination. Yet, brought together here, they spread the ideal which the artist is always trying to establish.

form. It was that constant searching for the correlation between material and spiritual beauty that made Greece what she was. No common artisan, making the commonest articles for daily use, but worked at them constantly with the thought

AMERICAN ART AND ARTISTS.

THE STUDIO AND THE STAGE
By HILLARY PAUL.
With parallel and contrasting illustrations.

In the discussion of this novel and ingenious theme, it may seem to the unprejudiced mind that the painter has been placed at a disadvantage. Through his judgment in selecting models whose exact depiction by the camera shall hold to strict accountability the correctness of the brush, the editor brings forward instances of nature which art finds it difficult to discover. If the studio had these opportunities which are now felicitously employed by the magazine, there would be more triumphs on canvas and fewer anxieties at the easel.

The young women who, in the illustrations of this paper, have embodied the ideas of several famous painters, are particular types, not general examples, of the graces of their sex. Such a complete and agreeable union of feminine form, color, mobility, beauty and variety of expression cannot be engaged by the most ambitious artist. The painting is a composite, while the photograph is an entirety. The canvases herewith reproduced may be, and no doubt are, studies of various models blended into a symmetric portrayal of thought in the alchemy of the artist's imagination. But the actresses whose abundance of mental intelligence and physical charm has enabled us to draw these decisive contrasts between life and art, contain the whole matter in themselves. They are extraordinarily endowed by nature as well as thoroughly equipped by training for the visual expression of sentiment. Their gifts of inheritance have been improved by a study of taste. The constant portrayal of simple and complex emotions necessitated by their profession, renders them qualified to represent with ease and thoroughness any theme that may be required. The stiffness of pose, awkwardness of line and dulness of expression that the painter has to combat in his hired model, would not confront his brush if it were engaged in delineating the graces of women whose business in life it is to depict every temperament save their own. Further than this, there is a considerable difference between the ease of sitting before the camera for two seconds, and the hard work of posing in the studio for a month.

Being thus assisted by nature, art and accident in the illustration of all the moods of womanhood, it may be observed that an actress who has increased her naive gifts by judicious education is hindered by no such difficulties in the expression of an idea as those that frequently beset the painter. In the reproductions of Paul's canvas and a modern photograph there can be no question

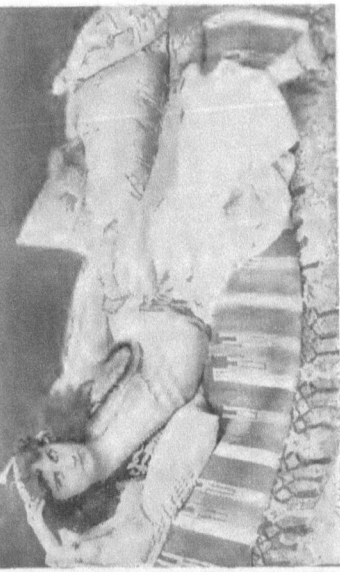

From a photograph of Miss Viola Allen, engraved by the painting by N. Sichel.

From a painting by Paul.

From a photograph of Miss Isabelle Urquhart.

From a photograph of Miss Jennie Goldthwaite, IN TUXEDO COSTUME.

AMERICAN ART AND ARTISTS.

of the general superiority in pose, line, drapery and expression of the player's "Iphigenia" over that of the painter. It may be urged with some reason that in this picture Miss Urquhart resembles Clytemnestra more than the hapless daughter, whose death was demanded by Diana. But in the maturity of the face we find a pathos of woe and eloquence of expression that seem as natural to the character as they would be incongruous in early girlhood. Miss Urquhart's pose is more unconsciously graceful, the carriage of the head is easier, the curve of the back is more subtly shown, and the right arm and hand are nearer to nature than in Paul's celebrated work. There is more poetry in the canvas than can be discovered in the photograph. But the actress has a tragic reality that the cunning of the artist was not quite able to convey.

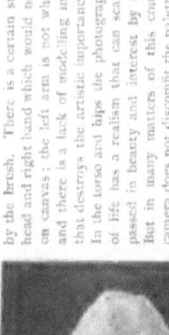

From a photograph of Miss Gladys Wallis.
SADIE.

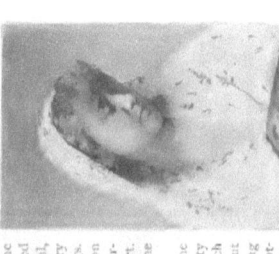

From a photograph of Miss Jennie Goldthwaite.
IN THE CAFÉ.

Miss Viola Allen, whose dramatic skill is employed in channels wholly separate and removed from those of her sister actress, is not so successful in imitating Sichel's "Summer." This lady, although one of the cleverest and most attractive performers on our stage, has not fully grasped the idea of the artist. In the poetic feeling of Sichel's brush we find memories of spring, while in the photograph we have suggestions of autumn. The painter has given us the bloom and beauty of womanhood softened by tender sentiment, but the actress offers us a sampler that is past and already touched by the early frosts of sorrow. As a composition, the photograph compares favorably with the painting, but in the expression of a theme so genial as this the brush is more eloquent than the camera.

A painter could have found no finer model than Miss Gokhiawiste for "In Turkish Costume," nor could a hundred charcoal studies have expressed the luxurious languor of the figure more admirably than it has been told by this engaging actress. Yet it is easy to note various tactics of the lens that might be amended

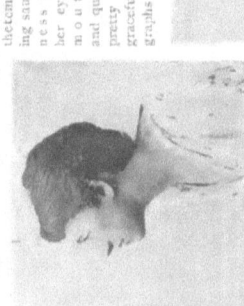

From a photograph of Miss Ada Lewis,
suggested by the painting by F. Thurman.
ALLEN.

by the brush. There is a certain stiffness in the head and right hand which would not be allowed on canvas; the left arm is not wholly graceful, and there is a lack of modelling in the drapery that destroys the artistic importance of the legs. In the torso and hips the photographic depiction of life has a realism that can scarcely be surpassed in beauty and interest by idealistic art. But in many matters of this composition the camera does not discomfit the palette.

Miss Gladys Wallis, the pocket Venus of the stage, could scarcely retain this subtile sensuality of expression long enough for the painter to catch it with that fidelity which the lens conveys. But although an artist might have failed in seizing the tempting sauciness of her eyes, mouth

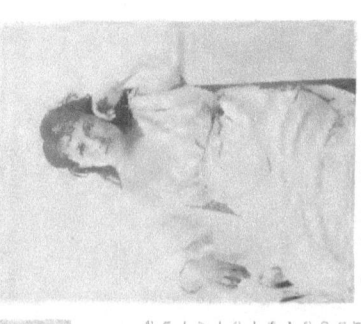

From a photograph of Miss Thea Akre,
suggested by the painting by M. Niewerkerke.
IN CRIMSON.

and quivering chin, he would depict the pretty girl's nose, hair and arms more gracefully. In this, as in all other photographs of the female figure, we observe that in small, evanescent things the camera comes nearer to reality than the brush. But having caught the exact spirit of an expression, it generally retires from a task that can be completed only by the painter. We have no artist who could arrive at the mischievous look in this young woman's half-closed eyes, or depict the alluring pout of her lip, or convey the diaphanous nature of her drapery so easily as these particulars are shown by photography. Yet the ensemble of the photograph is awkward and meaningless, two qualities that must un-

AMERICAN ART AND ARTISTS.

From a photograph of Miss Gladys Wallis.
TRANQUIL.

From a photograph of Miss Golden Wells, suggested by the painting by N. Sichel.
WOMAN OF FASHION.

From a painting by N. Sichel.
IN BONDAGE.

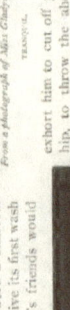

From a photograph of Miss Jennie Goldthwaite.
TIRED.

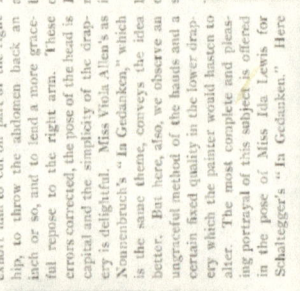

From a photograph of Miss Ida Lewis, suggested by the painting by G. Schalteggar.
IN GEDANKEN.

From a photograph of Miss Viola O. Urquhart.

consciously be avoided by anyone who made a lengthened study of the young actress.

In an art that relies on fancy as much as on fact Miss Geoldthwaite would not have been posed exactly in the attitude she assumed before the camera for her portrayal of "In Thought." Thinking she certainly is. But it is evidently not the reverie of girlhood that a painter would convey in carrying out such a theme. If this photograph were a charcoal sketch ready to receive its first wash of color, the artist's friends would exhort him to cut off part of the right hip, to throw the abdomen back an inch or so, and to lend a more graceful repose to the right arm. These errors corrected, the pose of the head is capital and the simplicity of the drapery is delightful. Miss Viola Allen's as Nourenbruch's "In Gedanken," which is the same theme, conveys the idea better. But here, also, we observe an ungraceful method of the hands and a certain fixed quality in the lower drapery which the painter would hasten to alter. The most complete and pleasing portrayal of this subject is offered in the pose of Miss Ida Lewis for Schaltegger's "In Gedanken." Here we discover a young woman who is beautiful alike in person and in mind, a graceful, slender arm against which the brow is easily resting, the requisite curve of the neck, a youthful form, and a face full of sensibility and imagination. Miss Lewis as "Ellen" is not so successful as the painter's study. Yet it is a most interesting head that she gives us, which only requires a finer gradation of lights and a better treatment of shadows to become as artistic to the eye as it is fascinating to the mind.

This is a very excellent illustration by Miss O'Neill of Leick's "Süsses Glück." The painter has drawn a more sensitive nostril than the actress shows in her photograph; but he has managed the pose, the soft shadows, the faint suggestion of muscles in the neck and the careless hair with no better skill than the camera has repeated. Miss Gladys Wallis in repose, after the lively expression of her earlier mood, is a suggestion of perfect *negligé* which a painter might carry into story-telling, but which we could not easily surpass in the feeling of lassitude. Miss Jennie Goldthwaite, fatigued by her effort at thinking lies on a neighboring lounge in an attitude that even the impressionistic artist would not waste time to consider. Nor is the smaller picture of Miss Wallis worth serious thought in its relation to art, inasmuch as the manifest awkwardness of the arms would be impossible in the studio. The final contest between the lens and the brush, in this instance, has resulted in another triumph of Miss Urquhart over the model who preceded her for Sichel's "In Bondage." Here we find the distinction between life and art very strongly marked, with the merits of the composition generally in favor of the actress. The realist and the idealist can choose between these rival treatments of a single theme.

By these parallel examples of real life and its artistic presentment it will be seen that, however clever the camera may be, our painters are in no serious danger of its rivalry. The studio model is amiable, beautiful and seductive, but seems to be in the bondage of love rather than of fetters.

AMERICAN ART AND ARTISTS.

BOSTON ART AND ARTISTS.

By William Howe Downes.

THE GIRL WITH THE WHITE SHAWL.
From Picture, Pennsylvania Academy, 1895, by Edmund C. Tarbell.

There can be no doubt that Boston possesses every claim to be considered one of the art centres of the United States. The honor and profit of it are somewhat vague and wholly incalculable compared with the glories and emoluments of leather, wool, and banking, but, such as it is, Boston has a right to it, as is to be proved by the facts and figures of the case—the existence of several hundreds of professional artists who make their living (heaven alone knows how) out of their art; the enormous activity of the city, increasing from year to year, in the way of art exhibitions; the multiplying numbers of clubs, societies, and associations, the establishment and growth of museums, and public and private collections of art; and the everlasting talk about art, which fills the newspapers and emanates in an incessant trickle from the lecture platform, and the women's countless clubs, which discuss everything under the sun. Behind all this, in the background, as it were, is the respectable if not at all thrilling history of art in Boston, beginning before the Revolution, and connected by many tangled threads with the art of England in the latter half of the eighteenth century. The career of Copley was, as we survey it from this distance of time, most remarkable in that he performed so much of his best work in a virtually isolated backwoods town, without advantages except of the most meagre description. Imagine what the "art atmosphere" of Boston must have been in the last century! Yet Copley managed to make a long series of portraits which to-day hold their own with the best portraits ever painted on this continent. Then came Colonel John Trumbull, Gilbert Stuart, and the rest of our American old masters, most of whom lived in Boston at some period of their lives. A second era of note in the art opened with Allston's ascendency, when a brilliant constellation of artists acknowledged his primacy—

"THE OLD CAVALRYMAN."
By Thomas Allen.

a circumstance which we of a later generation find it difficult to account for except on personal grounds. Roughly speaking, we may count the third period of art history in Boston as that of the William Morris Hunt epoch, which began about the time of the Civil War, and which disappeared from view with the deaths of Foxcroft Cole and Tom Robinson and Johnny Johnston. The flurry over George Fuller's work has been quickly

"INTERIOR OF A SMITHY."
From a painting by John J. Enneking.

AMERICAN ART AND ARTISTS.

forgotten, and he has had no followers; his works, with few exceptions, were even more faulty than Allston's, though they were not so closely based on the old masters. Both Allston and Fuller were superior men—intelligent, amiable, poetical—and imaginative, and their pictures will always be prized much in spite of their weaknesses. In the few pages allotted me here, I am to speak only of the accomplishments and traits of the living painters of Boston, and the many reproductions of their works which accompany these comments may be depended upon to give a better idea of their talents and scope than any verbal criticism.

There are at present in Boston twenty-five painters whose work may be said to fairly represent the best taste, though, and accomplishment of the profession in the New England capital; and although this computation is arbitrary, as all such computations must be, the list has been made with due regard to all the legitimate considerations which enter into this delicate problem of selection. Reputation, the degree of success in the outside world, the validity of popular esteem, the consensus of opinion, both professional and lay,—all these are entitled to due weight, as well as the intrinsic worth of the art work, and criticism concerns itself properly enough with much which makes no special personal appeal to the critic as an individual. It will always be apparent enough without explanation that the commentator, being neither a machine nor a deity, has his preferences and prejudices, which he need not seek to undermine. While he attempts to teach the public appreciation, he must learn appreciation himself; and the greater his experience in this line the deeper will be his respect for the efforts of all sincere workers, including those

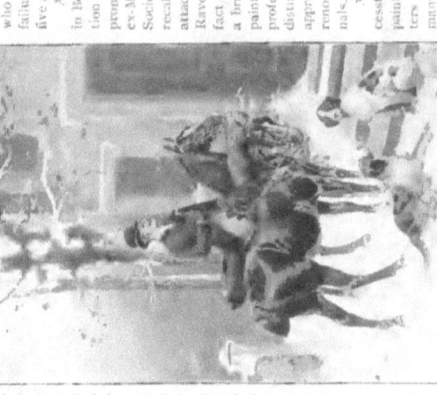

"WAITING."
By Ross Turner.

PORTRAIT OF A LADY.
By Frederic P. Vinton.

who have had to learn to smile at the north wind on the barren mountain-sides of failure and neglect. With this much by way of preamble, let us take up in order the five and twenty representative men and women whose work is the theme before us.

Among the portrait-painters the man who stands at the head of his profession in Boston to-day is, without doubt, Frederic P. Vinton. If there were any question as to the eminence of this artist in his specialty, it would be set at rest promptly by an acquaintance with his great portrait of Dr. Samuel A. Green, ex-Mayor of the city of Boston, and Secretary of the Massachusetts Historical Society. A certain straight-from-the-shoulder force in this magisterial work recalls vividly the weight of statement and the personal aggressiveness which attach to the portraiture of such Dutch painters as Van der Helst and Van Ravestein. This parallel hints at Vinton's characteristics as a portraitist. In fact he is a sober, truthful painter of what can be seen; he is a solid rather than a brilliant artist. He is candor itself, and he does not flatter his sitters. He has painted a long line of Massachusetts statesmen, judges, capitalists, orators, and professional men, and he has painted them well enough to be credited with a distinct contribution to the history of his time, a contribution which will be better appreciated as time goes by, and which will be secure to his name much respect and renown in our annals.

Another successful portrait-painter whose sitters have included many well-known people is J. Harvey Young, who has been painting portraits in Boston for nearly half a century, with an ever-increasing reputation. Among his distinguished subjects I need name only General Joseph Hooker, Prescott, the historian, Everett, Dr. A. P. Peabody, Horace Mann, Erastus Hopkins, William Warren, the actor, and John Holmes, the editor of the *Boston Herald*. The reproductions which are here

MINIATURE PORTRAIT
By Laura Hills.

From a painting by Scott Leighton.
"NOON AT THE POOL."

"THE OTHER SIDE."
From painting by Albert Groves.

AMERICAN ART AND ARTISTS.

given of several of his best works testify sufficiently to the admirable quality of his art.

Wilton Lockwood, known chiefly as a portrait-painter, is a much younger man, and relatively a late arrival. His paintings are highly artistic in style and sentiment, and they give evidence of the influence of Whistler, being sober in color, mysterious and retiring, with soft gray tones, relieved by touches of warm color as accents. There is much that is interesting and attractive and suggestive in Mr. Lockwood's figure compositions and portraits. His first exhibition in Boston, in 1895, at once drew the attention of amateurs of art to him as one of the most distinguished of contemporary painters.

Frank W. Benson's name has become familiar to lovers of art throughout the country, during the past ten years, as an artist who has captured numerous prizes at the exhibitions in all the principal cities. This has not been mere chance, nor is it to be attributed to a "pull." These rewards have in every case been given by the suffrages of artists and connoisseurs, and if they have made mistakes it is only because they are not infallible judges, and not because of any favoritism. In certain instances there was room for doubt as to the wisdom of the awards. There is no room for doubt regarding the serene and chaste beauty of Mr. Benson's best works. They have an unsurpassed grace of line and movement, an unsurpassed refinement and distinction, and much delicacy and harmony of color, which combine to make them distinctly decorative. Edmund C. Tarbell, who, with Mr. Benson, is teaching with marked success in the leading art school of New England, is another painter of conspicuous strength and ability. His figure paintings, whether of nude or draped form, are in every respect, except possibly their imaginative quality, the equal of the best that has been produced in this province of art in our country. Mr. Tarbell is essentially a painter whose perceptions of the visible world are singularly penetrating and keen; and few modern painters of any school have given a more striking interpretation to the phenomena of light and color in relation to the human figure.

A more intimate and narrative treatment of the human figure characterizes the work of Abbott Graves, whose happy faculty of invention and description is well illustrated by his pathetic and interesting picture of "The Silent Partner" and the suggestively dramatic "Saved from the Wreck." Mr. Graves believes in the story-telling picture, and it is due to him to say that he tells his stories well. He has until recent years been known chiefly as a painter of flower paintings, in which charming specialty he is unexcelled. But a broader and more congenial field opened before him when he began to paint the human figure, and his prompt recognition by the buying public, as well as by his brother artists, shows that he has not mistaken his calling. Another talented painter of the anecdotal genre which has so strong a hold on the general taste is I. H. Caliga, whose cabinet pieces, dealing with diminutive figures in interiors, are extremely well conceived and painted, with a sure grasp of character and a vivid suggestion of action. He has also painted a great number of portraits, both cabinet size and life size: one of the best is his portrait of his fellow-artist, Thomas Allen; but in general he is most felicitous in the portraits of women and children. Henry Sandham is well known as a painter of historical pieces of considerable importance and as an illustrator, in which capacity he has been a contributor to many of the leading magazines, notably the *Century*. His experience as an illustrator has naturally turned his thought to the invention of pictorial situations with a dramatic significance and episodic character. This has been well exemplified in some of his most ambitious canvases, such as the World's Fair picture of the Foundation of Maryland. The dominant note of these compositions is their human interest, which is unfailing; and a great

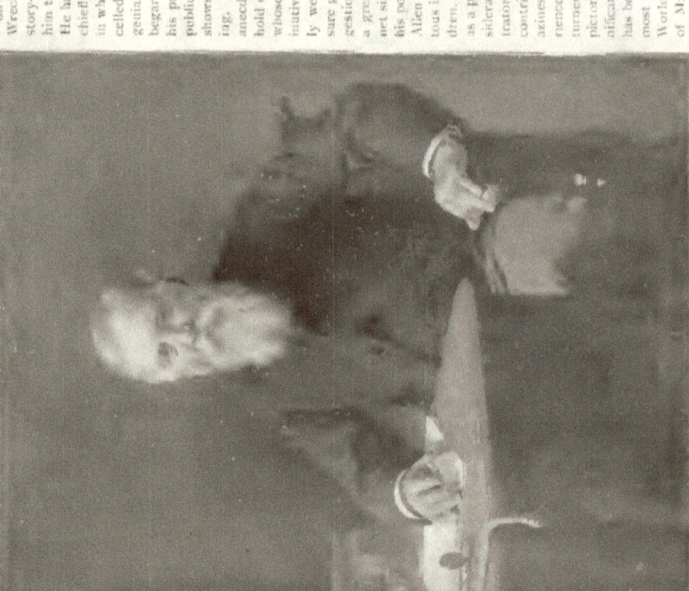

PORTRAIT OF PROF. C. C. LANGDELL, DEAN OF THE LAW SCHOOL, HARVARD UNIVERSITY.
By Frederic P. Vinton.

"A HALT ON THE HILL."

From painting by Scott Leighton.

"THE PROUD FATHER."

From painting by Scott Leighton.

From a painting by Alexander Pope. PORTRAIT OF MR. JOHN F. SPAULDING'S TROTTING STALLION "ARTHUR CLEVELAND."

AMERICAN ART AND ARTISTS.

factor in the production of this interest is the artist's understanding of the principles of design and light-and-shade.

An indispensable personage in the Boston artist world is John J. Enneking, the landscape painter, who, now that Inness has passed off the stage, looms up as one of the American masters of the first rank in his special field. Enneking has this supreme quality, which is never wanting in the equipment of a great artist, incomparable energy. The man is a wonder of productive vitality, and apparently never rests. His enthusiasm is something utterly indescribable. Truth, the greatest of merits in art as in life, shines forth from his inspired canvases. No one has ever so grandly interpreted the scenery of New England.

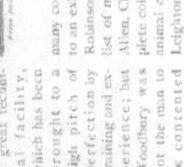

Marcus Waterman cannot be classified, because he is unique. His work has included Oriental subjects (painted in Algiers), scenes from the Thousand and One Nights, animal pictures, and landscapes from the luxuriant Vermont woods to the vast and lonely sand-dunes of Cape Cod. Into all his work he puts those rarest of qualities, originality and imagination. The originality is both of feeling and of style, of conception and of manner. The imagination is highly romantic. Something remote and strange and fascinating emanates from his compositions of Eastern life. His color is brilliant to the verge of audacity. His power of expressing sunlight is marvellous. The time will come when Waterman will be acknowledged one of the greatest of American painters.

Charles Herbert Woodbury paints both landscapes and marines, and occasionally introduces figures into his compositions. He is a painter of much talent; he started out as a youth with a great facility, which has been brought to a high pitch of perfection by training and experience; but Woodbury was not the man to be contented with an easy success, and he has tried to make his paintings the vehicle of expression for something of more general interest than a genteel bit of wall ornament, or a clever study from nature. Being a philosopher, he has the noble ambition to set forth something of permanent beauty and significance, of his very own coinage; and where he exhibited his "Mid-Ocean" in 1895, every man who has any of the old Northmen's blood in him took off his hat to Woodbury. There was a glimpse, only a glimpse—but enough—of that illimitable, mighty, awful Atlantic, flashed for a moment before our eyes and memories, and never to be forgotten. There is somewhat of the same sentiment of the elemental and typical forms and forces of nature in Woodbury's "The Forest," with its billowy foreground of drifted sand near the coast of Holland, and its mysterious ranks of pines beyond, forming a fit theatre for some stirring event, worthy of a page from George Sand.

"THE CHESS PLAYERS."
From painting by J. H. Cohen.

Boston, for many years has had a strong proportion of cattle and animal painters of note. "Too many cows," wrote one of the New York critics, nearly twenty years ago, referring to an exhibition of Boston paintings which contained works by Foxcroft Cole, Tom Robinson, Johnny Johnston, Albert Thompson, and W. M. Hunt. At this day the list of most successful cattle-painters would have to be made to include Thomas Allen, Charles F. Pierce, and A. H. Bicknell; and if one wished to make a complete collection of animal pictures, he would not leave out the spirited examples of animal compositions made by such men as Scott Leighton and Alexander Pope. Leighton devotes his brush chiefly to horses, and Pope to wild animals, which he paints in an ultra-realistic vein. Their works are not always marked by the most unimpeachable taste, but they are interesting by their earnest fidelity and naturalism.

"A LA THE FIRE."
By Henry Sandham.

From painting by A. H. Bicknell. "A NEW ENGLAND PASTURE."

From a painting, by Abbott Graves.

THE SILENT PARTNER.

NEAREST OF KIN.
From painting by Abbott Graves.

AMERICAN ART AND ARTISTS.

Allen is a very accomplished artist, and his pictures of Jersey cows, sheep, horses, and other domestic animals, knowingly set in admirable New England landscapes, are full of refinement, life, and beauty. Bicknell, earlier known in connection with historical pictures ("Battle of Lexington," "Lincoln at Gettysburg," etc.), and with portraits, later entered the field of landscape and cattle pictures with great and well-merited success. His cows are finely drawn, grouped, and colored; they have much character and vitality; and they are usually to be seen in landscapes of splendid extent and luminosity. Leighton's horses are esteemed, especially by the horsey; and it will not do to underestimate the weight of sportsmen's judgment on such matters. He is an earnest, honest, and skilful painter. Of Pope's menagerie one speaks with the respect due to a studious and sincere endeavor to record exact facts.

Boston has also had at all times a certain number of very able and successful marine-painters. Of those who at the present day carry on this interesting specialty, I have been content to choose William F. Haisall, W. F. Norton, and Walter L. Dean, as three good representative artists. These men have that thorough practical familiarity with the sea which can be gained only by a long experience of life on the ocean wave. Haisall is a native of England, ran away to sea as a lad, served his time before the mast, entered our naval service, and saw plenty of real work in the Atlantic blockading squadron during the war. His "First Fight between Ironclads" belongs to the United States Government. It is the only authentic picture of that revolutionary duel between the Monitor and the Merrimac in Hampton Roads. Haisall has painted many other historical compositions, such as "The Arrival of the Mayflower in Plymouth Harbor," etc., but his most stirring works are the episodes of the sailors' lives in storm and winter off the New England capes, a superb theme for one who knows it by actual personal experience. Dean and Norton are equally at home on the blue water, and their paintings of fishermen, yachts, and men-of-war, are full of spirit and truth. As a colorist, Dean promises to outrank any of the living marine-painters of our school. His color is singularly sweet, pleasant, and lucid. His "Peace," a large canvas depicting the Squadron of Evolution lying at anchor in Boston Harbor, in 1892, has been seen in all of the principal American cities.

Frank H. Tompkins is a competent portrait-painter, and a very interesting painter of figure compositions, nudes, etc. He has made the likenesses of many distinguished citizens, and has a rare faculty of bringing out his sitter's character. He does not flatter quite enough yet Tompkins has more than the ordinary stock of imagination, as one may judge by his figure-pieces, such as the memorably tender and lovely "Mother and Child," bought by the Boston Art Club before the artist returned from Munich. Tompkins is an intellectual painter, a man who thinks of something besides his palette. He is one of the few American artists who can say, *Nihil humani alienum a me puto.*

A figure-painter who enjoys a reputation extending considerably beyond the borders of New England, an artist whose dainty and minutely finished cabinet genres are vastly appreciated on account of their human interest, and their humor and their dramatic quality, as well as because of their skilful workmanship, is I. M. Gaugengigl, by birth a Bavarian, but for many years a Bostonian. Most of his pictures refer to bygone periods, when men wore more paintable costumes than they do at present. He has also met with success in the making of cabinet portraits.

Another water-color painter

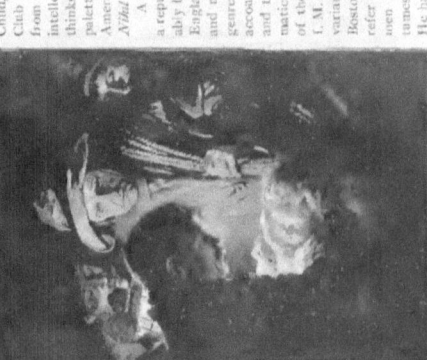

"THE MARTYRDOM OF ST. EUPHEMIA."

From a painting by Alexander Fisher.

AMERICAN ART AND ARTISTS.

By Henry Bacher.
WHEN CÆSAR WENT GREEN.

whose landscapes and flower-pieces are highly valued by good judges, owing to the beauty of their color, their delicacy, and decorative character, is Ross Turner, who has been conspicuous as a teacher. Nothing could be more pleasing than his Bermuda compositions, revealing the wealth of the local color, and the glare of the sunlight in those fortunate islands, unless it were one of his old-fashioned Salem flower-gardens a tangled mass of vivid blooms, brimful of sweetness and light.

It is not possible to go into particulars with respect to the army of water-colorists; but I will venture to name as conspicuously able and deserving practitioners, Frederic D. Williams and Henry DeMerritt Young. Mr. Williams's water-colors are most

work and illustrating, but space is wanting. A word should be devoted to the women painters. Every year we see more and more of these sisters of the brush and palette coming forward as doughty competitors with the men, and nowhere do they threaten more serious rivalry than in Boston, where such artists as Sarah C. Sears, Frances C. Houston, Sarah W. Whitman, Susan H. Bradley, Marcia Oakes Woodbury, Lilla Cabot Perry, Alice M. Curtis, and Laura C. Hills need only be mentioned to show that the democracy of art regards neither sex nor "previous condition of servitude." The pictures by Mrs. Woodbury, Mrs. Houston, Miss Curtis, and Miss Hills, which are given in

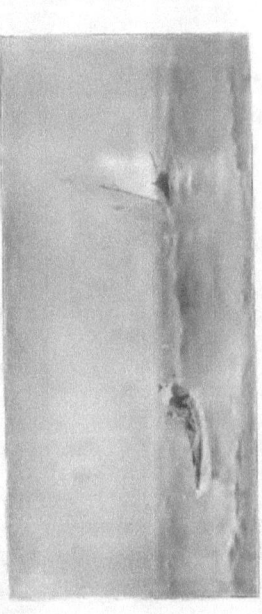

By Marcia Oakes Woodbury.
"THE STYLE SEARCH."

this connection, show well enough the trend of their talents. Mrs. Woodbury, who is the wife of the artist Woodbury, has distinguished herself by the inimitable and charming manner with which she has painted little children, and especially little Dutch children, who are, perhaps, the most unconscious models to be had. Mrs. Houston is an exceedingly clever painter of figures and portraits, whose work was specially praised in the 1896 Exhibition of the Society of American Artists. Miss Curtis is a landscapist of unquestionable superiority, and Miss Hills paints the best miniatures I have ever had the pleasure of seeing anywhere.

By Bertram T. Pratt.
"GOLD GLEAMS ON THE GEORGES."

delightful productions, for the most part landscapes painted on the Massachusetts coast, at Ipswich, or perhaps in France, where he has spent many years. Beautiful designs, sweetly and soundly colored, each one is completely thought out and amply satisfying. Mr. Young makes a specialty of the mountain and lake region of New Hampshire, to which he does justice, though this difficult class of motives has suggested more than one able artist. I would like to refer to S. P. R. Triscott, W. L. Taylor, E. H. Garrett, and others, known chiefly in connection with water-color

www.ingramcontent.com/pod-product-compliance
Lightning Source LLC
Chambersburg PA
CBHW032122230426
43672CB00009B/1825